the conquistadors

the conquistadors

First-person accounts of the Conquest of Mexico

Edited and translated by

PATRICIA DE FUENTES

Foreword by ROSS HASSIG

University of Oklahoma Press
Norman and London

Library of Congress Cataloging-in-Publication Data

The Conquistadors : first-person accounts of the conquest of Mexico /
  edited and translated by Patricia de Fuentes ; foreword by Ross
  Hassig.
      p.   cm.
    Includes bibliographical references and index.
    ISBN 0-8061-2562-4
    1. Mexico—History—Conquest, 1519–1540—Personal narratives.
  2. Mexico—History—Conquest, 1519–1540. 3. Indians of Mexico—
  First contact with Europeans. 4. America—Early accounts to 1600.
  5. Conquerors—Spain—History. 6. Conquerors—Mexico—History.
  I. Fuentes, Patricia de.
  F1230.F9   1993   93-13383
  972′.02′0922—dc20   CIP

1   2   3   4   5   6   7   8   9   10

contents

foreword

By Ross Hassig

The Conquest of Mexico in 1521 was a major
watershed in world history—the invasion, subjugation, and colonization of a "New World"
that had developed without influence from the
Old. The general outlines of the Conquest are
alive in the popular imagination, although the
details are often poorly known. Many books
recount the events, but the accounts of those
who actually participated in the Conquest often
conflict, or emphasize different matters, and
modern interpretations have inevitably privileged some accounts over others. To penetrate
the conflicting interpretations, nothing is better
than the words of the participants themselves,
and the seven accounts reproduced here are
among the best available: three record events
immediately before and after Cortés's conquest
of the Aztecs; the other four chronicle the events
of the Conquest. Of the major first-hand Conquest accounts, only the lengthy, but readily
available, chronicle of Bernal Díaz del Castillo
has been omitted from this collection. There are
many other important documents, but the first-
hand accounts published here are indispensable
for understanding the Conquest. Like all descriptions of intercultural contacts, however,
these accounts suffer from the misinterpreta-
tions of their authors.

To Spanish eyes, many native practices seemed
strange at best and abominably heathen at worst,

and many more were not understood by the conquistadors at all, so that their purposes and meanings were twisted in the Spaniards' minds as they sought to make sense of them. Often, this resulted in a condemnation of native practices even as the Spaniards unquestioningly accepted their own, despite marked similarities. For instance, the Spaniards were repelled by the human sacrifices that were calmly accepted by the Indians as part of their religion, but they had no difficulty in burning Indians alive or cutting off the hands of suspected spies, which horrified the Indians. The Spaniards also were disgusted by what they considered idolatrous worship of bloody and grotesque heathen gods, even as they venerated Christian saints many of whom were depicted crucified, decapitated, with their breasts cut off, and otherwise mutilated with swords, arrows, and hot pokers.

The Spaniards misunderstood the natives, which is reflected in their chronicles, but more than that, their accounts were biased because they were written for overt political purposes. For example, Governor Diego Velásquez de Cuéllar of Cuba authorized only the exploration of the coast and trade with the natives encountered, but Cortés, lured by visions of enormous wealth, flagrantly exceeded his authority, establishing a permanent town and embarking on an expedition of conquest into the interior. Cortés risked imprisonment in taking these actions, but he threw the entire issue into the political arena by disingenuously declaring that he had fulfilled the terms of Velásquez's charter, which freed him from further obligations. Unhindered by Velásquez's restrictions, he founded the town of Vera Cruz and established a town council that claimed authority directly from the king of Spain rather than from Velásquez. The town council then authorized Cortés to carry out his plans under their dubious authority.

Cortés's only hope of sustaining that transparent ploy was to seek royal patronage, which, he reasoned, would be forthcoming if he succeeded and was able to flood the crown with wealth from the New World. Accordingly, his letters to the king during the Conquest emphasized the great odds against which he struggled and the great feats that he and his men performed. At the same time, he minimized or ignored the contributions of his Indian allies. Cortés's account also is peppered with assertions about observing all the required legalities in dealing with the natives. Though often improbable, these claims were intended for royal consumption, to sway the king toward Cortés's position and away from the more legitimate claims of Governor Velásquez. Thus, even though Cortés's account was written the closest to the events described of all the major chronicles, and therefore offers some of the best evidence about the Conquest, it is also one of the most suspect.

Not all the chronicles suffer from Cortés's biases, but that does not mean the writers attempted to be objective. Virtually all the participants stood to gain financially and politically if the king recognized their contribution to the Conquest. Thus, their accounts were not simply histories intended to record events but were, in effect, petitions for royal patronage in which the authors invariably placed their own actions in the best possible light. These accounts remain important historical documents, but they are nevertheless flawed by their self-serving purpose.

It is precisely the chroniclers' self-aggrandizement that has caused so many difficulties in reconstructing the history of the Conquest. When he landed, Cortés was accompanied by a few hundred men, yet he and his men decisively defeated an empire of millions in just a few months of combat. Taken at face value, the Spanish actions were so incredible (in the word's original sense) that they defy common sense, and heavy reliance on Spanish accounts has led to an overemphasis on such intangibles as European cultural superiority, Cortés's psychological dominance, and the superiority of European writing that gave the Spaniards a better grasp of their symbolic system. When the Indian factors are discussed, they are frequently the inferior inverse of the above, augmented by the presumed effects of losing faith in the native gods and a ritualistic perspective on war that made the Aztecs unable to overcome the Europeans.

However the Conquest is explained, today's climate has turned against the earlier idea that the conquistadors were heroes. The pendulum has swung the other way to the extent that many inadvertent results of the Conquest, such as the devastating introduction of smallpox, have been reinterpreted as conscious acts by the Spaniards, even though, in fact, they were as ignorant of the processes of infection as were the Indians. Such reevaluations of the Conquest have had important consequences because today the Conquest chronicles are no longer taken at face value. We recognize that they express somewhat doctored reactions to what the Spaniards encountered, that they represent the Spanish side. The Indian perspective remains largely ignored.

Native perspectives often are neglected because of the paucity of indigenous descriptions of the Conquest. Even those that exist were written well after the fact, and often by people who were not participants in the events they described. Nor are they free from allegations that the authors were trying to mold history. But they often include matters that the Spanish accounts do not. For instance, only through native accounts do we know that the Spaniards who failed to flee Tenochtitlan with Cortés did not die that night, but returned to their quarters, where they were besieged for some days before being killed. The native accounts do not encompass the entire sweep of the Conquest; they focus primarily on events in and around the Valley of Mexico. Only Spanish accounts detail the Conquest throughout its entire time span; thus they serve as our primary sources, although the sketchier Indian accounts are a necessary palliative for the extreme claims of the Spaniards.

The Spanish accounts offer a glimpse into a world that no longer exists; indeed, a world that began changing as soon as Cortés stepped ashore. They record the reactions of outsiders to the previously unknown, indigenous civilizations, which had their own views of the world, their own forms of society, and their own arts and technologies, which had arisen independent of the Old World. Moreover, these chronicles provide indispensable accounts of what happened during the Conquest—at least from the Spanish perspective. Although the writers often contradict each other, they record both when and where various things happened, helping to disentangle the historical record and render it intelligible.

However unbalanced their view, the Spanish chronicles are indispensable because they are the most comprehensive accounts of the Conquest. How important they are depends on how we view the conquest of Mexico, but even in today's revisionist climate, they remain an essential, though distorted and Eurocentric, view of one of the great turning points in world history.

introduction

European man at the beginning of the sixteenth century was absorbed with the conquest of space. In a sense this conquest began much earlier, with the Crusades, when the East was revealed to the European world. In the thirteenth century Marco Polo became the first traveler to trace a route across the longitude of Asia, and to speak of India as a country seen and partially explored. In Polo's own lifetime there existed several *portolani* or coast charts, based on the practical experience of pilots and mariners, and by the fourteenth century the *portolani* showed the known world on the basis of collected fact rather than theological conjecture.

A long list of Italian and Portuguese discoveries followed, and by the middle of the fifteenth century Henry the Navigator had established the trade routes of northwest Africa. At the end of the fifteenth century Columbus attempted the western route to Asia. The Spanish caravels under his command, bobbing over the seas as improbably as so many washtubs, opened the way to the discovery of an entire continent whose existence had not been suspected. Under Magellan in 1518, five Spanish vessels set out to accomplish the circumnavigation of the globe, an achievement equally as great as the discovery of America.

Columbus, of course, miscalculated the distance separating India from Europe across the western sea. When he came to the Caribbean islands he reported: "I reached the Indian Sea, where I discovered many islands, thickly populated . . ." The designation of *las Indias* (the Indies) given to these islands applied as well to later discoveries on the mainland, and to this day the Spanish refer to their fellow countrymen residing in Latin America as *Indianos*.

It is with the early *Indianos* that the present volume is concerned; more specifically, those whom the passion for travel and adventure, the desire for fame and fortune, impelled yet further west, to the discovery and conquest of Mexico.

From the European point of view this was one of the most remarkable adventures of all time, and the participants themselves were well aware of it. In the chronicles and histories they wrote —and how fortunate for us that the Spanish had also a passion for recording everything—they did not attempt to disguise their feeling of uniqueness. Often they displayed a self-conscious identification with the heroes of classical antiquity, especially the Roman; at other times they fancied themselves protagonists of the *caballerías* or tales of chivalry that were the popular reading of the period. But the Spanish, who are able to laugh at themselves, produced their own corrective to this solemn pretentiousness, in Cervantes' delightfully absurd figure of Don Quixote.

The conquistadors felt no embarrassment about saying they wanted to make a fortune. The gold they sought would buy a life of ease, which was every man's aspiration. When they became discouraged, wrote Francisco de Aguilar, Cortés "gave us very good talks, leading us to believe that each one of us would be a count or a duke, and one of the titled. With this he transformed us from lambs to lions, and we went out against that large army without fear or hesitation."

At the same time they were religious almost to the point of fanaticism. They believed in God, and feared the Devil more than death itself. To serve God it was necessary to destroy the works of the Devil—the temples and hideous idols— and to extirpate human sacrifice and the sins of anthropophagy and sodomy.

Cortés himself felt called upon to preach to the Indians wherever he went, reasoning with them that their gods were worthless; evangelization, however, was the special province of the missionaries who accompanied all expeditions. By a papal decree of Alexander VI issued in 1493, it became mandatory that the natives of the new lands discovered and taken possession of in the name of the Spanish sovereigns were to be properly instructed in the Catholic faith, "for the salvation of these souls, and so that the barbarous nations may be humbled and converted to the Faith."

The conquistador's conscience was clear in the knowledge that he was on a sacred mission, for in the most literal sense he was helping to free the Indians from the tyranny of the Devil. Furthermore, he had been absolved of guilt before so much as setting foot in Mexico. In the royal license authorizing the expedition it had been promised that the Crown would secure the Pope's indulgence and absolution for all the conquistadors.

If there were excesses and abuses, wrote Ruy González to the king thirty years later—denying the imputations of Fray Bartolomé de las Casas —"why should all the conquistadors pay for these sins? Let those pay who commited them. . . ."

The quest for fame and fortune did not seem, at the time, incompatible with religious conviction. Such doubts were to manifest themselves much later. Yet the ambition of the conquistadors did not make them totally insensible to their surroundings. Clumsily written as some of the chronicles are—limited in vocabulary, blunt in expression, full of ambiguities—they nevertheless articulate the conquistadors' enchantment with the land and its graceful people. These Spaniards were generous, too, in their praise of Indian valor, and they looked upon the Indian warrior as a worthy adversary. Their admiration of native skill and artistry was constantly reiterated and they were also aware, though a little dimly, of the high degree of civilization attained by the people of Mexico.

In the chronicle of Juan Díaz, which is the opening selection of the present volume, we see through the eyes of the early explorers the wonders of the New World. Juan Díaz shipped with Captain Juan de Grijalva in 1518, as chaplain of the expedition. A year later he was to sail with Cortés, but the account he wrote describes the voyage of exploration led by Captain Grijalva, a voyage that laid much of the groundwork for the Cortés expedition.

Governor Velázquez of Cuba, entrepreneur of these expeditions, was disappointed in the material results of Grijalva's efforts, and he then commissioned Hernán Cortés to lead an armada to the newly discovered lands. Velázquez was again to regret his choice of captain, but for quite different reasons. In effect, Cortés cheated Velázquez of his share in the enterprise by some adroit but entirely legal measures taken as soon as he reached the coast of Veracruz. This matter is gone into in detail by Andrés de Tapia, the second of the soldier-chroniclers presented in this volume. Tapia's chronicle begins with the assembling of the armada in Cuba, and ends with Cortés' campaign against Pánfilo de Narváez in 1520.

After founding the city of Veracruz, Cortés
left a hundred and fifty settlers there and set out
with the rest of the men to conquer Moctezuma's
kingdom. The extent of that kingdom, its physi-
cal nature, resources, and exact location were
matters on which Cortés had very sketchy information, but he was not a man to be daunted by
the unknown. His little Spanish army was accompanied by several hundred Totonac Indians from
Cempoala, a city-state not far from Veracruz.
The Totonacs, weary of being oppressed by the
Mexicans (or Aztecs), were one of the first of
the Indian peoples to be persuaded by Cortés
to support the Spanish cause. As the various
chronicles of the period testify, no small measure
of Cortés' genius lay in his ability to manipulate
people, and he never used armed force where
diplomacy could better serve his purpose.

In the chronicles of both Andrés de Tapia and
Fray Francisco de Aguilar, which are presented in
this volume, there are first-hand accounts of the
march from Veracruz to the great city of Mexico-
Tenochtitlan, and the impressive welcome that
Moctezuma gave the Spaniards. The splendors
of the Mexican city made many of the soldiers
rub their eyes in wonder, and even today their
accounts capture the imagination like one of the
tales of Scheherazade.

All was blissful for the Spaniards: the conquest
of Tenochtitlan was effected without bloodshed,
Moctezuma and the other lords gave fealty to
the Spanish king, and Cortés and his men seemed
to have become the new lords of the land. However, a series of circumstances led to an upris-
ing on the part of the Mexicans, and a determined
effort to annihilate the intruders. Cortés and his
men were forced to abandon the city, for they
were hopelessly outnumbered, and their retreat
could be cut off whenever the Mexicans chose to
remove the bridges leading from their island city

to the mainland. On the night the Spaniards made their escape, the *Noche Triste* (June 30, 1520) more than half their army was slaughtered by the Mexicans.

There were no heroes that night, for when the alarm was given and the Indians began to pursue them, the Spaniards stumbled over one another in their terror, intent on mere survival. A chilling description of their flight is given by Fray Francisco de Aguilar, whose chronicle is fourth in order of appearance in this volume.

Cortés and his remaining forces made their way back to Tlaxcala (an independent "republic" as the Spaniards called it, inasmuch as it was governed by a council) and there they spent the next six months preparing for the reconquest of Tenochtitlan.

These plans and preparations, as well as the actual siege of Tenochtitlan, are told most authoritatively by Hernán Cortés himself; therefore, his letter or dispatch to Charles V of Spain, dated May 15 of 1522, has been included in this volume.

After a terrible siege that lasted more than ten weeks, and in which the most hardened Spanish soldiers were amazed at the Mexicans' stoicism, the last sector of the city fell on August 13 of 1521. The backbone of the Mexican empire was broken. The lands once dominated by Moctezuma and his ancestors became the Province of New Spain, "one of the best provinces of the New World, and the most habitable," wrote the sixteenth-century historian, Antonio de Herrera.

With phenomenal energy, Cortés, as governor general, directed the formation of the new colony. It was his conviction that "this noble land" should grow and prosper, and there was not a phase of its development that failed to receive his attention. From the Aztec tribute lists he learned what sections of the country provided metals, and to these regions he despatched Spaniards to open mines. He sent to Spain for seeds and plants in order to add the crops and fruit trees of the Old World to those of the New. Every caravel also brought livestock, and in a very few years cattle ranches flourished on American soil. In particular, Cortés requested friars who were men of exemplary lives, so that they might inspire the same respect among the Indians as had their own priests.

It was not long, however, before administrative duties palled on Cortés and he longed for action. He had been sending other men on further conquests, notably Pedro de Alvarado, Cristóbal de Olid, and Gonzalo de Sandoval, but in 1524 Cortés abandoned the governorship of New Spain, leaving it in the hands of treacherous and incompetent subordinates, and set out on the overland route to Honduras. He was scarcely heard of for two years.

In his absence conditions became chaotic, there was a stream of complaints to the Spanish court, and his enemies made the most of his disappearance to accuse him of negligence, fraud, and even murder. In the face of these charges the Crown was obliged to order a *residencia,* an official investigation, and to appoint an interim governor.

The investigation dragged on, while royal governors came and went, until it was decided that New Spain was to be governed by an *Audiencia*—a judicial and administrative court composed of four jurists called *oidores*—presided over by Nuño Beltrán de Guzmán. We shall return to Guzmán in a moment.

Cortés at this point found it advisable to go to Spain and clear his name in person before Charles V. He outfitted two ships, offering free passage to any of his friends who wished to make the crossing, and took with him the conquistadors

Gonzalo de Sandoval and Andrés de Tapia; also one of Moctezuma's sons who had become a Christian, and many other Mexican and Tlaxcalan nobles. He took Indian dancers and acrobats, all kinds of animals including the opossum, rich examples of Indian craftsmanship, and fifteen hundred silver marks, thirty thousand pesos of gold, and valuable jewels.

Charles V was chronically in need of funds, and Cortés' gifts had precisely the calculated effect. The court was dazzled. Cortés received enormous grants of land in New Spain, and other privileges, but not the coveted governorship. He returned to Mexico as captain general and as a member of the hereditary nobility, with the title of Marqués del Valle de Oaxaca. However, he never regained his former authority, and New Spain continued to be governed by *Audiencias* until 1535, when the first viceroy was appointed.

Nuño de Guzmán and the other members of the first *Audiencia* had been plundering New Spain with scarcely any attempt at discretion. Their tyranny and corruption, and especially their illicit slave trade, reached such proportions that the Spanish court was inundated with protests, one of which was formulated by the Bishop of Mexico. Nuño de Guzmán brazenly accused the clergy in general of obstructing the *Audiencia's* functions for venal motives, and these charges and counter-charges threw the Council of the Indies into confusion. But it became evident that a new *Audiencia* must be appointed, and an investigation made of the activities of Guzmán and his *oidores*.

Nuño de Guzmán then considered it prudent to leave the city. He announced that it was his duty to the king to go and quell a revolt of the Indians of Michoacan, who were killing Spaniards, and that it was his pleasure to further serve the king by exploring the regions beyond this province.

On this expedition Nuño de Guzmán killed, burned, tortured and terrorized the Indian population all the way from Michoacan to Culiacan in the northwest. As a result of the subsequent inquiry conducted by the second *Audiencia,* the full particulars of the expedition were brought to light and preserved in the testimony of several of Guzmán's henchmen. His punishment, in the opinion of his contemporaries, did not fit the crime; after a year in prison he was ordered to appear in Spain before the Council of the Indies, and through his influence at court the charges against him were dropped.

Nuño de Guzmán had not come to Mexico until 1526, seven years after the arrival of Cortés. He was sent by the Crown to govern the province of Pánuco, which Cortés considered part of his own conquest. Guzmán and Cortés became strong rivals, equally ambitious and astute, equally voracious for power, but with the difference that Cortés had the forbearance to hold his peace in the interests of the general welfare. Guzmán, on the other hand, used every available weapon to destroy Cortés, and contributed largely to his loss of power and authority in New Spain.

Hernán Cortés, whose star had risen so swiftly and almost as quickly extinguished itself, was condemned at the age of forty-four to live out his days in a subordinate role. His vast land grants made him very wealthy, but, as he had written Charles V, "I have more regard for being rich in fame than rich in possessions." Thwarted in his attempts to regain the governorship of New Spain, he poured his energies and fortune into mining and agriculture, and the exploration of the Pacific coast. He built shipyards at Tehuantepec and Acapulco, where he outfitted several armadas. One of them, which he led himself, reached the peninsula of Lower California, but the land was found to be arid and inhospitable. On these expeditions he spent three hundred thousand gold castellanos in the hope of discovering another new world and regaining his prestige. He died in Spain in 1547, embittered by the conviction that his king, whom he had served as no other subject had, denied him the recognition he deserved.

PATRICIA DE FUENTES

Mexico City
1963

the conquistadors

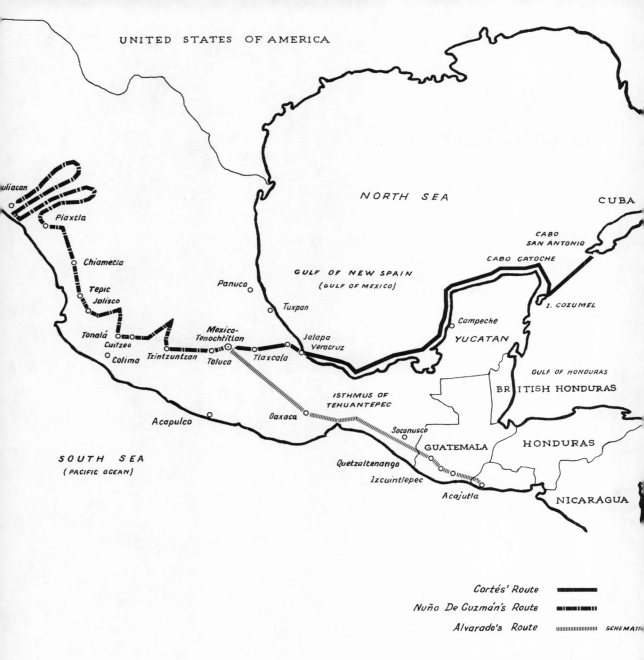

UNITED STATES OF AMERICA

Culiacan

Piaxtla

Chiametla

Tepic
Jalisco

Tonalá
Cuitzeo
Colima

Tzintzuntzan
Toluca

Mexico-
Tenochtitlan
Tlaxcala

Acapulco

SOUTH SEA
(PACIFIC OCEAN)

NORTH SEA

GULF OF NEW SPAIN
(GULF OF MEXICO)

Panuco

Tuxpan

Jalapa
Veracruz

ISTHMUS OF
TEHUANTEPEC

Oaxaca

Saconusco

Quetzaltenango

Izcuintlepec
Acajutla

CABO
SAN ANTONIO

CABO GATOCHE

CUBA

I. COZUMEL

Campeche

YUCATAN

GULF OF HONDURAS

BRITISH HONDURAS

GUATEMALA

HONDURAS

NICARAGUA

Cortés' Route ▬▬▬▬▬
Nuño De Guzmán's Route ▬▬▬▬▬
Alvarado's Route ||||||||||||| SCHEMATIC

Routes of the Conquistadors

the chronicle
of
juan diaz

Juan Díaz shipped to the Indies in 1512. He was
a secular member of a militant religious order, the
Mercedarians, the first order to be sent from
Spain to the New World. After several years of
missionary work in the islands of the Caribbean,
he was chosen in 1518 to accompany Juan de
Grijalva, captain of the second expedition to
Yucatan. This was in the year following Hernández de Córdoba's discovery of that "island" (as it
was then believed to be) and in the year preceding the expedition led by Hernán Cortés. Díaz
also sailed with Cortés, and later took part in
Pedro de Alvarado's conquest of Guatemala.

The document Juan Díaz left us is a first-hand
account of the Grijalva expedition. Though the
original manuscript has disappeared, Díaz' chronicle was preserved in an Italian translation, inserted in one of the later sixteenth-century
editions of the "Itinerary" of Varthema. The
nineteenth-century scholar Joaquín García Icazbalceta translated the Díaz account into Spanish
and published it in his ten-volume *Collection of
Documents for the History of Mexico*. The present English translation has been made from the
García Icazbalceta text (see bibliography).

Juan Díaz was outspoken in his contempt for
Captain Juan de Grijalva, and this opinion was
shared by many of his contemporaries. Unavoid-
ably Grijalva was compared with Cortés and
found lacking in the boldness and enterprise that
characterized the great conquistador. Grijalva

faithfully carried out the *capitulaciones*, or stip-
ulations, of his agreement with Diego de Velázquez, governor of Cuba and entrepreneur of the
expedition, and these conditions limited his activities to exploration and bartering for gold. He
carried no authorization to settle the land.

When Grijalva returned to Cuba, no doubt
proud of his accomplishment (he had explored
the Gulf coast from Yucatan as far north as Ta-
miahua, near the present Tampico, and had
established friendly relations with many of the
Indian peoples), Governor Velázquez abused him
for not having settled in such a rich land, despite
his instructions to the contrary. Velázquez had
already received a full report from Pedro de Alvarado, whose ship had sped back to Cuba ahead
of the fleet, and before Grijalva's return Velázquez was busy outfitting a new and larger armada.

Itinerary of the Armada of the Catholic King to the island of Yucatan, the year 1518, whose Commander and Captain General was Juan de Grijalva. Written for His Highness by the First Chaplain of the Armada.

On Saturday, the first day of May of the year 1518, the captain of the armada left the island of Fernandina,[1] from which point he initiated his voyage. On the Monday following, the third day of the month of May, we sighted land and on nearing it we saw, on a point, a white building and some thatch-roofed houses, also a lagoon which the sea formed inside the land. And because it was the day of the Holy Cross, we called this land Santa Cruz.

Seeing that this side was full of reefs and sand bars, we approached the opposite shore where we could see the white building more clearly. It was a small tower[2] that looked the length of a house of eight spans and the height of a man. There, about six miles from land, the armada anchored.

Soon there appeared two craft called canoes, each manned by three Indians. They came to within a bombard throw of our ships but would not come nearer, nor were we able to speak to them nor find out anything from them, except that by signs they gave us to understand that on the following morning we would be visited by the cacique,[3] which in their tongue means the lord of the place.

The next morning we sailed out to explore a cape that could be discerned, and the pilot said it was the island of Yucatan. Between that point and the tip of the island of Cozumel where we were we discovered a gulf, which we entered, and going close to shore, we coasted this island. We saw fourteen more towers, all shaped like the first, but before we had left the first tower the two Indian canoes returned, bringing the cacique or lord of the place, who boarded the flagship and said through the interpreter that he would be honored to have the captain go to his town where he would be well attended. Our men asked him for news of the Christians left on the island of Yucatan by Francisco Fernández, captain of the first armada, and he replied that one was living and the other had died. And after our captain gave the cacique some Spanish shirts, the Indians returned to their town.

We set sail and followed the coast looking for this Christian who had been left with a companion to gather information on the island's nature and condition, and were able to keep but a stone's throw from shore because the sea was quite deep on this side. From the point referred to we counted fourteen towers of the manner already described, and almost at sunset we saw a white tower that looked very large; we sailed close to it and saw many Indians of both sexes who were watching us. They remained there until the fleet hove to at a crossbow's throw from the tower, which seemed to us very large, and we could hear a tremendous roar of drums because of the many Indians that inhabit this island.

Thursday, the sixth day of the month of May, the captain ordered one hundred men armed and readied, who boarded the shallops and went ashore, taking a cleric. They thought that many Indians would come against them, so they proceeded in formation at the ready toward the tower, but no one was there nor could they see anyone in the vicinity. The captain climbed the tower together with the standard bearer, who set the flag in the place appropriate to the service of the Catholic king. There the captain took possession in the name of His Highness and had it certified by the scrivener. In sign and testimony of this possession the captain's writ was affixed to one of the sides of the tower. This tower was eighteen steps high, with a solid base, and measured one hundred and eighty feet around. At the top was a small tower of the height of two men, and inside were bones and ash, and certain figures that are the idols they worship, and from the nature of these it is presumed the people are idolatrous.

While the captain and a number of our men were at the top, an Indian who was accompanied by three others went inside, leaving the others to guard the doorway. Inside he placed a bowl with very fragrant perfumes that seemed like liquidambar. This Indian was an aged man, and the toes of his feet were cut off.[4] He offered much incense to those idols inside the tower, singing a chant that was almost of an even tenor. From what we were able to comprehend we thought he called to those idols of theirs.

They gave the captain and several of our men some cane tubes a span in length, which on being burned gave forth a very pleasant odor.[5] Then the tower was at once put in order and mass was held. After mass the captain ordered certain articles proclaimed immediately in the interests of His Highness' service, and then that same Indian arrived who seemed to be the priest of the others. Eight more Indians were with him, bringing poultry, honey, and certain roots called maize[6] from which they make bread. The captain told them he wanted only gold, which in their tongue is called *taquin*, and made them understand that in exchange he would give them wares that he had brought for this purpose.

These Indians took the captain and ten or twelve others and gave them to eat in a refectory with stone walls and thatched roof, in front of which was a well where all the men drank. By nine o'clock in the morning not an Indian remained in the place, and thus they left us alone. We entered that same town whose buildings were all of stone, and among these were five with towers on top, all but three of them very finely worked. The bases on which they are built are solid and occupy a great deal of space, and diminish to a small space at the top. These buildings seem to be old, although there are new ones also.

This village or town had its streets cobblestoned in a concave form, raised on the sides with a hollow down the center, and along that hollow the pavement was of large stones. The whole length of the street had many houses belonging to the townspeople, made of stone foundations with mud walls and thatched roofs. The people of this place seem, from their buildings and houses, to be a very skillful people, and if it were not for several buildings that seemed to be new, one might assume they were buildings made by Spaniards.[7]

This island seems to me a very good one, and ten miles out as we approached it we perceived such sweet odors that it was something to marvel at. Aside from this there is much sustenance to be found on the island; that is, many beehives and much wax and honey.[8] The hives are like those of Spain, only smaller. There is nothing else on the island from what they say. Ten of us penetrated three or four miles inland and saw towns and habitations separated from one another, very beautifully arranged. There are trees called *jarales* on which the bees feed; there are also hares and rabbits, and the Indians say there are pigs,[9] deer and many other wild animals on this island of Cozumel, which is now called Santa Cruz, as well as on the island of Yucatan, to which we crossed the following day.

Friday, May 7, exploration of the island of Yucatan commenced. On this day we left the island of Santa Cruz and crossed to the island of Yucatan, traversing fifteen miles of gulf. On reaching the coast we saw three large towns about two miles apart, with many stone houses and very large towers, and many thatched houses. We should have liked to enter these places had the captain permitted us; but since he refused, we sailed the coast this day and night, and the next day almost at sunset we saw in the distance a town or village so large that the city of Seville could not be better or larger; and in it could be seen a very large tower. Many Indians were running along the shore with two banners which they raised and lowered, signaling us to approach; but the captain did not wish to. This same day we came to a beach which was near a tower, the highest we had found, and a very large town could be seen. On the land were many rivers. We discovered a wide inlet encircled with timbers, made by fishermen, where the captain went ashore; but we could find no way of continuing along the coast nor going ahead, so we hoisted sail and went out the way we had come in.

Sunday following. This day we turned back along the coast until again sighting the island of Santa Cruz, where we landed in the same place or town as before, because were in need of water.

There was no one about when we landed, and we took water from a well since we could not find river water. We took on provisions of *managi*, which are tree fruit of the size and flavor of melons, and also sweet potatoes, which are roots like carrots, and ungulates that are animals called *schirati* in Italy. We stayed until Tuesday, when we hoisted sail and made for the island of Yucatan on a northerly course. We sailed along the coast and saw a very beautiful tower on a point that is said to be inhabited by women who live without men; it is believed they are of the Amazon race. Other towers apparently with towns were seen nearby, but the captain would not permit us to land.

On this coast could be seen people, and many columns of smoke one after the other. We went along it looking for the cacique or lord, Lázaro, a chieftain who showed much respect to Francisco Fernández, captain of the other armada and the first to explore this island and enter the town.[10] In the town and seat of this chieftain there is a river called the Lagartos, and because we were very short of water the captain ordered us to go ashore and see if there was any there. None was found, but the land was reconnoitered. It seemed to us that we were close to this chieftain, and we went along the coast and came to him. We anchored about two miles from a tower that was at the edge of the sea, and one mile from where the chieftain lives. The captain ordered one hundred men readied to go ashore, with five guns and certain harquebuses.

All that night and next morning many drums sounded on land, and great shrieking, as of men on the alert, for they were well prepared. Before dawn we went ashore and approached the tower, and there the artillery was emplaced and all the men stayed at attention. The Indian spies were close by watching us. The tenders returned for the men still aboard ship, who were another hundred, and as day broke a squadron of Indians came toward us. Our captain ordered the men to remain still, and the interpreter to tell them that we did not want war but only to take on water and wood, after which we would leave. Then certain messengers came and went, and we thought the interpreter was deceiving us; for he was a native of this island and town, and on seeing that we guarded him and he could not leave he began crying, which aroused our suspicions. Finally we had to move in formation around another tower that was up ahead. The Indians told us not to advance, but to go back and take water from a rock we had left to the rear, where there was very little and it could not be gathered. We continued our way skirting the town, the Indians holding us off as much as they could, and so we came to a well where Francisco Fernández, captain of the other armada, took water on the first voyage.

The Indians took the captain a cooked turkey and many raw ones, and the captain asked them if they had gold to trade for other wares. They brought a wooden mask with gold leaf and two other pieces like disks of gold of little value, and they told us to leave, that they did not want us to take water. At dusk they came to feast with us, bringing maize, which is the root they make bread with, and some cakes of this root. Nevertheless they still asked us to leave, and all that night they remained on watch and kept careful guard. The next morning they advanced in three squadrons, armed with many bows and arrows, and they were dressed in colors. We were at the ready. One of the chieftain's brothers and a son came to tell us to leave, and the interpreter replied that on the following day we would go and that we did not want war, and so we stayed.

Late in the day the Indians returned within sight of our army, and all the men were desperate because the captain would not let them fight the Indians. The latter again spent the night on guard, and next morning formed ranks and told us once more to leave. So saying, they placed a brazier with burning incense in the middle of the field, telling us that if we did not leave before the incense was consumed they would make war on us. And when the incense was burned out they began shooting many arrows at us. The captain ordered the artillery fired, at which three Indians were killed, and our men pursued the Indians until they fled to the town. We burned three straw huts and the crossbowmen killed some Indians.

Here a grave accident occurred: some of our men followed the banner and others the captain, and because we got scattered among great numbers of the enemy forty Christians were wounded and one killed. In truth, such was the Indians' determination that had it not been for our artillery fire they would have given us a hard time, but we were able to retreat to our camp where the wounded were attended to, and not another Indian appeared. Quite late, however, an Indian came bringing a gold mask, and said they wanted peace. All of us begged the captain to allow us to avenge the death of the Christian, but he refused; instead he made us go aboard that night.

After we were on board we saw no more Indians except one who had come to us before the battle and was, so he told us, a slave of that chieftain or lord. This Indian gave us signs of a place with many islands where there were caravels and men like ourselves, except that they had large ears, and he said they had swords and shields, and that there were many other provinces there. He told the captain he wanted to come with us but the captain would not take him and this displeased us all.

The land we coasted from the twenty-ninth of May when we left the town of the chieftain Lázaro was very low and did not satisfy us at all, because the island of Cozumel, called Santa Cruz, was better. From here we reconnoitered to Potonchán,[11] where Francisco Fernández, the captain of the other armada, left the men that were killed, and which is a place thirty-six miles more or less from this other chieftain.[12] And along here we saw many mountains and many Indian barks, called canoes, with which they thought to make war on us. But as they approached a ship we fired two artillery shots at them, which put so much fear into them that they fled. From the ships we saw stone houses, and at the edge of the sea a white tower, where the captain refused to let us land.

On the last day of May we found at last a very good harbor which we called Puerto Deseado because until then we had not found any. Here we stopped and all the men went ashore, and we made an arbor, and some wells from which we got very good water. We cleaned and repaired one of the ships, and spent twelve days in this harbor because it is very pleasant and there is much fish, which is all of one kind, called *jurel*, and very good. In this place we also found rabbits, hare, and deer. An arm of the sea enters this harbor, on which the Indians sail in their barks, which they call canoes.[13] From this island they cross to the mainland of India, according to three Indians taken by the general of Diego Velázquez, who affirmed the above-said.

The pilots declared that the island of Yucatan divides here from the rich island of Valor, which we discovered. Here we took on wood and water, and continuing our voyage went on to discover another land which is called Mulua, and to finish reconnoitering it. We began on the eighth day of June, and, as the armada went along the coast about six miles away from land, we saw a very large stream of water coming from a principal river, which cast fresh water six miles into the sea. Because of the current we could not go up the river, which we named the Grijalva River. We were being followed by more than two thousand Indians and they were giving us war signals. As soon as we reached this port one of the dogs threw itself into the water and when the Indians saw it they thought it was performing a great feat, and went after it until they killed it. They also shot many arrows at us, so we fired an artillery shot and killed an Indian.

Next day there crossed toward us from the other shore more than a hundred canoes or barks, in which there could have been three thousand Indians, who sent one of the canoes ahead to find out what we wanted. The interpreter told them we were looking for gold, and that if they had some and wanted to give it we would offer good exchange for it. Our men gave these Indians in the canoe certain cups and other utensils from the ships to make them happy, for they were people of good will. One of the Indians we had taken in a canoe at Puerto Deseado was known to these who came now, and they brought some gold and gave it to the captain.

On the day following, the cacique or lord came in a canoe and asked the captain to come aboard. He did so, and the chieftain told one of his people to dress the captain. The Indian dressed him with a breastplate and bracelets of gold, lace-shoes ornamented in gold, and on his head he placed a gold crown which was of very delicate leaves of gold.

The captain ordered his men likewise to dress the chieftain, and they dressed him with a green velvet doublet, pink hose, a frock, some *espadrilles* and a velvet cap. Then the chieftain asked to be given the Indian that the captain had, and the latter refused. So the chieftain told him to keep him until the next day, when he would give his weight in gold; but the captain did not wish to wait.

The river here comes from some very high mountains, and this land seems to be the finest there is under the sun. If it is to be colonized, a town of importance should be built. The name of this province is Potonchán. Its people are very adept, for they have many bows and arrows and use swords and shields. Here they brought the captain certain small gold bowls and gold wrist and arm bands. All the men wanted to enter this chieftain's territory, believing they could get more than a thousand pesos in gold from it, but the captain refused.

From here the fleet continued along the coast until sighting a river with two mouths, and it was named the San Bernabé because we reached that place on the day of Saint Barnaby. The interior of this country is very high, and the river is presumed to have much gold. As we sailed along this coast we saw many columns of smoke one after another, set in the manner of signals, and farther on there appeared a town where, according to a brigantine that had gone scouting ahead, many Indians were seen following the ship, and they had bows and arrows, and shields gleaming with gold, and the women wore gold bracelets, necklaces and tassels. This land is low along the coast, and high and mountainous in the interior. We coasted it all that day looking for some cape but were unable to find any.

Within sight of those mountains we found ourselves at the end or tip of an islet situated off the center of the range and about three miles distant from it. We anchored and all went ashore on this islet, which we called Isla de los Sacrificios. It is small, measuring some six miles around. We found several buildings of lime and sand which were very large, and a section of a building of this same material constructed like an old arch that is found in Mérida;[14] also some buildings whose bases were the height of two men, and ten feet wide and very long. Another building made like a tower was fifteen paces wide, and round, and on top was a base of marble[15] like those of Castile, with an animal like a lion on it,[16] also made of marble, and it had a hole in the head in which they put the perfumes. This lion had its tongue hanging out of its mouth, and near it was a stone basin with dried blood that must have been a week old. There were two posts the height of a man, between which were some articles of clothing embroidered like the Moorish silks called *almaizares*. On the other side was an idol with a plumed head, its face turned to the aforementioned stone, and behind this idol was a pile of large stones. Also between the posts, near the idol, were two dead Indians of tender age wrapped in a painted mantle, and behind the clothing lay another two Indians who seemed to have been dead about three days. The first two had been dead some twenty days. Near these dead Indians and the idol were many skulls and bones, and many pine fagots, and some wide stones on which these Indians were killed. And there was also a fig tree and another called *zuara*, which bears fruit.

When the captain and the men had seen all this, the captain wished to be informed whether this was done as a sacrifice, so he sent to the ships for an Indian who was of this province. As he came down the path toward the captain, this Indian fell suddenly in a faint, thinking he was being taken to be killed. Upon reaching the tower he was asked by the captain why this thing was done at the tower, and the Indian replied that it was a form of sacrifice. As we understood it, the victims were beheaded on the wide stone and the blood ran into the basin; then the heart was cut out and burned, and offered to that idol. The thighs and upper part of the arms were cut off and eaten. They did this to their enemies taken in war.[17]

While the captain talked, one of the Christians unearthed two alabaster jars worthy of being presented to the Emperor, which were filled with stones of many kinds.[18] Here we found many fruits, all of them edible.

Next morning we saw many people with banners on the mainland, and the general sent Captain Francisco de Montejo in a boat to find out what they wanted. When he arrived the Indians gave him a great number of colored mantles of various kinds which were very beautiful, and Francisco de Montejo asked them if they had gold to barter, to which they replied that they would bring it in the afternoon, and with this he returned to the ships.[19]

That afternoon a canoe came out with three Indians who brought mantles like the others, and they said they would bring more gold the next day, then they left. On the following morning they appeared on the beach with some white banners and began calling the captain, who went ashore with certain of his men. The Indians brought him many green branches to sit on, and all of them including the captain seated themselves. Then they gave him some pipes with certain perfumes similar to liquidambar and benjamin, and these were followed by many dishes of ground maize, which is the root they make bread from, and very well made cakes and pies of fowl, which were not eaten because it was Friday. Afterward they brought many cotton mantles, finely painted in diverse colors.

We stayed here ten days, and every morning before dawn the Indians were on the beach making arbors so that we might be shaded; and if we did not come quickly they were angry with us, for they were very well disposed toward us, and would embrace us and shower us with attentions. We made one of these, named Ovando, the cacique and gave him authority over the others, and he showed such affection for us that it was something to marvel at.

The captain told them we did not want anything but gold and they replied that they would bring it. Next day they brought gold cast in bars, and the captain told them to bring more of this. On the following day they came with a beautiful gold mask, a figurine of a man with a half mask of gold, and a crown of gold beads with jewels and stones of various colors. Our men asked them for cast gold, and the Indians showed it to them and said it came from the foot of the mountain range, for it was to be found in the rivers that flowed from it, and that an Indian leaving here would arrive there at noon, with time until nightfall to fill a cane tube the thickness of a finger. To gather it they dived to the bottom and brought out handfuls of sand from which they picked the grains of gold, keeping these in the mouth. From this it is believed that there is much gold in this land. These Indians melted it in a vessel wherever they found it, and for bellows they used cane tubes, with which they lighted the fire. We saw it done this way in our presence. The aforesaid chieftain brought our captain a gift of a young man about twenty-two years old, but the captain would not accept him.

These are people who have great respect for their lord, because when they did not provide shade for us quickly, the chieftain would beat them right in front of us. Our captain took their side, prohibiting us from trading our wares for their mantles, and for this reason they came to us on the sly, without any fear—one of them would approach ten Christians with no misgivings—bringing gold and excellent mantles, and we would keep the latter and give the gold to the captain.

There was a very important river here where we had our camp, and our men, seeing the quality of the land, thought to settle by force, which troubled the captain. But it was more his loss than anyone else's that he lacked the enterprise to possess himself of such a land, where it is estimated that in six months no one could have found less than two thousand castellanos, and the king's share would have been more than two thousand; each castellano is worth a ducat and a quarter. And so we left this place very disgruntled by the captain's refusal.

When we were leaving, the Indians embraced us and cried over us. They brought the captain an Indian girl so finely dressed that had she been in brocade she could not have been richer. We believe this land to be the richest in the world in stones of great value, of which many samples were brought back, particularly one that was brought for Diego Velázquez and is presumed because of its workmanship to be worth more than two thousand castellanos. I do not know what more to say of these people, because even discounting much of what was seen it is scarcely believable.

From here we set sail to see if at the end of the mountain range the island terminated. The current was very strong. We sailed in that direction to a place situated below the mountains, which we called Almería after the place in Spain which has abundant foliage. Four canoes or barks came out toward the brigantine that was with us, and they told the ship to proceed because they were pleased at her arrival, and in fact were so insistent about it that they seemed almost to be weeping. But because of the flagship and the other ships which were sailing behind, nothing was done nor did we reach them.

Farther on we met fiercer people, and when they saw the ships twelve canoes with Indians came out from a big town which looked from offshore no lesser than Seville, in size and in the quality of its stone houses and towers. These Indians advanced against us with many bows and arrows, and came straight out to attack us with the intention of taking us prisoner, thinking they were numerous enough to do so. However, on coming closer and seeing how large the ships were, they retreated and began shooting their arrows at us. Seeing this the captain ordered the artillery and crossbows to fire, at which four Indians were killed and a canoe sunk. The rest then fled, not daring to continue the attack. We wanted to enter their town but our captain refused.

Late this day we saw a great miracle. A star appeared over the ship, after the sun had set, and it moved off emitting continuous rays of light until it settled over that large town, leaving a trail in the sky that lasted three hours or more. And we saw other very clear signs too, by which we knew it was God's wish that we settle in that land. On approaching the town, after seeing this miracle, the current was so strong that the pilots would not venture forward but decided to go back, and we turned about. With the current as strong as it was, and the weather not very good, the first pilot pointed the bow seawards. After we had altered course we thought to pass to San Juan, the town of the chieftain named Ovando, but the lateen yard of one of the ships broke and we yawed all the way to port, where we went to take on water.

In two weeks we covered only one hundred and twenty miles from our starting point at the Grijalva River. We reconnoitered another harbor, which we called San Antonio, and which we entered because we were in need of water for the galley. Here we spent a week repairing the broken yard and taking on the necessary water. We could see a town in the distance but the captain would not let us go to it; moreover, one night eight of the ships dragged and collided against the others, damaging some of the rigging. Nevertheless we wanted to stay there, but the captain refused, and on leaving the harbor the flagship hit a shoal and broke a timber. As we saw that she was flooding, we landed thirty of the men, and when they had been landed we saw some ten Indians from the other side, and they carried thirty-three hatchets. They called to the Christians to come near, making signs of peace with the hand, and according to their custom they bled their tongues and spit on the ground as a sign of peace. Two of our Christians went to them, and they asked for the hatchets, which were copper,[20] and the Indians gave them willingly.

Since the flagship was damaged it was necessary to unload everything in her, as well as all the men. And thus at the aforesaid port of San Antonio we built ourselves some straw huts which proved very useful because of the stormy weather. For we had decided to stay there to repair the ship, which took two weeks, during which time the slaves we had brought with us from the island of Cuba went about on land and found many fruits of different kinds, all edible. The Indians of those parts brought cotton mantles and poultry, and twice they brought gold. But out of fear of Christians they did not come confidently, whereas our slaves came and went unafraid to the towns and into the interior.

Here, near a river, we saw that a canoe or bark of Indians had crossed from the other shore bringing a youth, and they were beheading him and taking out his heart before the idol. Also one of the flagship's boats that crossed from the other bank saw a grave in the sand, and on digging they found a young boy and girl who seemed but a short time dead. The bodies wore around their necks some gold chains and pendants that might have weighed about a hundred castellanos. These bodies were wrapped in cotton mantles.

Four of our slaves left camp and went to the town, where the Indians received them kindly, giving them fowl to eat and lodging them. They showed them certain packloads of mantles and much gold, and told them by signs that they had prepared these things to take them the next day to the captain. As they saw it was late and time to return, they told the slaves to return to the ships, giving them each two brace of poultry. Had we had the right kind of captain we should have got more than two thousand castellanos here; but as it was we could not barter our wares, nor settle the land, nor make any headway with him.

When the ship had been repaired we left the harbor and headed for sea. Then one of the ships' mainmasts broke and had to be repaired. Our captain told us not to worry, and although we were gaunt from the hard voyage and scarcity of food, he said he wanted to take us to Potonchán where, as we have said, the Indians killed the Christians brought by Francisco Fernández, captain of the other armada. And so in good spirits we began readying our weapons and setting up the artillery.

We were more than four miles out from the town of Potonchán, so a hundred of us rowed ashore and went to a high tower that was a crossbow's shot inland, where we stayed to wait for day. There were many Indians at the tower, and when they saw us rowing in they gave a shout and got into their canoes, then started circling our boats. Our men fired some artillery shots, whereupon the Indians took to land and abandoned the tower, and we occupied it. Then our boats came back with the rest of the men who had remained aboard ship. When they had all landed, the captain began getting our opinions, and everyone was eager to go in and avenge the death of the aforementioned Christians and burn the town. However, it was later decided not to enter, and we set sail, heading for the town of Lázaro. Here we went ashore for provisions of water, wood, and maize, which is the root mentioned before from which they make bread, and which lasted us the entire crossing.

We crossed from this island bearing for the port of San Cristóbal,[21] and met another ship which Diego Velázquez had sent out for us, thinking we had settled some place. This ship had given up the search, but there were seven more ships that had been looking for us for twelve days. So when Diego Velázquez learned that we had arrived and had not settled, there was trouble about it. He ordered the men to remain in this province, and supplied their living necessities, for he wanted us, God willing, to join the new expedition.

After the voyage here referred to, the captain wrote the Catholic Sovereign that he had discovered another island called Ulúa, in which he found highly civilized people who dress in cotton clothing, live in stone houses, and have law and order and public places devoted to the administration of justice. They worship a large white marble cross with a gold crown on top, and they say that the one who died on it is more magnificent and resplendent than the sun.[22] They are a very skillful people, and their skill is observed in some vases of gold and outstanding cotton mantles with finely woven figures of birds and animals of various kinds. The inhabitants gave these things to the captain, who sent many of them to the Catholic Sovereign, and everyone in general considers them highly skilled works. And it is noteworthy that all the Indians of this island are circumcised, from which it is surmised that Jews and Moors are to be found close by;[23] furthermore it was avowed by these Indians that nearby were people who used ships, clothing and weapons like the Spanish, that a canoe made the trip there in ten days, and that it is a journey of some three hundred miles.

This ends the Itinerary of the Island of Yucatan, which was explored by Juan de Grijalva, captain of the armada of the king of Spain; written by her chaplain.

the chronicle
of
andres de tapia

In spite of the terrible hardships and the disappointments they had suffered, nearly all of the men who had sailed with Grijalva were ready to join the third expedition, which was led by Hernán Cortés. The conquistadors had to buy their own equipment, and they received no pay until such time as the profits or booty from a campaign were divided among the participants; nonetheless they were willing to risk their lives in the most dangerous undertakings. And no matter how often the search for gold and pearls proved fruitless, they felt that the next land, or the next, could very well be the fabled one.

When Cortés was ready to sail in 1519, he had taken on between five and six hundred men. The Mexican scholar Manuel Orozco y Berra estimated that there were 633 when the armada landed on the island of Cozumel. Some of these, however, returned to Cuba after the fleet had reached Veracruz.

Sailing to Yucatan for the first time was a young man of twenty-four who was to distinguish himself in the Conquest. His name was Andrés de Tapia, and he became one of Cortés' most trusted captains, taking a prominent part in all the campaigns. Bernal Díaz del Castillo mentioned him frequently in his *True History of the Conquest of New Spain,* and regarded him as a man of the calibre of Pedro de Alvarado, Cristóbal de Olid, and Gonzalo de Sandoval.

Tapia also acquitted himself creditably as a

writer, and his precise account, written in a vigorous style, contains incidents and observations that are not to be found in any other writings of the Conquest, although several passages of Tapia's narrative are distinctly recognizable in López de Gómara's *General History of the Indies.*

Tapia's chronicle begins with the assembling of the armada in Cuba, and tells of the landing in Cozumel, the founding of Veracruz, Cortés' deliberate sinking of the ships, the battles against the formidable army of Tlaxcala, the entrance into Moctezuma's city of Tenochtitlan, and Moctezuma's imprisonment by Cortés. And although the chronicle ends rather abruptly with the campaign against Pánfilo de Narváez in 1520, we are left with a vivid sense of having participated in all of these extraordinary events.

Relation of some of the things that happened to the Very Illustrious Don Her-
nando Cortés, Marqués del Valle, from the time he determined to go in search
of land on the Mainland of the Ocean Sea, and who left the island of Cuba,
which is in the Indies, and went to the port of Villa Rica de la Veracruz, which
is the first name he gave to a city he settled and founded in what he later called
New Spain.

The aforementioned marqués[1] bore a pennant of blue and white colors charged with a red cross in the center; and its motto read: *Amici, sequamor crucem, et si nos fidem habemus, vere in hoc signo vincemus.*

The marqués left the aforementioned island of Cuba less well provisioned for the voyage than he should have liked. He sailed the length of the island to a port named Macaca, where he had a certain bread made from the roots they call yucca, which are cultivated in mounds of earth and are like turnips. These roots are poisonous and toxic until shredded and cooked in a certain manner, and after they are scraped and crushed and baked they make bread and rea-sonable sustenance.

From this port he dispatched several ships to the point of the island, and sent a ship to another island called Jamaica. This ship carried goods from Castile and some gold to purchase bread and salt pork, which at that time were more plentiful on this island than in Cuba. He also had news of a ship belonging to a resident of Cuba, that was carrying a cargo of this bread and taking it to sell in another part of the island where gold was mined. The marqués ordered some of his company to go after the ship and bring it by force or persuasion to the point of the island where his ships were waiting. It was done just as he or-dered, and in this manner he obtained some provisions for his armada, paying the value of the ship and her cargo with some gold jewelry.

After this the marqués was lost for fifteen or twenty days among some shoals and keys, and finally got to the city of San Cristóbal of the port of Havana, which is on the island of Cuba, where he negotiated with an individual who loaned out the customs revenues of the island, and with another who was col-lector for certain indulgences, receiving bread and salt pork in payment since gold is not mined in this part.

He completed his stores with this and a few other provisions bought later from these residents,[2] which he went to pick up at another port, called Guani-guanico, that is also on the island of Cuba.

At the port of Guaniguanico the Marqués del Valle assembled his men and fleet and distributed what stores there were. He assigned the captains to their ships, giving them instructions as to the command of their men and the course he thought the ships should follow. And as soon as his fleet had cleared the island a storm hit and set the ships adrift, but by following the course he had given them they met at a small island in the sea near the mainland, which the natives call Açuçamil.[3] Of all the ships there was only one missing, which we shall mention later.

This island has about two thousand people, and is some five leagues from end to end, and one and a half or two leagues across. Its people worshipped idols to which they made sacrifices, especially to one that was on a high tower at the edge of the sea. This idol was made of baked clay and was hollow, set with lime against a wall with a secret entrance behind it, where it looked as though a man could enter and invest himself in the idol. This must have been so, because as we later understood it the Indians said that the idol spoke. We found in front of the idol, at the foot of the tower, a cross made of lime that was an *estado*[4] and a half high with a merloned stone wall, where the Indians said they offered quail and the blood of quail, and burned a resin in the manner of incense.[5] They said they did this when they needed rain, whereupon it would rain.

It was understood by signs, or as well as could be understood, that on the mainland across from this island were three or four bearded men like ourselves. The Marqués del Valle gave an Indian some jewelry and articles for barter, with a letter to take to these Christians. With this Indian he sent a brigantine and her captain, and four boats, and because the Indians said the Christians were near the coast he wrote in the letter that the boats would wait for them five days and no longer. They waited a week, and the Indian returned to them and made signs as if to indicate the Christians did not want to come, so they all returned to the island.

Then the marqués ordered all the men aboard and gave the signal to hoist sail. No sooner was this done than the wind suddenly turned so contrary that it was necessary to take to the harbor and disembark again.

On another day the one who writes this was on board ship with several companions when we saw a canoe in the distance. This is the name given to the bark the Indians navigate, which is made of a tree trunk that is hollowed out. Seeing that the canoe was heading for the island, we left the ship and went along the shore concealing ourselves as much as possible until we reached the place where the canoe was landing. We saw three naked men, their parts covered, their hair tied in back like women, and their bows and arrows in their hands. We made signs to them not to be afraid, and one of them came forward but the other two looked afraid and as though they wanted to run back to their boat. The first spoke to them in a tongue we did not understand, and came toward us saying in our Castilian: "Gentlemen, are you Christians, and whose vassals are you?"

We said yes, and that we were vassals of the king of Castile. He was over-joyed and begged us to give thanks to God, and as he did so himself he wept. After we had risen from our prayer we walked toward camp taking his two Indian companions with us. On the way he told us that ten years before while sailing a ship bound from the island of Santo Domingo to some part of the Main near the Pearl Islands, their vessel split open and thirteen of the men took to the skiff. They put a sail on it and ran wherever the wind carried them. The ship sank with the rest of the men aboard, but the Lord guided him and his com-panions to this land, and he had taken great pains to please an Indian lord into whose hands he had fallen. Another Spaniard had taken as wife an Indian woman of rank, and the others had been killed by the Indians. He felt regret over his companion, the other Spaniard, whom he had asked repeatedly to come with him but who refused, pointing out that his nose and ears were pierced, and his hands and face tattooed. For this reason he did not call him when he came away.

The marqués was very pleased with this Spaniard,[6] who served as interpreter. Through him he summoned the Indians of the island and preached to them and made admonitions, begging them to tear down their idols, which they did willingly it seemed. They asked him for images, so he gave them several of Our Lady the Virgin Mary. He also had crosses erected in various parts of the island, and at the tower where the idol was, and he gave the Indians whatever things he had that they seemed to like. Then he left the island, and we learned afterward that whenever a ship passed there the Indians went out to meet it in a canoe, carrying an image of Our Lady, and were given of whatever was on board.

After leaving the island the marqués sailed his armada somewhat close to the mainland, in search of the missing ship, and by following the course he had set [for the voyage from Cuba] he found the ship in a cove. Strung along her rig-ging she had a large number of hare and rabbit skins, and some deer hides both large and small. The Spaniards of this ship said that when they arrived they saw a Spanish dog running on the shore and barking at the ship. The captain and some of the men landed and saw it was a greyhound bitch of good size. She came up and greeted them happily, then returned to the woods and began bringing them rabbits. They hunted with her during the time they were there and had prepared a supply of jerked rabbit and deer meat.

From here the marqués sailed to the point he called De Las Mujeres, because all the idols that were there on some salt flats were fashioned like women, and he was there two days waiting for the weather to clear. While on my ship I saw some of the men catch a fish they call a *tiburón*,[7] which is a kind of shark. It turned out that this fish had eaten all the men's meat rations, which were salt pork and had been tied to lines over the sides of the ships and left to soak. We caught the shark with a hook and some lines drawn through the eye of the hook, but could not use the tackle to raise it without listing the ship, so we killed it in the water, from the skiff, and hauled it on board in pieces. Inside its body were more than thirty sides of pork, a cheese, two or three shoes, and a tin plate. The plate appeared to have fallen overboard with the cheese from the ship commanded by Pedro de Alvarado, whom the marqués had made captain of one of the ships of his armada. There were thirteen ships, and the men in all the armada numbered about five hundred and sixty. The largest of the ships was a hundred *toneles*,[8] and three were of sixty to eighty *toneles*, while the rest were smaller. As for the meat that was taken out of the fish, we ate it because it was more unsalted than the other and tasted better.

From here the fleet sailed to a river that runs through the province of Tabasco. He left the larger ships out at sea and put the men and artillery in the smallest skiffs, with which he started up the river. He was intercepted by certain Indian warriors, and talked to them through the interpreter, promising not to take anything of theirs nor allow any harm to come to them if they received him in peace and listened to the reasons for his being there. They asked for a day's leave to give their reply, and the marqués waited with the men and skiffs on a tiny islet formed by the river.

As it turned out, they had asked for deferment in order to take out their belongings. The next day about ten o'clock the marqués took his men in the boats toward land. The Indians were arrayed for war with their bows and arrows and spears, and began shooting toward the boats. The marqués demanded several times to be received in peace, adding that he begged them insistently because he knew they would otherwise be destroyed; but they refused, and threatened to kill us if we came ashore. And so we landed and their town was taken, and the marqués and his men took quarters in a courtyard where there were rooms used by the people who served the idols.

Upon retiring that night he placed guards in the camp, and in the morning sent three patrols out on some wide roads leading in from villages, to look for fruits and things like plants to eat. The patrols followed the roads as far as some tilled fields belonging to the townspeople. There they encountered some Indians who fought with them, and they brought a few back. At camp these Indians told us how they were gathering to give us battle and fight with all their might to kill and then eat us. Also, as we understood through the Spanish interpreter already mentioned, it was agreed among them that if the Christians defeated them they would thenceforth serve them as lords.

The marqués talked to these Indians and sent them as messengers, assuring their people that if they wished not to fight they would receive very good treatment and be regarded as his children. The messengers did not return with an answer, but some warriors moving about in the canals and estuaries were saying to our men that in three days all the warriors in the land would be gathered and would eat us; and so they gathered and appeared one morning.

The marqués and all his men heard mass and went out against them. Since the land is crossed with canals, and there are deep estuaries along the route we were to take, the marqués, with ten of the thirteen horses he had, went along the left of the estuary to see where he could find cover of trees from which to attack the enemy from the rear or the flank. The foot soldiers headed straight forward over the canals, and as the Indians knew the terrain and are more nimble than the Spaniards, they crossed over quickly, and from the other side shot many arrows and spears at us, and stones from slings. Although we killed some of them with certain field pieces we had, and with the crossbows, they did us much damage because they were so numerous. We found ourselves in great danger and were out of touch with the marqués, for with so many dangerous crossings he had not found the way to reach the enemy.

Just as the Indians had us foot soldiers surrounded on all sides, there appeared at their rear a man on a dapple-gray horse, and the Indians began to flee and leave us alone a while, thanks to the damage the rider was doing them. We, thinking it was the marqués, rallied ourselves and killed some of the enemy, but the horse did not appear again for the moment. Turning back on us again, the enemy began to abuse us as before, and again the horseman appeared and attacked them, closer to us this time so that we all saw him. Once more we charged and the horse disappeared as before. And still he came again, which made three times that he appeared and that we saw him, believing him to be one of the marqués' company.[9]

The marqués and his nine horsemen returned to our rear and told us how they had been able to cross over to us. We told him how we had seen one of the horsemen and he said: "Onward companions, for God is with us." Once he was out of the canals he charged into the enemy, the foot soldiers behind him, and in this way we routed them. Many were killed and the rest fled to take refuge in the impassable parts of the canals.

The marqués returned to camp with his men, and sent some of the prisoners we had taken to tell the enemy that he regretted the losses he had caused them and would still regard them as friends if they wished to come give their fealty. Then certain dignitaries came, bringing fowl that we call here Indies hens, and fruits of the land and other provisions, and they gave fealty to the marqués. He begged them to remove their idols and put crosses in their place, and this was done insofar as we could see. The lords sent fruits to the ships, and maize, which is a grain they nourish on, and gave the marqués twenty of the women they kept as slaves, to grind bread for us. Then, after the Palm Sunday procession, and mass in the courtyard of the idols, we boarded our ships. We learned from the Indians that there had been as many as forty-eight thousand of them fighting us, for their way of counting is by eight thousands[10] and they said they had assembled a full six times eight thousand.

On leaving here we had good weather down the coast to the port of San Juan, as it is called by the Spaniards, which we reached on Good Friday. The marqués took most of the men ashore, leaving watches aboard, and in the name of our lord the king of Castile he founded a city to which he gave the name of Villa Rica de la Veracruz.

Here some Indians of this region came to speak to him, but our Spanish interpreter did not understand them because the language is very different from that spoken where he had been. They gave us things to eat, fruits and maize bread such as they eat themselves. Of the twenty Indian women that had been given him, the marqués had divided some among certain gentlemen, and two of them were in the same company as I was. When certain of these Indians happened to pass, one of the women spoke to them, so we found she spoke two languages and our Spanish interpreter could understand her. We learned from her that as a child she had been stolen by some traders and taken to be sold in the land of Tabasco where she was brought up.[11]

And so we had another interpreter, through whom the marqués summoned several of the Indian dignitaries in the vicinity and asked them about the lord or lords of that land. They told him that all of it pertained to a great lord named Moctezuma.[12] Each town had its lord or governor, but all of these served him and were vassals of his. He and his ancestors, as newcomers to this land he ruled, had come in the guise of religion and had settled on an island where the city of Mexico now stands, and which was surrounded by water and deep canals, so that in some parts they planted in a certain fashion.[13] As they gained power they made war on the natives of the land, and from those who surrendered peaceably, without offering resistance, they took certain tribute and *parias*,[14] whereas those they defeated by strength of arms and who refused to give themselves peaceably, they took as slaves, regarding everything they possessed as their own. Besides making use of their persons, their wives, and children, anything that was found to have been left in their homes was taken by the collectors who came for the revenues of the lords.

On this coast there were several such towns and provinces. When the marqués was informed of this he endeavored to speak with some of the natives living in this subjection, and they complained to him and asked for his help. He offered to do everything in his power for them, saying he would not allow them to receive harm.

He sent several light ships to search the coast and see if there was any harbor. At this the Indians stationed there by Moctezuma's orders went into service as his messengers, going and coming in a very short time although it is seventy leagues from the port of San Juan to the city of Mexico where Moctezuma was. He ordered that the marqués be given a present of gold and silver which included a gold disk and another of silver, each the size of a cartwheel, though not very thick, which they say were made to represent the sun and the moon.

The marqués gave certain of his own garments, and caps and hose, and necklaces of colored glass beads to be taken to Moctezuma. He also gave what he had to the messengers and lords who came to see and speak with him.

Here he learned of a mutiny planned by some of his men, and had certain gentlemen of his company arrested and placed under guard in the ships, then taken to a small harbor ten leagues down the coast, which was a better place for a Spanish settlement because there were hills and good streams nearby. The marqués and the rest of the men went by land, and on the way they found a city that also complained to him of the abuses of Moctezuma and his collectors. He told these people that although he regarded Moctezuma as a friend he would not allow him to abuse them nor any others who wished to be his friends. And so he sent word to Moctezuma by his servants, begging him not to do injury to the natives of the land.

Arriving at the harbor where the ships had been sent, the marqués established the Spanish town he had founded [first] at the port of San Juan.[15] At half a league and a league from here he found Indian towns that also complained to him of the abuses they suffered from certain collectors who had just come to ask for tribute and order them to do things they were not accustomed to. The marqués told them what he had said on other occasions, assuring them that he would be their friend and would not allow harm or injury to be done them. With this support they decided to strike at the collectors and the people who accompanied these, and they bound and cudgeled many of them. Some fled to where the marqués was, and since he was not averse to the discord between them he saved them from being killed but did not entirely take over authority. Later he had several of them freed and sent to Moctezuma to tell him that he had arrived in this land and found people of Moctezuma's whom the natives had tried to kill, and he had protected them; also that he had heard they had come to ask for tribute when there was no obligation to pay it, but that as a newcomer to the land he did not know which of the two was right or wrong and was only informing him of what had happened. In this way all these people revolted against Moctezuma and became the good friends of the marqués and the Christians.

When the marqués saw that among his men were persons who did not bear him good will, and that these, together with some others who showed a desire to

return to Cuba, represented a goodly number, he spoke with several of the ships'
mates, asking some to scuttle their ships and others to come and tell him that
their vessels were unseaworthy. When they did so he said to them: "Then if they
are not seaworthy bring them to the coast and smash them, that we may be free
of their maintenance."[16]

And so they scuttled six or seven ships, and in one of the others, which was
the flagship he had sailed, the marqués loaded all the gold and other things of
that land he had been given, and sent them to the king of Castile, our lord, who
then was king of Romans and emperor elect.[17] There were Spanish persons
in the marqués' company who had set in motion a plan to steal one of the small
ships and go out to rob what was being taken to the king. On learning of it the
marqués arrested some of them and executed the guiltiest. Others he pardoned,[18] and had it said in his camp that he wanted to send the best remaining
ship to Cuba, on which the men who did not want his company would be permitted to leave. And so some of the men came to ask permission to go, and he
gave them permission, saying: "Because I am determined to make my way in
this land or die here, all the rest of the ships are to be scuttled, but for those
who do not share my views there remains this ship on which they may leave."
Then he scuttled them, and after they were scuttled he sank the remaining one
also. And thus it was made evident who were the ones that did not want his
company.

Now, there was one Diego Velázquez who was governor of the island of Cuba,
and who had been sent there by the Admiral Diego Colón[19] as his lieutenant
governor. Diego Velázquez, with the help of the Marqués del Valle and others,
had conquered this island and then negotiated in Castile with members of the
king's council to obtain a royal concession, which they gave him, and which carried the order to govern the island and not cede it to the admiral. This Diego
Velázquez, who became wealthy with the government of Cuba, sought the
friendship of Don Juan de Fonseca, Bishop of Burgos, who was then president
of the Council of the Indies, and also designated Indian towns for the use of certain members of the king's council. Velázquez' wife had died, the bishop wanted
to marry him to a relative of his, and it had been discussed and agreed, so Diego
Velázquez believed he had great influence in the royal council.

When he learned that a certain Francisco Hernández de Córdoba and another
resident of the city of Trinidad, which is on the island of Cuba, had sent a ship
of theirs to cross over to some islands called the Guanahí[20] with the intention of
bringing workers for the mines, and that a storm had carried them[21] to a part of
the mainland where they discovered populated land on a part of the coast
below the island of Cozumel, Diego Velázquez decided to send an armada by

the same route the other ship had taken. As captain he sent a relative of his, or one who claimed to be, whose name was Juan de Grijalva.

Juan de Grijalva landed with his men where the other ship had been, and there they fought with the natives of the land. One of his men by the name of Juan de Guitalla was killed, and the captain was hit on the mouth by an arrow, losing a tooth. At great risk they boarded the ships again and sailed down the coast, but on seeing that it was populated the captain did not venture to stay. While this captain was away there were talks between Diego de Velázquez and the present Marqués del Valle, who was then a resident of the island of Cuba, to the effect that the marqués was to go in search of Grijalva, for which purpose they began enlisting men. As Diego Velázquez saw that the marqués was liberally investing his own fortune and enlisting more men than seemed necessary, he grew wary and tried to prevent the marqués' departure. The marqués was well liked by the men who had joined him, and Diego Velázquez was powerless to stop him. And so the marqués sailed from the port of the city of Santiago, Cuba, not as well provisioned as was necessary, and, as we have said, went the length of the island gathering supplies, ships, and men.

Diego Velázquez did not admit publicly that the marqués was embarking against his will, nor did the marqués make public that he was an enemy of Velázquez, though he would say to his friends: "Where would be the justice in turning over to Diego Velázquez the land I discover, after I have spent a fortune handsome enough to retire to Spain, and after the peril and hardship of going out in its quest."

For this reason Diego Velázquez made it appear that he had a claim to the marqués' enterprise, though he had actually not spent much on it. In fact when I arrived at the Cuban port of the city of Santiago and told Diego Velázquez that I was there to serve him and wished to go on the expedition with the Marqués del Valle, he said to me: "I do not know what Cortés' intentions are toward me, but I think they are bad, because he has spent everything he had and is in debt, and has gathered in his service as many attendants as if he were one of the lords in Spain. Nevertheless I shall be pleased to have you go in his company, and since it is no more than two weeks since he left this port you will soon overtake him. Also I shall be pleased to aid you and any others who wish to go."

Several of us joined together, and his aid consisted in granting each of us an order of payment for forty pesos, redeemable in equipment at a shop he owned. In spite of his saying I was his nephew and making me all kinds of promises, I received less for the forty pesos gold than my companions and I got for ten pesos at other shops. And yet he made each of us sign a note for the forty pesos and we signed them and afterward paid them.

What I have said in this chapter is by way of explaining why an armada of

Spaniards was later sent against the marqués and his companions. It should also be known to whoever may read this that when the ship was leaving for Spain with the things we had collected up to that time, we joined unanimously to tell the marqués what we feared might happen as a result of the confederacy and friendship between Diego Velázquez and the Bishop of Burgos, and by mutual agreement we wrote a letter to His Majesty the Emperor. It was signed by almost all the marqués' company, and began by giving an account of events to date. We then went on to swear in the interest of the royal service that inasmuch as we believed that Diego Velázquez, through the favor of the Bishop of Burgos, would obtain or might already have secured from His Majesty some decree that would prove detrimental to the royal patrimony, asking for the government or other prerogatives in this territory, and that His Majesty might grant it in the belief that the same conditions prevailed here as in other parts of the Indies heretofore discovered, we would nevertheless obey as royal command any letters or decrees of His Majesty or the royal council that were presented to us. As to the execution of the decree, we hereby petitioned, and would continue to petition until receiving assurance that His Majesty was informed of our account and of how we had labored and would yet labor in his service, that nothing be done contrary to what we were writing him, and that His Majesty not grant favors without knowing what he was granting. Furthermore, we were ready to die holding the land in his royal name until we saw a reply to this letter we were writing him.

After the ship had left for Spain there was fighting among the natives, and when the people of a town called Tizapacinga did not cease their attacks on the others when the marqués had sent word for them to cease, he went with some of his men to punish them, and although they took up arms against him he put down the revolt. Then he left the number of men he thought necessary for the safety of the city he had established, and with all the rest started inland along the route he was told led to Moctezuma's city.

By this time the Indian vassals in Moctezuma's service had left so they would not have to show the way, and the natives of this region falteringly led us as best they could. For twenty leagues or more after leaving the territory of these people who had become our allies,[22] we crossed uninhabited badlands where there were salt lakes and where we suffered from hunger, but more from thirst, until we reached a town called Zacotlán. The marqués asked the lord of this town whether he was a vassal of Moctezuma, to which he replied: "And who can there be who is not a vassal of that lord?"

The Marqués del Valle had crosses erected everywhere that he stopped, and after doing so here, he left ahead of the rest of the company to reconnoiter the land, taking eleven horsemen and a few of the swiftest foot soldiers. At the rise of a hill he sent word to the captain of the foot soldiers to come up quickly, while he and the horsemen advanced toward eight Indians who were there spying. As the Spaniards tried to capture one of them to find out where they were from, the Indians with two blows of their swords killed two horses, and also wounded two Spaniards, and so defended themselves that not one of them was taken alive.

There the marqués waited for us because it was already late, and we arrived at sunset and heard what I have just told. The marqués stationed his sentries and slept there that night. Next morning he broke camp, and at about eight o'clock there came toward us such a great number of warriors that I am certain they were more than a hundred thousand, although according to some opinions they were many more. Some of them were waiting for us in the deep parts of the ravines that crossed the way, and in trying to get through we would find ourselves in their midst. We were helped some by our Indian friends who came with us from the seacoast, of whom we have already spoken. The marqués and the horsemen always fought in the vanguard, and he would return from time to time to keep his men in formation, making them keep closed ranks. There were Indians who would attack a horse and rider to seize the horseman's lance.

Fighting in this manner, the marqués that day reached an idol house that had two or three little buildings around it, where the Spaniards put their baggage, going out to fight in the order the marqués commanded. We were at this hill eighteen days, and the order of battle was as follows:

The Indians usually came out to fight with us in the morning, sometimes later, and at other times at sunset, and after they had done this the first three days they decided to find out what damage they were doing us by coming to speak with the marqués. They told him they regretted very much that we were being troubled in their country, for it was not their wish, but the people fighting us were of another nation who lived in some mountains which they pointed out to us, and though they had asked these people not to fight us they had not listened. These [spies] usually came to us in this manner and brought maize bread and some poultry and cherries, and then they would ask: "What damage have those wretches done you?" The marqués would thank them and tell them we were suffering no harm at all but that he was sorry for the injuries received by the others. With this [the spies] would leave, and we could see them mingling with the people who were fighting us.[23]

Therefore they tried their fortune at all hours of the day, and seeing that this did not profit them in the least they attacked our camp several times by night, but were beginning to flag a little. The marqués, seeing they were weakening, went out against them in various directions where we had seen hearth fires at night that might be towns, and we always found towns and people in them to fight. They also came looking for us, though not so often.

It happened that at the time we arrived there the marqués was taken with a fever and decided to purge himself. He had with him a lump of physic pills he had had made in Cuba, but since there was no one who knew how to melt it and make the pills, he broke some off and swallowed it in hard pieces. Next day as he was beginning to purge we saw a great number of warriors coming, and he got on his horse and went after them and fought all day. At night we asked him how he had made out with the purgative and he said he had forgotten he had taken it, so the next day he purged as though he had just taken the purgative.

The marqués was quartered in the idol tower, as we have said, and sometimes at night during his turn to sleep he looked out from there in all directions for signs of hearth fires. He saw at a distance of more than four leagues, near some rocky hills and among thickets, a great number of hearths which led him to think there were many people there. Next day he divided his men, leaving in camp those he thought necessary, and two or three hours after dark he began feeling his way toward the cliffs, because it was a dark night.

About a league from camp the horses were struck with something like gripes and fell to the ground where we could not budge them. When the first one fell and they told the marqués, he said: "Then have his owner go back to camp with him." The second time he said the same, and some of the Spaniards began saying to him: "Sire, this is a bad sign, and it would be better to wait for daylight; then we can see our way." But he said: "Why do you heed omens? I shall not give up the march, because I sense that much good will come of it this night, and the devil is trying to obstruct it with these difficulties." Then his horse fell like the others, and we halted a while. Leading the eight horses on foot, we walked until we lost our sense of the direction of the cliffs and got into some rough country with rocks and gullies, and guided by a small light in some hut we went toward it and took two women. Some Spaniards the marqués had stationed on a path took two Indians, and these led us toward the cliffs, which we reached at dawn. The horses were well now, and when we came to a town near the cliffs, called Zimpanzingo, the people were taken unawares because we had not come by the road. The marqués commanded that no Indian be killed nor anything of theirs taken, and as they came out of their houses he made signs for them not to be afraid, at which they hesitated somewhat, for they were still in flight.

When the sun started coming out the marqués went to a hill to survey the land, and saw all of the city of Tlaxcala, which was visible from there, and he called the Spaniards and said to them: "See what little object there would have been in killing the few Indians in this town, when over there must be a multitude of people."

Three or four days before this, certain Indians had come to the camp bringing five other Indians to the marqués, and saying to him: "If you be a god that eats meat and blood, eat these Indians and we shall bring you more. And if you be a kind god, here are plumes and incense. And if you be a man, here are turkeys and bread and cherries."

The marqués said to them as always: "My companions and I are men like yourselves. And it is my hope that you will not lie to me, for I shall always tell you the truth. So in truth I beg you not to be foolhardy or fight, that no harm shall come to you."

Later in the day, when they had left, a great number of people were sighted crossing along a hill, and after a while fifteen or twenty Indians came to the marqués in the company of some messengers, saying they had come to see how we fared and what we planned to do.

The marqués said to them through our interpreters: "I have warned you in speaking to me not to lie to me, for I never lie to you. But now you come as spies and speak falsely." One by one he took them aside and they confessed it was so, and that on this night a great number were to attack and kill us. He had the hands cut off some of them and sent them on their way, saying he would like-wise to all who were found to be spies, and that he was setting out to fight their people.

He had his men form ranks, then ordered bell straps harnessed to the horses. Night was falling when he set out in the direction in which he had seen the people crossing. On hearing the din, and after having seen their spies with their hands cut off, they began to flee and the marqués pursued them for two hours in the night. This episode should have gone before.

The Indians had seen the good turn we did in not killing them, so later when the marqués sent for their lords, and waited with all his men by a large fountain in the town, some of them came bringing quantities of food. They said they were very grateful for having received no harm. From then on they would serve us in whatever way was ordered of them, and would summon the lords of all the land.

The marqués made it clear that although they brought him food he knew they were the ones who were fighting us, but he forgave them everything, and begged them to be friends in order to avoid further harm to themselves, since they could see how little harm they did us. He then returned to his camp, and ordered that henceforth no harm be done any Indian.

Reaching camp in good spirits, he said: "I believe, thanks be to God, that we have today ended the war with this province, and that from now on they will be our friends. It is time to go on to the land of that great lord we have been told about."

He called for an Indian of rank who had come with us from the coast as captain of a company of warriors. Teuche, as he was called, was a judicious man who, according to what he told us, was practiced in Indian wars. He said to the marqués: "Sire, do not trouble yourself going on from here. As a youth I went to Mexico, and am experienced in the wars. I know that you and your companions are men and not gods; that you hunger and thirst and weary as men do. Let it be known to you that beyond this province lie so many people, that one hundred thousand men will fight you now, and when these are dead or vanquished, that many again will come forward, and again and again by the hundred thousand, and you and yours, though you be invincible, will die wearied of fighting. For as I have told you, I know you are men, and all I can say is that you should think carefully about what I have said. But if you determine to die, then I shall go with you."

The marqués thanked him and told him that in spite of everything he wanted to go on, for he knew that God, Who made heaven and earth, would help us, and he too must believe this.

Before this there had been talk among the Spaniards, and they had been saying that we should ask the marqués not to go on but to return to the coast, where little by little an understanding could be reached with the Indians, and time would tell what was best to do. Some of the men had already spoken of this in secret to the marqués.

One night when he was in the idol tower, around which were some huts used by the Spaniards, he heard a few of the soldiers talking inside one of the huts, and they were saying: "If the captain wants to be a madman and go where he will be killed, let him go alone. Why should we follow him?" Others said that if they followed him it would be like Pedro Carbonero who went into Moorish territory to make a raid and was kept there with all his men and killed.

The marqués had two of his friends called, and said to them: "Listen to what they are saying here. Whoever dares say it, dares carry it out. Therefore we should make haste to go on to the land of Moctezuma."

There came Indians of Tlaxcala, the province we were then in, and they said to him: "We have done all we could to kill you and your companions, but our gods are worthless to help us against you. We have determined to be your friends and serve you, and because in this province we are surrounded on all sides by our enemies we beg you to protect us against them, and to come to our city of Tlaxcala to rest from the labors we have given you."

The marqués had crosses put in the camp and the idol tower and other places, then we broke camp and marched toward the city of Tlaxcala. There we were quartered in some temple rooms, and the marqués had markers set out to indicate our limits, and ordered us not to cross or leave them. And in truth we obeyed him, for even to go to a gully which was a stone's throw from there we asked his permission.

On all sides of their province the Tlaxcalans were bounded by their enemies, the vassals of Moctezuma, and others who were his allies. Every time Moctezuma prepared for a feast and sacrifice to his idols, he sent his men out to fight this province and capture people for sacrifice, since the Tlaxcalans also killed many of their enemies. But it seemed very certain that if Moctezuma and his vassals and allies wanted to join forces in attacking this province, they could quickly crush it and put an end to the war between them. Therefore I [later] asked Moctezuma and some of his captains why, with these enemies completely surrounded, they did not finish with them in a day, and they answered: "We could easily do so. But then we would have nowhere to train our youths except in far places. Also we wish to have people at hand to sacrifice to our gods."[24]

In this province they had no salt, but had to barter dearly for it with their neighboring enemies. Nor did they have gold, nor cotton clothing, except by barter. The marqués and his men stayed here a while, during which time the natives came to live with the Spaniards and showed that the friendship was a true one.

Whenever the marqués spoke with them he urged them to give up their idols. They would reply that as time passed they would see our way of life and better understand our natures and the things we told them, and might become Christians. The marqués had crosses placed wherever he thought they would be prominent, and with the Indians' permission made a church in the house of a principal idol, where he put images of Our Lady and several saints. Sometimes he preached to the Indians, and they favored our way of life, many more coming each day to live with us.

The marqués left Tlaxcala after gathering as much information as he could of the territory ahead, and the Indians said they would go with him to show the way as far as they knew it. They also said that about four leagues from here was an enemy city called Cholula which was a state in itself and a friend and ally of Moctezuma. And so the Spaniards set out for this city accompanied by forty thousand warriors who by order of the marqués marched at a distance from us.

The morning of the day we arrived at the city of Cholula, ten or twelve thousand men in squadrons came out to meet us, bringing maize bread and turkeys. Each squadron advanced toward the marqués to bid him welcome and then withdrew. The Cholulans earnestly begged the marqués not to allow the Tlaxcalans to enter their territory, so the marqués ordered them to go back, but the Tlaxcalans said: "Beware of the people of this city, who are traders and not men of war, and who have one heart and show another, resorting to trickery and lies. We dislike having to leave you, for we gave ourselves as your friends." In spite of this the marqués ordered that all their men were to go back, but that if some of the notables wished to stay they could be quartered outside the city with a few men to serve them, and that is the way it was done.

As we entered the city the rest of the men came out in their squadrons, greeting the Spaniards they met, who were marching in formation. After the squadrons came all the ministers who served the idols. They were dressed in sleeveless robes, some of which were closed in front like surplices, with heavy cotton fringe at the edges, and other kinds of dress. Many of them were playing flutes and trumpets, and carrying certain idols that were covered, and many incense burners. They approached the marqués first and then the other men, perfuming them with a resin[25] they burned in the censers.

In this city they had a principal god who at one time had been a man. They called him Quetzalcoatl. He is said to have founded this city, and to have commanded them not to kill men, but instead to build edifices to the creator of the sun and the heavens, in which to offer him quail and other things of the hunt. They were to wish no harm and do no harm to one another. Quetzalcoatl is supposed to have worn a white vesture like a monk's tunic, and over it a mantle covered with red crosses. They had certain green stones there, one of them a monkey's head, which they said had belonged to this man, and they regarded them as relics.

The marqués and his men stayed here several days, and he sent certain men as volunteers to explore a volcano we could see on a high ridge five leagues away, and which gave out much smoke. They were to look out from there in all directions and bring back news of the disposition of the land.[26]

Certain persons of rank came to this city as messengers of Moctezuma and made their speeches over and over again. Sometimes they said there was no reason for us to go on, and where would we go anyway, since they had no provisions for us to eat where they lived. At other times they told us Moctezuma said that if we went to see him he would die of fright. Also they said there was no road by which to go. When they saw that the marqués was undisturbed by all this, they made the people of the city tell us that where Moctezuma lived there were great numbers of lions and tigers and other wild beasts that he let loose any time he wanted to, and that they were enough to tear us to pieces and eat us.

When they saw that none of this served to deter us, Moctezuma's messengers plotted with the people of the city to kill us. The way they proposed to do it was to take us to the left of the road leading to Mexico, where there were dangerous crossings formed by the waters flowing from the ridge where the volcano was. Since the earth there is soft and sandy, a little water can make a big ravine, and some of them are more than a hundred *estados* deep. They are also so narrow that there is timber tall enough to make bridges across the ravines, and these exist, because we later saw them.

As we were preparing to leave, an Indian woman of this city of Cholula, the wife of one of the notables, told the woman who was our interpreter along with the Christian, that she would like her to stay there because she was very fond of her and would be grieved to see her killed. Then she told her what they were plotting and thus the marqués learned of it and delayed his departure two days. He repeatedly told the Cholulans that it caused him no surprise or anger when men fought, even if they fought against him; but that he would be greatly displeased if they told him lies, so he warned them not to lie in their dealings with him, nor to resort to treachery. They assured him they were his friends and always would be, and that they would never lie to him. Then they asked him when he wished to leave, and he said that on the following day. They said they wanted to assemble many men to send with him, but the marqués said he wanted only some slaves to carry the Spaniards' baggage.[27] They still insisted on giving him warriors, and he refused, repeating that he wanted only enough men to carry the baggage.

Next day there came unbidden many men with weapons of the kind they use, saying they were slaves and bearers, though it later turned out that they were among the bravest of their warriors. The marqués said he wished to take his leave of all the lords, and asked that they be summoned. There was no one lord of this city, but only captains of the republic, since it was in the nature of a dominion and they governed themselves in that way. The dignitaries then arrived, and the marqués took about thirty of them, those who looked most important, into a courtyard of the house where he was lodged, and he said to them: "In everything have I spoken the truth to you, and I have given orders to all the Christians of my company to do you no harm, and no harm has been done you, yet with evil intention you asked that the Tlaxcalans be kept from entering your territory. And although you have not given me to eat as you should, I have not allowed so much as a chicken to be taken from you. Also I have asked you not to lie to me. But in payment for these good deeds you have conspired to kill me and my companions, bringing men to fight me as soon as we have reached the bad terrain over which you plan to lead us. For this wickedness you shall all die, and as a sign that you are traitors I shall destroy your city so that no edifice remains. It is needless for you to deny this, for I know it as well as I am saying it to you."

They were astonished, and kept looking at one another. There were guards to keep them from escaping and there were also men guarding the people that would carry our baggage, who were outside in the large courtyards of the idols. The marqués then said to these dignitaries: "I wish to have you tell me the truth, though I already know it, so that these messengers and all the rest may hear it from your mouths and not think that I have accused you falsely."

Five or six were taken aside, and each confessed separately, without torture of any kind, that it was as the marqués had said. When he saw that they were in agreement with one another he brought everyone together again and they all confessed that it was so, and said among themselves: "He is like our gods, who know all; there is no use in denying it to him."

The marqués had Moctezuma's messengers brought, and said to them: "These people wanted to kill me, and they say that Moctezuma was behind it, but I do not believe it because I hold him as friend and know that he is a great lord, and a lord does not lie. I believe they wanted to do me this injury by treachery, as scoundrels that they are, and people who have no lord; and for this they shall die. But you have nothing to fear, for besides being messengers you are the envoys of that lord I regard as friend, who I have reason to believe is very good, and nothing will I hear to the contrary."

Then he ordered most of those lords killed, leaving a few of them fettered, and ordered the signal given the Spaniards to attack the men in the courtyards and kill them all, and so it was done. They defended themselves the best they could, and tried to take the offensive, but since they were walled inside the courtyards with the entrances guarded, most of them died anyway.

This done, the Spaniards and Indians in our company went out in squads to different parts of the city, killing warriors and burning houses. In a short time a number of the Tlaxcalans arrived, and they looted the city and destroyed everything possible, making off with a great amount of plunder.

Certain priests of the devil climbed to the top of the principal idol's tower and would not give themselves up but stayed there to be burned, lamenting and complaining to their idol how wrong of him it was to forsake them. So everything possible was done to destroy this city, but the marqués ordered us to refrain from killing women and children. The destruction took two days, during which many of the inhabitants went to hide in the hills and fields, and others took refuge in surrounding enemy country.

At the end of two days the marqués ordered the destruction ceased, and within another two or three days, it later appeared, many of the natives of the city must have gathered together, for they sent word to the marqués begging for pardon and for permission to reoccupy the city, offering themselves under protectorate of the Tlaxcalans. The marqués pardoned them and told them that their intended treachery had caused him to mete that punishment and aroused the desire to wipe out their city without leaving a trace. In the future he would do thus wherever he found that they had evil intentions against him while pretending good will, for he considered it more wicked than if they came right out to fight him. And so the city was reoccupied and he was promised their friendship from then on.

From here he despatched Moctezuma's messengers, whom he had treated always with great honor, sending word to Moctezuma of what he had done in Cholula and the reason for it; also that the Cholulans had accused Moctezuma of being implicated, which the marqués did not credit, and he would soon be on his way there. After the messengers had gone the marqués left the city, taking the route thought best by the men who had gone to the volcano.

The first night he slept four leagues from Cholula at the foot of the volcano, and next day ascended the ridge. At the top[28] he found people who came out to meet him and bring food, and some shelter of straw huts the Indians had made for them to rest in, and there he slept that night. The mountains were heavily wooded and he thought there might be many people, so he took his men to an open space. There he summoned the people's leaders and captains and said to them: "Let it be known that these men who accompany me do not sleep by night; if they sleep at all it is a little during the day. By night they are at arms, and whoever they see afoot or entering where they are, they kill at once. And I am powerless to prevent it, therefore make it known to all your people and tell them that after the sun sets no one is to come where we are or he will die, for I should be sorry for any that might be killed."

That night he ordered all his men to be on the alert, and placed sentinels and listening posts. Some Indians came to spy on what we were doing and the sentries killed them, and not a word was said of this by our side or theirs.

Next day the marqués descended the ridge, and four leagues from there he found a large town on the shore of a great lake. There he took quarters and they made straw houses where his men could be sheltered together, and brought much food. The marqués spoke with the lord and some of the nobles of this town, who said they were vassals of Moctezuma. In secret they complained to him about Moctezuma, saying he committed many grave abuses in demanding tribute and things which they were neither obliged to do nor pay.

Here some messengers of Moctezuma came with their embassy of persuading the marqués not to go to see Moctezuma, and he told them he would not fail to see him because he wanted very much to speak with him and had made the journey for no other reason than to meet and speak with him. These Indians made him believe that there was no way to go except by water, and that they made the passage in very small canoes, so he decided to make some barks. But in the four days he was there he learned that there was a road, though it was dangerous because one had to cross the water over a stone causeway that had wooden bridges at intervals.

The marqués and his men left this town, where he had as usual warned the

Indians not to come near the Spaniards' quarters after sundown, and went to spend the night in another town on the shore of this lake. There some spies approached in small canoes, and our sentries shot blindly at them with their crossbows, so they did not come ashore. Next day the marqués and his men began following a narrow stone causeway that entered the lake and had bridges at intervals, as we have said. He spent the night in a town built on the water, taking precautions against any attempt to cut off the bridges or causeway, and every two hours or so messengers arrived.

When day came he continued on the causeway until reaching land, and went to spend the night ten miles from Mexico in a town on the edge of a salt lake, where he stayed one day. It was the town of a brother of Moctezuma, and from the time that we entered Moctezuma's territory we were always given of whatever food they had.

From this town the marqués and his men followed another causeway that crossed the lake, all the way to Mexico, and Moctezuma came out to meet him, after first having sent a nephew with many men and provisions. Moctezuma came down the center of the street, and all the rest of the people along the sides of the walls, according to the custom. He had the marqués lodged near the chamber of the idols, in a courtyard whose halls were more than large enough to take care of all the marqués' men and many of the Tlaxcalan and Cholulan Indians who had come with the Spaniards to serve them.

A short time before the marqués entered Mexico he learned that the Spaniards he had left on the coast had gone to the town of a vassal of Moctezuma to ask to be given food, and that the townspeople had fought them and killed a horse and a Spaniard, wounding most of the others. After resting from his march into Mexico, but still apprehensive for his life and that of his men, he was walking about his quarters when he saw a doorway that seemed recently closed off with stone and mortar. He had it opened and on entering found a large number of rooms, some of them containing great quantities of gold in jewels and idols, and magnificent featherwork. He had gone in with two of his servants and came out again without having touched anything.

Then in the morning he alerted his men, fearing it was planned to remove one or two of the bridges over which we had entered so that we could not escape with our lives. He went to Moctezuma's palace, where there were many things worthy of notice, and ordered his men to follow him in twos and fours. Moctezuma met him and took him into a hall where he had his dais. About thirty of us Spaniards went in with him, while the rest stayed at the door to the building. In a courtyard of this building the marqués said to Moctezuma through the interpreters: "You well know that I have always held you as a friend, and have begged you through your messengers to deal honestly with me. I have never deceived you in anything, but now I learn that the Spaniards I left on the coast have been ill-treated by your people, who have killed one of them and wounded many of the others. Some of the Indians captured by the Spaniards say that this was done by your command, so in order that I may make an investigation you must go as my captive to my quarters where you will be attended and well treated. In the event that you are in any way guilty I shall look after your person as though you were my brother. I must do this to you because if I should overlook the matter it would anger the men who are with me; they would say I was indifferent to their being ill-treated. Therefore command your people not to be alarmed by this, and be advised that you will pay with your life for any disturbance, for it is in your power to allay it."

Moctezuma was greatly perturbed, and said with all the gravity imaginable: "My person is not one to be taken captive, and even if I should consent, my people would not tolerate it." And so they disputed for more than four hours, until finally it was agreed that Moctezuma would go with the marqués, so he took him to his quarters and put him under the guard of a captain. By day and by night there were Spaniards constantly in Moctezuma's presence, and he never told his people he was a prisoner but continued despatching matters pertaining to the government of his country. Often the marqués went to speak with him, and through the interpreter would beg him not to be pained at being there, and gave him all the gifts he could. One day he said to Moctezuma: "These Christians are troublesome; in going about this house they have discovered a certain amount of gold and taken it. Do not be vexed by it."

Moctezuma answered generously: "That belongs to the gods of our people. Leave the things like plumes and other pieces that are not gold, and take the gold. I shall give you all that I have. For you must know that from time immemorial my ancestors believe that a people from whom we all descend came to this land from very far, and they came in ships, then went away again leaving the land populated. They said they would return, and we have always believed that some time they would come to rule and command us. Our gods and diviners have always affirmed it, and I think that now it is fulfilled. I regard you as our lord and thus shall I have all my vassals and subjects regard you."

He summoned many of the lords of the land and said to them: "You know it has always been our belief that we are not the true lords of these lands, and it seems this must be the lord whose vassals we are. Therefore, as you have given me your fealty, so give it now to him, and I shall give mine."

Then one after the other, with Moctezuma first, made his discourse offering himself as vassal and servant of the marqués and placing himself under his protection. It was a sight to behold, and they shed many tears, saying: "It seems that in our time the fates wished to see fulfilled what so long ago was prophesied."

The marqués reassured and comforted them, promising that Moctezuma would continue to rule his land as before, and would be as much a lord or more because there would be other lands won and put also under his command. And Moctezuma said to him: "Have some of your men go with these servants who will show them a house with gold jewels and personal ornaments of mine." And the one who writes this, with another gentleman, accompanied two of Moctezuma's servants to the house of birds, as it was called, where they showed us a hall and two other chambers full of gold and silver, and green stones, though not of the finest. I had the marqués called, and he went to see it and had it taken to his quarters.

After Moctezuma saw the Spaniards' manner of conversation he seemed to enjoy himself very much with them, so all of them tried to give him as much pleasure as possible. His servants came to wait on him and every time he ate they brought more than four hundred dishes of food in which there were fruits, greens, rabbit, deer, quail and turkey, and many kinds of fish cooked in different ways. Under each of the dishes that his attendants thought he might eat came a burning brazier. They always brought him new plates to eat from, and he never ate more than once from the same plate, nor used the same clothing more than once. Also he bathed his body twice every day.

At this time Moctezuma advised the marqués about a nephew of his named Cacama, lord of a city on the shore of this lake, and of many other towns and lands. Being a restless young man, this nephew was seeking war, and Moctezuma thought it would be advisable for the marqués to take precautions. The marqués did so, entrusting the matter to certain Spanish gentlemen.

Moctezuma had a house of many rooms and courtyards where he had robes and mantles and other things. In some of the courtyards of this house he kept separate cages of lions and tigers, ounces, wolves, and foxes. In other courtyards, in a different type of cage, he kept many kinds of falcon and hawks and all manner of birds of prey. And it was a sight to see the amount of meat fed to all these birds and beasts, and the number of people for their care. Also in large earthenware vessels there were many snakes and vipers, and all of this was merely a form of grandeur. In this house of beasts he kept men and women monsters, some crippled and others dwarfed or hunchbacked.

He had another house where he kept all the kinds of waterfowl one could think of, and other kinds of fowl, each kind to itself. Without fail, more than six hundred men were kept occupied in the care of these fowl. There was, besides, a place where the sick birds could be cured. In the house of these waterfowl Moctezuma kept men and women who were white all over: their bodies and hair and eyebrows.

The courtyard of the idols was so large that there would be space enough for the houses of four hundred Spanish people. In its center was a tower with one hundred and thirteen steps of more than a span each, and this was solid. At the top were two rooms, higher than a pike and a half, and here was the principal god of all the land.[29] He was made from all kinds of seeds, which had been ground and kneaded with the blood of virgin boys and girls. These they killed by cutting open their breasts and taking out the heart, and from there they took the blood and kneaded it with the seeds into a mass thicker than a man and as high. At the time of their feasts they adorned the figure with the kind of gold jewelry they wore when they dressed for great festivals. They wrapped the figure in very thin mantles, making a bundle, then with many ceremonies they made a beverage[30] and put it with this figure inside the room at the top of the tower. They say they also gave some of this beverage to the one they elected captain-general when there was a war or something of great importance. They put these things between the outer wall of the tower and another inner wall, leaving no opening so that it seemed there was nothing there.

Outside the hollow wall were two idols on large stone bases the height of a measuring rod. The idols were nearly the height of three measuring rods, and the girth of an ox. They were of polished granite covered with mother-of-pearl, which is the shell that the pearl grows in. Over this they used a glue in the form of a paste to incrust gold ornamentation, and designs of men, serpents, birds, and other figures made of large and small turquoises, emeralds, and amethysts, so that all of the mother-of-pearl was covered except in some places where they left it to make a design with the stones. These idols wore thick gold serpents, and for necklaces some ten or twelve human hearts made of gold. For faces they had gold masks with mirror[31] eyes, and at the nape of the neck hung another face like a human head without flesh.

There were more than five thousand men in the service of this idol, some of them superior to the rest in rank as well as dress. They had their high priest whom they devoutly obeyed, and whom Moctezuma as well as all the other lords held in great veneration. They arose promptly at midnight for their sacrifice, which was the letting of blood from the tongue and the arms and thighs —sometimes from one place and sometimes from another—and wetting straws in the blood and offering them before an enormous oakwood fire. Then they went out to the idol tower to offer incense.

At a crossbow's throw from this tower, and facing it, were sixty or seventy very tall beams set on a platform made of stone and mortar. Lining the platform steps were many skulls set in mortar, with their teeth bared. At each end of the row of beams was a tower made of mortar and skulls with bared teeth, apparently built without any other stones. The beams were a little less than a measuring rod apart, and from top to bottom as many poles as there were room for had been fitted across, each pole holding five skulls pierced through the temples. The one who writes this, together with Gonzalo de Umbría, counted the poles and multiplied them by the five skulls hung between beams, and found there were 136,000 skulls, not counting the ones on the towers.[32] This courtyard had four entrances, and at each entrance a large high room full of weapons; the entrances were at the east and west, and north and south.

Moctezuma, when he was imprisoned by Cortés, sent for the lord of the coast town that had fought the Spaniards, giving the messengers a special seal that he wore around his arm, and saying to the marqués: "Have two of your men go with these messengers I am sending, and they will bring the one who has done injury to your people." Moctezuma did this because the marqués asked him to, and he said to the messengers: "Go and summon Qualpupoca (as this lord was called), and if he should not want to come by the persuasion of my seal you are to muster warriors from my territory and descend upon him and destroy him and take him by force. You are not to return without him, and are to take good care of these Christians."

They went, and they brought him, and he confessed to having done that injury to the Spaniards when he had said that Moctezuma had commanded him to do it. The marqués ordered all the arms taken out of the arsenal we have mentioned, which were bows and arrows, spears and slings, and wooden swords with flint blades. There were about five hundred cartloads, and he had them burned together with Qualpupoca, saying it was necessary to burn them so that Qualpupoca could be burned.

The marqués had sent some of his men to survey several parts of the country, and other men to subdue a region eighty leagues from Mexico which Moctezuma said had revolted. Still others had gone to collect gold, which they did in this manner: Moctezuma sent his messengers throughout the land in the company of the Spaniards, and when they arrived in a town they would say to the lord, "Moctezuma and the captain of the Christians beg you to give of your gold to send to the captain's country." And so they gave it liberally, each as he wished.

Therefore on this day that the marqués went to the courtyard of the idols, he had few of his men and, walking about the courtyard, he said to me: "Go up in that tower and see what is there." I climbed it, and some of the ministers of the people went up with me. I came to a curtain of several thicknesses of hemp, on which were many little metal bells, and as I started to go in they made such a racket that I thought the building was falling. The marqués came up as though to pass the time, and eight or ten Spaniards came with him. And because the mantle that screened the doorway made the room very dark we cut at it with our swords and let in the light. All the walls of the chamber were stone, with carved images of the same stone. The images were of idols, and in their mouths and over parts of their bodies were quantities of blood two or three fingers thick.

When the marqués had seen the stone carvings and looked about at what there was to be seen, he was saddened. He sighed, saying so that we all heard him: "Oh God! Why do You permit such great honor paid the Devil in this land? Look with favor, Lord, upon our service to You here."

He called the interpreters, because some of the priests of those idols had come at the sound of the bells, and he said: "God Who made heaven and earth made you and made us and all men. He grows what sustains us. And if we have been good He will take us to heaven, but if not we shall go to hell, as I shall tell you at greater length when we understand one another better. Here where you have these idols I wish to have the images of the Lord and His Blessed Mother. Also bring water to wash these walls, and we will take all this away."

They laughed as though it were not possible to do such a thing, and they said: "Not only this city but all the land holds these as gods. This is the house of Uchilobos,[33] whom we serve, and in comparison with him the people hold for nothing their fathers and mothers and children, and will choose to die. So take heed, for on seeing you come up here they have all risen in arms and are ready to die for their gods."

The marqués told a Spaniard to go see that Moctezuma was well guarded, and to send thirty or forty men to the tower. Then he said to the priests: "It will give me great pleasure to fight for my God against your gods, who are a mere nothing." And before the men he had sent for arrived, angered by some words he heard, he took up an iron bar that was there and began to smash the stone carvings. On my faith as a gentleman I swear by God that, as I recall it now, the marqués leaped supernaturally, and, balancing himself by gripping the bar in the middle, he reached as high as the idol's eyes and thus tore down the gold masks, saying: "Something must we venture for the Lord."

Moctezuma was informed of this, since his quarters were nearby, and he sent word to the marqués asking to be allowed to come, and meanwhile not to harm the idols. The marqués sent for him under guard, then Moctezuma suggested placing our images on one side and leaving his gods on the other, but the marqués refused. Moctezuma said: "Then I shall do everything in my power to have what you want done; but you must let us have the idols to take wherever we wish."

The marqués let him have them, saying: "See how they are but stone, and believe in God Who made heaven and earth, for by His works shall the Master be known." The idols were taken down from there with marvelous skill and ingenuity, then the walls of the chamber were washed.

It seemed to the marqués that there was little space inside considering the size of the structure, so he had the front wall bored. There the jar of ceremonial water was found, and the mass of ground seeds and blood. It was broken up, and the gold jewelry removed. There was also some gold in a tomb that was on top of the tower. The marqués had two altars made: one on one side of the tower that was divided in two hollows, and another on the other side. On one he placed an image, of wood, of Our Lady, and on the other Saint Christopher, for we had no other images then. From then on mass was celebrated here.

A few days later the Indians came bringing handfuls of corn that was green and very wilted, and they said: "Since you have taken away the gods whom we asked for rain, now make yours give us rain or we shall lose our crops." The marqués assured them it would soon rain, and asked all of us to pray for it. So the next day we went in procession to the tower, where mass was held, and the sun was shining brightly. But by the time we left it was raining so hard that our feet were covered with water as we crossed the courtyard, and the Indians marveled greatly.

In this manner we stayed on, the marqués keeping us so close to our quarters that no one stepped a musket-shot away without permission. Everyone was at peace and there were no quarrels, and Moctezuma was always giving the Spaniards gold rings or swordguards, and beautiful women, and an abundance of food.

At this time Moctezuma called the marqués to show him a mantle on which were painted eighteen ships, five of them wrecked on the coast and turned over in the sand. This is the way the Indians have of conveying news accurately. He told the marqués that the ships had been wrecked eighteen days ago on the coast, almost a hundred leagues from the port. Then another messenger came with a painting that showed certain ships anchoring in the port of Veracruz, and the marqués feared it was an armed force sent out against us.

He had me called, as I was just back that day from settling a war between certain lords of Cholula and Tlaxcala who were fighting over some boundaries, and he ordered me to go to Veracruz by some back way, to find out what had happened to the men he had left there. Walking by day, and with Indians to carry me by night, I reached Veracruz in three and a half days. The captain there had already sent messengers to the marqués, together with three Spaniards he had captured of our opponents. When the marqués was informed that it was an armada of Diego Velázquez, governor of Cuba, carrying more than a thousand men not counting those that were lost in the five ships that had been wrecked, and that they had very good artillery and ninety horse, and more than a hundred and fifty crossbowmen and musketeers, he decided to go after them, sending spies and runners ahead. Then he left for the coast, taking with him several of Moctezuma's favorite nobles and leaving about fifty men in Mexico to guard Moctezuma, under the command of Pedro de Alvarado who later was governor of a province called Guatemala.

Since there was only a small number of us at the port we went to the top of a ridge to watch for the marqués and join him when he arrived. At this time some of the Spaniards in his company mixed in with the Indians that were supplying our opponents with grass and food. Naked, and with their bodies stained like the Indians, they were able to go in and hear and see what the enemy was doing. And so it was that the captain in command of these Spaniards told the Indians that he had come solely to free Moctezuma and to capture the marqués and kill him, and therefore they should help him because he would be leaving this land and taking us with him as soon as he killed the marqués. This did a great deal of harm, and the Indians served him by Moctezuma's orders and also served the marqués because some of them by now felt well disposed toward him.

With about two hundred and fifty men that he had with him, the marqués encamped in an Indian town near his opponents, who were in another town, and sent messengers to the enemy captain, whose name was Pánfilo de Narváez. This captain, at the petition of some of his own men, sent word to the marqués that he and his company were willing to let the marqués have part of that land and would guarantee that they would not go against him in any way and that he could remain at his convenience until such a time as the king issued his commands. By this it is understood that he was to remain with his men as governor of the land they chose to give him.

The marqués conferred with the most responsible of his men and it was the opinion of some of them that he should accept the proposition. He ended by making a counter proposition, sending the messengers back to Narváez asking whether it was acceptable to him, and saying that if it were not he would consider the truce ended as soon as the messengers returned.

After sending off Narváez' messengers and his own, the marqués set out with his men and marched almost ten leagues that day. On the way some deer and wild pigs came out and were speared by the horsemen. We encamped two leagues away from our opponents, where our messengers came to tell the marqués that Narváez and his men were laughing and mocking at the idea of going over to our side when our forces were so small. The messengers also confirmed the number and quality of our opponents' artillery, and told how the captain was making gifts of our property to his own men.

There near a river, in the presence of the messengers, the marqués called all his companions together and talked to them, saying: "I am but one man and can speak for no more than one man. Offers have been made me that were advantageous only to myself; and because they were disadvantageous to you I have not accepted them. You have heard what they say, therefore the matter rests with each one of you. Whether it is your inclination to fight or to seek peace, speak your mind and no one shall hinder you from doing as you wish. These messengers of ours have told me in confidence how it is being said in the enemy camp that you are deceiving me in order to place me in their hands, therefore say what is on your minds."

Nearly all of us satisfied him as to our loyalty, then we begged him affectionately to give his own opinion. Pressed by all of us to speak first, he said almost angrily: "There is a saying in Castile, and it is this: 'May the donkey be killed or else the one who goads him.' That is my opinion. For I see that anything else we might do would be a great disgrace to us all. Nor would we safeguard everyone's life by giving in to the enemy; on the contrary, some would be endangered. However, let us hear your sentiments in response to mine, for each of you is entitled to give his opinion."

Unanimously we gave a shout of joy, saying: "Hurrah for our captain and his good judgment!" Then we picked him up and carried him on our shoulders until he had to beg us to let him go.

It had been raining and we were wet, and eager to roast the deer and pigs the horsemen had killed, but when we pitched camp a league away from the enemy the marqués ordered us not to make a fire so that we should not be seen. After posting double watch we tried to rest a while but were unable to because we were wet and there was a cold wind. The marqués awakened, or rather, since he could not sleep he called without sounding the drum and said to us: "Gentlemen, you know it is quite usual for the military man to say 'attack the enemy at dawn'; so if we have been perceived, that is the hour they will expect us. And if they have not perceived us, in any event we cannot sleep and may as well use the time fighting and enjoying the benefit of our victory rather than waste it suffering in the cold."

So we arose, and he gave us another talk saying there was still time for us to decide whether or not to fight. When we responded that we would win or die he started the march, and within a mile of the enemy quarters our runners caught one of the two sentinels the other Spaniards had posted, but the second got away. On asking the one we caught what was happening at his camp, he told us they had heard from some Indians that we were on the way and were prepared to come out to meet us at dawn. He also told us the disposition of the men and artillery, and he was telling the truth. The marqués ordered us not to harm him, because some of the men wanted to hang him for the truth.

His companion that got away gave warning at their camp, and they, thinking we would stop and rest the remainder of the night to attack at dawn, gave the order for the men to retire again and go out on the field at dawn. However, their captain and certain gentlemen were armed and awake, talking about our rashness and calling us madmen.

The marqués had ordered eighty of us to go straight to the captain's quarters without stopping for anything, and to try to capture or kill him. To this end he gave a command to one of the gentlemen who was his *alguacil mayor*,[34] in these words: "You shall go where Pánfilo de Narváez is to be found, and I command you to seize him or kill him because it thus serves the interests of the king our lord." And some of us laughed very much over this.

It had been raining, and was still raining when we approached the enemy, so their gunner had the touchholes of the artillery covered with wax. Also because of the rain we caught the sentries unawares, and they ran crying "To arms, to arms," with our men after them sounding the drum-call to arms. The marqués had sent the eighty men to quickly attack the captain's quarters while he stayed in back of us disarming and seizing our opponents, since it happened that both calls to arms had sounded together and their men came toward us thinking we were their own, and asking "What is it?" and in this way they were caught.

The marqués had the foresight to cut the cinch straps of the horses that were all saddled and ready to ride out on the field. When some of the enemy tried to bridle the horses they fell as they mounted, or soon after, because of the broken straps. The eighty of us who had gone ahead went to the captain's house, where he had about thirty men with him. In front of his quarters were ten or twelve fieldpieces, and in the excitement and commotion a gunner and some others were removing stones or tiles from the touchholes and priming the guns over the wax. We saw that when they fired them they would not shoot, so we closed in and took the guns and then went for the captain and those who were with him. Some more of his men ran forward, breaking through us and reaching his side. Now we had them hemmed in but could not attack them inside, so we set fire to the house and they surrendered, and we seized the captain and some others.

Then, since our victory was not yet known, the marqués ordered the cry given, and his men began shouting loudly: "Hurrah for Cortés who carries the victory!" At this, about four hundred of the enemy fortified themselves at a high idol tower, and the horsemen, most of whom had mended their cinch straps, mounted and rode out into the countryside.

It also happened that when we had captured the artillery some of the pieces were knocked down and others taken away by our men. A young cavalier chanced to find eight kegs of powder and half a cask of pitch, and since he no longer saw the guns, and heard it said that the enemy were fortifying themselves and going out in the field to await the morning for an attack, he thought they had taken the missing guns. Eager as he was to see victory for our side, he got in between the powder kegs saying to some companions: "Stay clear and I'll burn this powder so our enemies don't find it and injure us with their artillery." With a burning straw torch in his hand he tried to light the powder, but since he could not because it was in kegs he broke one open with his sword and, entrusting himself to God, stuck the flame inside and threw himself to the ground. But it happened that the seaman who had brought the kegs from the ship took seven kegs of powder and one of espadrilles, thinking it was powder because it had the same marking as the others. So when the young cavalier put the flaming straw in the barrel and found it would not burn, he started to open another, at which point the marqués came by. He had been fighting and could not find any more enemies, and he asked "What is that?" I told him what was happening, and he said: "Oh my boy, do not do that or you will be killed and so will many of our men who are hereabout." So saying, he got in among the kegs and stamped out the fire with his feet and hands.

After taking the powder to a small idol house where he had some of the enemy imprisoned in the care of a captain, he sent for several of the guns and battered at the tower where the Spaniards were until they surrendered. He then ordered the captain in charge of the prisoners to kill all of them if he saw any signs of a skirmish or the approach of those in the field. He gave this order loud enough to be heard by the enemy general and the rest of the prisoners. The general sent out a countersign ordering and requesting them to give their allegiance to the marqués in order to spare his life and those of the captives, and thus they came and gave themselves up as prisoners. The marqués had them all disarmed, then made them give their oath or promise, and two days later ordered their arms returned. The captain and a few others remained under arrest.

the third
letter of
hernan cortes

Whereas in the chronicle of Andrés de Tapia we observe Hernán Cortés as the courageous and resourceful leader in action, in the dispatches written by the great captain himself we are privileged to know his mind in the full range of its powers; a mind working calmly, logically toward a desirable and foreseeable end. Consequently, his prose is as unhurried as though it had been composed in the tranquil surroundings of a monastery rather than under pressure of difficult circumstances.

The dispatches, addressed to Charles V of Spain, were very soon published abroad and reached a wide audience of Europeans who read avidly of these incredible adventures among exotic peoples. There were five dispatches, although there are other letters extant, and they are known conventionally as the *Cartas de Relación* of Hernán Cortés. The second and third of these were published in Seville in 1522 and 1523 respectively; they were then published in Nuremberg in Latin, the international language of cultivated men, and subsequently appeared in Venice in Italian translation, in Antwerp in a Flemish edition, in Augsburg in a German edition of 1550, and a French translation. Since the sixteenth century there have followed numerous other editions and translations of the letters.

Included in the present volume is the third letter, translated by Francis A. MacNutt, which opens with the details of Cortés' preparations for reconquering Tenochtitlan. His account of the siege and fall of the city constitutes the major part of the dispatch. The destruction of the Mexican empire accomplished, a metamorphosis takes place and there emerges Cortés the empire builder, or Cortés the creator and visionary. He envisions and proceeds to raise a new city of palaces over the rubble of the old. But this is to be merely the administrative center of a constantly expanding territory capable of producing immeasurable wealth for the Spanish Crown and those of its subjects willing to settle and work the land.

third letter

Sent by Fernando Cortés, Captain and Superior Justice of Yucatan, called the New Spain of the Ocean Sea, to the Very High and Most Potent and Invincible Lord, Don Carlos, August Emperor and King of Spain, Our Lord, concerning the things transpired and very worthy of admiration in the conquest and recovery of the very great and marvellous city of Temixtitan, and of the other provinces subject to it which had revolted. In which city and provinces the said Captain and Spaniards obtained great and signal victories, worthy of perpetual memory. Likewise, relation is made how the South Sea has been discovered; and many other and great provinces, very rich in mines of gold, and pearls, and precious stones, and information is even had that there are spices.

Very High and Most Powerful Prince, Very Catholic and Invincible Emperor, King and Lord. With Alonzo de Mendoza, native of Medellin, whom I sent from this New Spain on the fifth of March of the past year of 1521, I despatched a second account to Your Majesty of everything that had happened here; this I finished writing on the thirtieth of October of the year 1520, but on account of very contrary winds and the loss of three ships, one of which I had prepared to send with the said account to Your Majesty, and the two others to bring help from the island of Hispaniola, there was much delay in the said Mendoza's departure, as I more fully wrote by him to Your Majesty. In the closing part of that despatch I told Your Majesty how, after the Indians of Temixtitan had expelled us by force, I had marched against the province of Tepeaca, one of its vassals which had rebelled against us, and that, with the Spaniards who remained, and our friendly Indians, I had made war on them, and reduced them to the service of Your Majesty. I also said that the past treachery and the great sufferings and deaths of the Spaniards were so fresh in our hearts, that my determination was to return against the inhabitants of that capital, who had been the cause of all; that I had begun to build thirteen brigantines, with which to do them all the damage I could from the lake, if they persevered in their wicked intention; that while the said brigantines were being made, and we and the friendly Indians were preparing ourselves to return against the enemy, I had sent for reinforcements of people, and horses, and artillery, and arms, to the island of Hispaniola, where I had written regarding it to Your Majesty's officials who reside there, sending them monies for the necessary outlay and expenses. I also assured Your Majesty that, till we were victorious over the enemy, I would neither think of rest, nor would I cease to use all possible solicitude to accomplish it, disregarding whatever danger and hardship might overtake me; and that with this determination I was preparing to leave the said province of Tepeaca.

I likewise made known to Your Majesty how a caravel, belonging to Francisco de Garay, Lieutenant Governor of the island of Jamaica, had arrived in great distress at the port of Veracruz, carrying about thirty men, who said that two other ships had sailed for the river of Pánuco, where the natives had routed one of Francisco de Garay's captains; and it was feared if these landed there, that they would suffer injury from the natives along the said river. I likewise wrote to Your Majesty that I had immediately determined to send another caravel in search of the said ships, to let them know what had happened.

After writing this, it pleased God that one of these ships should reach the port of Veracruz, on board of which there was a captain with about a hundred and twenty men. He learned there how Garay's former party had been routed. The captain who was routed assured them that they could not land at the river of Pánuco without sustaining much harm from the Indians. While they still lay in the said port, with the determination to go to that river, a storm with violent wind arose which drove the ship out to sea, breaking the cables, and driving it into a port, called San Juan, twelve leagues higher up the coast, where, after disembarking all the people, and seven or eight horses, and as many mares which they had brought, they beached the ship, which leaked badly. As soon as this was made known to me, I wrote to the captain immediately, telling him that I was much grieved at what had happened to him, and that I had sent orders to my lieutenant at Veracruz that he and his people should be given a very good reception and whatever they might need, and also to ascertain their plans; and that, if all or any of them wished to return in the ships which were lying there, he should give them permission and facilitate their departure. The captain and his men determined to remain, and join me, but we know nothing about the other ships thus far, and, as so long a time has already elapsed, we much doubt of their being saved; may God have taken them to a good port!

Being about to leave the province of Tepeaca, I learned that two provinces, called Cecatami and Xalazingo, subject to the lord of Temixtitan, had rebelled, and on the road from the city of Veracruz thither, which passes that way, they had killed some Spaniards. To render that road secure, and to administer chastisement to them in case they did not submit peaceably, I sent a captain with twenty horsemen and two hundred foot soldiers, ordering him, on the part of Your Majesty, to require the natives of those provinces to submit peaceably as vassals of Your Majesty, as they had done heretofore, and to use all possible moderation with them; but, if they would not receive him peaceably, to make war on them. I told him when he had done that, and quieted these two prov-

inces, to return with his men to Tascaltecal, where I would wait for him. He left
in the beginning of the month of December 1520, and pursued his road to those
provinces which were about twenty leagues distant.

Having despatched this business, Very Powerful Lord, I left Segura de la
Frontera, in the province of Tepeaca, at mid-December of that year, placing a
captain with sixty men there because the natives besought me greatly to do so;
and I sent all my people on foot to the city of Tascaltecal, where the brigantines
were being built, which is nine or ten leagues from Tepeaca, while I with
twenty horsemen went that day to sleep in the city of Cholula. The inhabitants
desired my coming on account of the sickness of small-pox,[1] which also affected
the natives of these countries, and those of the islands. Many of their caciques
having died from it, they desired that by my action, and with their approval,
others should be appointed in their places. We were very well received by them
on our arrival, and, having finished this business to their satisfaction in the
manner I have stated, and having explained to them my purpose to make war
on the province of Mexico and Temixtitan, I besought them, that, inasmuch as
they were vassals of Your Majesty, they should stand firm in their friendship
with us, as we would with them till death. I besought them also to aid me with
people during the war, and to treat well the Spaniards who would be coming
and going through their country, which as friends they were obliged to do.
They promised to do this, and having stayed two or three days in their city, I
left for Tascaltecal, a distance of six leagues, and, on my arrival there, all the
Spaniards and those of the city met me with great rejoicing at my coming. The
next day all the chiefs of the city and provinces came to speak to me, and told
me how Magiscatcin, who was the principal lord of all of them, had died of that
illness, the small-pox, and that they knew I would be much grieved by it as
he was my great friend. His son, about twelve or thirteen years old, survived,
to whom all the lordship of his father now belonged, and they prayed me to
recognise him as his heir. And I in the name of Your Majesty did this, at which
all of them remained very satisfied.

When I arrived in this city, I found that the master workmen and carpenters
had used great diligence with the joining and planking of the brigantines, and
that they had accomplished a very reasonable amount of work. I immediately
arranged to send to Veracruz for all the iron and nails they had there, together
with the sails and tackle and other needful things for them; and, as we had
no pitch, I ordered certain Spaniards to make it in a neighbouring forest. All
provisions for the brigantines were thus ordered to be ready in time, so that,
please God, I might, on arriving in the province of Mexico and Temixtitan, send
for them from there, a distance of sixteen leagues from the city of Tascaltecal.

During the fifteen days I remained there, I did nothing but urge on the master workmen, and the preparation of arms for our march.

Two days before Christmas, the captain, who had gone to the provinces of Cecatami and Xalazingo, arrived with the people on foot and horseback, and I learned how some of the natives had fought them, but that, at the end, some of their free will, and some by compulsion, had sued for peace. They brought me some lords of those provinces, whom, notwithstanding that they were entirely to blame for their rebellion and the death of the Christians, I pardoned, because they promised me that from henceforth they would be good and loyal vassals of Your Majesty. Thus, that undertaking was finished, in which Your Majesty was well served, not only in the pacification of those natives, but also in insuring the safety of all the Spaniards who will have to come and go through these provinces, to and from the city of Veracruz.

The second day after Christmas, I held a review in the city of Tascaltecal, and found forty horsemen and five hundred and fifty foot-soldiers, eighty of them cross-bowmen and musketeers, with eight or nine field-pieces, but very little powder. I divided the horsemen into four troops of ten each, and formed nine captaincies of sixty Spanish foot each. All being assembled for this review, I spoke to them as follows: They already knew that they and I had come to serve Your Sacred Majesty by settling in this country; and they likewise knew how all the natives of it had acknowledged themselves as vassals of Your Majesty, and how they had persevered as such, receiving good deeds from us and we from them, until, without any cause, all the inhabitants of Culua including the people of the great city of Temixtitan, and those of all the other provinces subject to it, had revolted against Your Majesty; yet more, they had killed many of our relatives and friends, and had expelled us from their country. That they should remember how many dangers and hardships we had endured, and how it was profitable to the service of God and Your Catholic Majesty to return and recover what was left, inasmuch as we had just causes and good reasons on our side. One cause was because we fought for the spread of our Faith, and against barbarians; another was because we served Your Majesty; another was for the security of our lives; and another because we had many natives, our friends, to help us. All these were strong motives to animate our hearts; for the same reasons I told them to cheer up and be brave. In the name of Your Majesty, I had made certain ordinances for maintaining discipline and regulating the affairs of the war, which I then immediately published. I enjoined them to likewise comply with these, because much service would be rendered by so doing, to God, and Your Majesty. They all promised to do so and to comply with them, declaring they would very gladly die for our Faith and Your Majesty's service, or return to recover the loss, and revenge so great a treachery as had been done by the people of Temixtitan and their allies. I, in the name of Your Majesty, thanked them for it. After this we returned to our camp on the day after the review in good spirits.

The next day, which was the feast of St. John the Evangelist, I had all the chiefs of the province of Tascaltecal assembled, and told them that they already knew I was about to leave the next day to enter the country of our enemies; that they must see that the city of Temixtitan could not be captured without the brigantines which were being built, and that hence I prayed that they would furnish everything necessary to the workmen and the other Spaniards I left there, and would treat them well as they had always treated us. I said also that they should be prepared, if God should give us the victory, whenever I should send from the city of Tesaico[2] for the joinings, planks, and other materials for the brigantines, to send them. They promised to do so, and they also wished to send some warriors with me at once, declaring that when the brigantines started they would go with all their people, for they wished to die where I died, and to revenge themselves on the Culuans their mortal enemies.

Next day which was the twenty-eighth of December, the Feast of the Innocents, I left with all my people in good order, and we marched six leagues from Tascaltecal to a town called Tezmoluca,[3] belonging to the province of Guajocingo, whose natives have always kept the same friendship and alliance with us as the natives of Tascaltecal; and there we rested that night.

In my other account, Very Catholic Sire, I said that I had been informed that the natives of Mexico and Temixtitan were preparing many arms, constructing earth-works and fortifications, and gathering forces for resisting our entrance into the country; for they already knew that I intended to return against them. I was aware of this, and knowing how dextrous and crafty they were in matters of war, I many times pondered how we could surprise them; for they knew that we had information of three roads or entrances, by each of which we might advance into their country. I determined to enter by the road of Tezmoluca, because as its pass was the roughest and steepest of all, I felt sure that we would not encounter much resistance there, nor would they be so much on their guard.

The next day after the Feast of the Innocents, having heard Mass, and recommended ourselves to God, we left the town of Tezmoluca, I leading the vanguard, with ten horsemen, and sixty light foot-soldiers, all able men of war. We pursued our road, leading up to the pass with all possible order, and sleeping four leagues from Tezmoluca on the top of the pass which is already within the limits of Culua. Although great cold prevailed, we made ourselves comfortable that night with large quantities of wood we found there, and on the next morning, a Sunday, we set out to follow our road, descending the pass to the plain. I sent four horsemen and three or four foot soldiers to reconnoitre the country, and, on our march descending the pass, I ordered the horsemen to go ahead and after them the archers and musketeers, and thus the rest of the people in their order; because, however unprepared we might take the enemy, we were certain they would come to attack us on the road, having some trap or other device prepared to injure us. As the four horsemen and the four foot soldiers were advancing, they found the road obstructed by trees and branches cut and thrown over it, with many large, thick pines and cypresses, which seemed to have been but just cut down; and, thinking the road further on might not be so much obstructed, they continued ahead, but the further they proceeded the more obstructed by pines and cypresses they found it. The whole pass was well wooded, and had many dense shrubs, so they marched with much difficulty; and, seeing the road in that condition, they became much alarmed, fearing that behind each tree the enemy lurked. On account of the thick woods, the horses could be little used, and the further they proceeded the greater became their alarm.

When they had already gone some distance in this manner, one of the four horsemen said to the others, "Brothers, let us go no farther. If you agree, it would be better to return, and inform the captain of the obstacles we have found, and of the danger in which we are, as we cannot make any use of the horses; but if not, let us go ahead inasmuch as I have offered my life till death, as well as all of you, for accomplishing this march." The others replied that this counsel was very good, but it did not appear to them wise to return to me until they had seen the enemy or ascertained how far the road went. So they set out again, and, when they saw that it continued a long way, they halted, and sent one of the soldiers to tell me what they had seen.

When I came up with the vanguard and the horsemen, we pushed ahead on that bad road, recommending ourselves to God; and I sent to order those of the rear-guard to hurry up and not be alarmed, as we would soon reach level ground. When I joined the four horsemen, we advanced in spite of many obstacles and difficulties. After marching half a league, it pleased God we should come down to level ground, where I halted to await the people. These I told, when they arrived, that all should give thanks to Our Lord, Who had brought us safely thus far, whence we could first behold all the provinces of Mexico and Temixtitan which are on the lakes and in their neighbourhood. Although we were glad at beholding them, we felt some sorrow, remembering the losses we had sustained, and we all vowed never to quit the country without victory, even if we died there. With this determination, we all advanced as merrily as if it were a pleasure party. The enemy having already observed us, instantly made many and great smoke signals all over the country, so I again exhorted and cautioned the Spaniards that they should behave as they had always done and as was expected of them, and that no one should stray aside but all should march in good order close together. Already the Indians began to yell at us from some hamlets and small towns, calling on the entire land for the people to assemble and attack us at some bridges and difficult places near by there. We made such haste, however, that we were already down in the plain before they could collect; and, marching thus, we met certain squadrons of Indians on the road in front of us, and I ordered fifteen horsemen to break through them, which they did without any loss to ourselves, killing some of them with their lances. We followed on our road toward the city of Tesaico [Texcoco], which is one of the greatest and finest to be found in all these parts, and, as the people on foot were somewhat tired, and it was getting late, we slept in a town called Coatepeque (which we found deserted) which is subject to the city of Tesaico and three leagues distant from it.

That night we bore in mind that, as this city and its provinces, called Aculua-can, is very great, and contains many people, possibly more than a hundred and fifty thousand men were ready at the time to attack us, so I, with ten of the horsemen, took the watch and guard of the first quarter, and ordered the people to be well on the alert. The next day, which was Monday, the last of December, we followed our road in the usual order, and at a quarter of a league from the town of Coatepeque, while we were all advancing amidst perplexity, discussing with each other as to whether the Tesaicans would be hostile or friendly, rather believing that it would be the former, four principal Indians met us on the road bearing a banner of gold on a pole,[4] which weighed about four marks of gold, giving us to understand by this sign that they came peaceably; God only knows how much we desired peace, and how much we stood in need of it, being as we were so few and so cut off from help in the midst of the forces of our enemies. When I saw the four Indians, one of whom was known to me, I halted our people and met them. After we had greeted one another, they said they came on the part of the chief of that city and province, who is called Guana-cacin.[5] They besought me, on his part, to do no injury to his country nor to permit any to be done; because the people of Temixtitan were to blame for the past injuries I had sustained and not they, and they wished to be Your Majesty's vassals and my friends, as they would always preserve our friendship; and they invited us to enter the city, where by their deeds, we should recognise their sincerity. I answered, after welcoming them through the interpreters, that I rejoiced in their peace and friendship, and that, though they excused themselves for the war waged on me in the city of Temixtitan, they also well knew that in certain of their subject towns, five or six leagues from the city of Tesaico, they had killed five horsemen, forty-five of my foot-soldiers, and more than three hundred Indians of Tascaltecal, and had taken much silver, gold, and other things from them; also that, inasmuch as they could not excuse themselves from this fault, the penalty would be the restoration of our property; and that on this condition—although they well deserved death for having killed so many Christians—I would make peace with them, since they offered it to me, but otherwise I would have to treat them with the utmost severity. They answered that the lord and chief of Temixtitan had taken all those things, but they would search for what they could, and return it to me. They asked me if I would come that day to the city, or would lodge in one of the two towns similar to suburbs, called Coatinchan and Guaxuta,[6] which extend unbrokenly for about a league and a half from it. The latter, as it transpired afterwards, was what they wished. I told them that I would not stop until I reached the city of Tesaico; and they said we would be welcome and they would go ahead and prepare quarters for the Spaniards and myself. On reaching these two towns, some of their chiefs came out to meet us and bring us food.

About noon, we reached the body of the city where they had prepared our quarters in a very large house, which had belonged to the father of Guanacacin, lord of the said city. Before we entered our quarters, I assembled our people, and proclaimed by the public crier that no one under penalty of death should leave the quarters without my permission. The building was so large that double the number of Spaniards could have lodged comfortably in it. I did this so that the natives of the city might be reassured and return to their homes, because it seemed to me that we did not see a tenth part of the people usually found in the city, nor any women and children; which was an alarming sign. On the day we entered the city, which was New Year's Eve, I disposed our quarters, and, still somewhat disquieted on account of the few people, and seeing these so uneasy, the thought struck us that they refrained from showing themselves and going about the city on account of fear, which somewhat quieted our apprehensions. Towards evening, certain Spaniards mounted some lofty terraces, from whence they could observe the whole town, and they saw that all the natives were abandoning it, some putting their effects in canoes (which they call *acales*) on the lake, and others going up into the hills. Although I immediately ordered their departure to be stopped, it was already so late that night overtook us, and, as they used such great haste, it was useless. Thus the chief of the city, whom I longed, as for my salvation, to have in my hands, escaped wtih many of the other chiefs to the city of Temixtitan, which by the lake is six leagues from there, taking away all their possessions. For this reason, and to save what they wanted, those messengers had come to see me as I have said above, so as to delay me somewhat, that upon entering the city I might do them no harm; and that night they thus abandoned not only us but also their city.

Three days thus elapsed in this city without any encounter with the Indians, for they neither dared to attack us, nor were we disposed to go out far searching for them, as my final intention was, that if ever they should wish to come seeking peace, to receive them, and to always require this of them. At this time the lords of Coatinchan, Guaxuta, and Autengo,[7] which are three of their large towns, and are, as I have said, incorporated and joined to the said city, came, weeping, to ask me to pardon them for having absented themselves from their country, saying that they had never fought with me, at least not of their own free will, and promising hereafter and henceforth to do all that I might command them in the name of Your Majesty.[8] I told them, through the interpreters, that they had already known the good treatment I had always shown them, and that, in leaving their country and the rest, they had done wrong; but, inasmuch as they promised to be our friends, they must inhabit their homes, and bring back their wives and children, and I would treat them according to their deeds. They went back, as it seemed to us, not very well content.

When the lord of Mexico and Temixtitan, and all the other lords of Culua (when this name of Culua is used it must be understood as meaning all the country and provinces of these parts subject to Temixtitan), knew that the lords of these provinces had offered themselves as vassals of Your Majesty, they sent them certain messengers to tell them that they had behaved very badly; and that, if they had done it from fear, they should realise that the Culuans were many, and had sufficient power to kill me and all the Spaniards and all the Indians of Tascaltecal, which indeed they would very soon accomplish; but that, if they had done it to save their lands, they should abandon them and come to Temixtitan, where they would receive larger and greater towns for their residence. The chiefs of Coatinchan and Guaxuta bound these messengers, and brought them to me; and they immediately confessed that they had come from the lords of Temixtitan, but that it had been to ask those chiefs to act as mediators, since they were my friends, in making peace between them and myself. But the men of Guaxuta and Coatinchan denied this saying, and added that the people of Mexico and Temixtitan desired nothing but war. Although I believed they spoke the truth, nevertheless, as I wished to entice the people of the great city into friendship with us, because on them depended peace or war with the other provinces which had revolted, I ordered those messengers to be liberated, and told them to have no fears, for I would send them again to Temixtitan. I prayed them to tell those lords that, although I had reason to do so, I did not want war with them, but rather to be friends as we had been before; and in order to assure them still more and to win them over to the service of Your Majesty, I sent them word that I well knew that the principal persons who had led them into the past war were already dead; that the past was the past, and that they ought not to provoke the destruction of their lands and cities, as I would be much distressed by it. With this I set the messengers free, and they went away, promising to bring me the answer. The lords of Coatinchan and Guaxuta and I remained better friends on account of this good action than before, and I pardoned them their past errors and thus they left well satisfied.

Having been seven or eight days in the city of Tesaico without hostilities or any encounter, fortifying our quarters, and ordering everything necessary for our defence, and for attacking the enemy, and, seeing they did not attack me, I sallied out from the city with two hundred Spaniards, amongst whom were eighteen horsemen, thirty archers, ten musketeers, and three or four thousand friendly Indians. I followed the shore of the lake till we reached the city called Iztapalapa, which is two leagues by water from the great city of Temixtitan, and six from Tesaico; it contains about ten thousand households, and half, or even two-thirds, of it is built on the lake. Its lord, Moctezuma's brother, whom the Indians, after the latter's death, had selected as sovereign, was the leading one in making war on us, and expelling us from the city. For this reason, as well as because I had learned that the people of Iztapalapa were very badly disposed towards us, I determined to march against them. When their people perceived me, about two leagues before arriving there, some warriors immediately appeared on land, and others in canoes on the lake; thus we advanced over those two leagues, skirmishing, both with those on land and with those on water, till we reached the said city. Almost two-thirds of a league outside the town, they had opened a causeway, which was like a dyke between the fresh and salt-water lakes, as Your Majesty may see from the map of the city of Temixtitan I have sent. When the dyke was opened the water of the salt lake began to rush with great impetus into that of the fresh-water lake, although the two lakes are more than half a league apart; while we, not noticing the trap in our eagerness for victory, passed all right and continued our approach, until we entered, mixed up with the enemy, into the city. As they were already warned of our approach, all the houses on land were deserted, and all the people took refuge with their property in the houses on the lake, and those who fled also retreated to them, fighting us very stoutly. But Our Lord was pleased to so strengthen His own that we pursued them until we drove them into the water, sometimes breast high, and at other times swimming; and we captured many of the houses in the water. More than six thousand souls, men, women, and children of the inhabitants, perished, for our Indian allies, seeing the victory which God gave us, had the sole idea to kill right and left.

As night came on, I collected my people, and set fire to some of the houses; and, while they were burning, it seemed that Our Lord inspired me, and recalled to my mind the dyke I had seen on the road, and I figured to myself what a great danger it was. I determined to leave the city, it being already far into the night and quite dark. When I reached the water, which may have been about nine o'clock at night, it was so deep, and flowed with such impetus, that we passed it running full tilt, but some of our friendly Indians were drowned, and all the plunder that had been taken in the city was lost. I assure Your Majesty that, if we had not passed the water that night, or had waited three hours more, none of us would have escaped, because we should have been surrounded by water, without having an outlet anywhere. When day broke, we saw that the water of the one lake had filled that of the other and was running no more, and that all the salt lake was covered with canoes filled with warriors, expecting to take us there. I returned that day to Tesaico, fighting sometimes with those on the lake, though we could do them little harm, as they would immediately retreat in their canoes.

On arriving at Tesaico, I found the people I had left there all safe, and without having had any encounter; and they were very glad at our coming and our victory. The day after we arrived a Spaniard, who had been wounded, died, and he was the first white man the Indians had killed in this campaign. The next day, certain messengers, from the city of Otumba and four other cities near to it, which are four or five leagues from Tesaico, arrived in this city. They came to beg me to pardon them for any fault of theirs in the past war, because all the power of Mexico and Temixtitan gathered in Otumba when we retreated routed, believing they could finish us. The people of Otumba saw plainly that they could not clear themselves from blame, although they excused themselves, saying they had been commanded; but, to incline me the more towards leniency, they told me that the lords of Temixtitan had sent other messengers, asking them to adhere to their party and not to conclude any friendship with us, otherwise they would fall upon them and destroy them. They declared, however, that they would rather be vassals of Your Majesty, and obey my commands. I answered that they knew very well how blameworthy they were for what had happened, and, to secure my pardon and belief in their professions, they would first have to bring me, as prisoners, those messengers of whom they spoke, and all the natives of Mexico and Temixtitan who remained in their country; and that I would not otherwise pardon them; and that they should return to their homes with their people, and then prove by their deeds that they were good vassals of Your Majesty. Although we exchanged many other arguments, they were unable to get anything else out of me, and returned to their country assuring me they would always do what I wished, and from henceforward they have always been, and are, loyal and obedient in Your Majesty's service.

In the other account, Very Fortunate and Most Excellent Prince, I told Your Majesty that, when they routed and expelled me from the city of Temixtitan, I took with me the son and two daughters of Moctezuma, the lord of Tesaico, Cacamacin, his two brothers, and many other chiefs whom I held prisoners, and that all of them had been killed by the enemy (although they belonged to their own nation and some of them were their chiefs), except two brothers of Cacamacin, who by a happy chance were able to escape. When I reached the province of Tascaltecal, one of these two brothers, called Ipacsuchil,[9] otherwise called Cucascacin, whom I had already, in the name of Your Majesty and with the approval of Moctezuma, appointed lord of the city of Tesaico and the province of Aculuacan, escaped, and returned to the city of Tesaico, where they had elected for chief another of his brothers called Guanacacin,[10] whom I have above mentioned. It is said that he had Cucascacin, his brother, killed in the following manner: On his arrival in Tesaico, the guards seized him and informed Guanacacin their lord, who communicated the news to the lord of Temixtitan. As soon as the latter heard that the said Cucascacin had come back, he could not believe he had escaped from us, but suspected he must have gone there in our interest to furnish us some information; so he immediately sent order to Guanacacin to kill Cucascacin, his brother. Guanacacin obeyed without delay. The younger of the brothers still remained with me, and being quite a lad, our conversation made more impression upon him, and he became a Christian, taking the name of Don Fernando.[11] When I left the province of Tascaltecal for Mexico and Temixtitan, I left him there with certain Spaniards, and I shall relate hereafter to Your Majesty what afterwards happened there.

The day after my return from Iztapalapa to the city of Tesaico, I determined to send Gonzalo de Sandoval,[12] alguacil mayor of Your Majesty, in command of twenty horsemen, two hundred foot soldiers, musketeers, archers, and shield bearers, for two very necessary objects: first, to escort out of this province certain messengers I was sending to the city of Tascaltecal to learn in what state the thirteen brigantines, which were being made there, were, and for some other necessary things, as well for the people of Veracruz, as for my own company; and second, to make sure of that region, so that the Spaniards might come and go in safety; for at that time we could neither go out of the province of Aculuacan without passing through the enemy's country, nor could the Spaniards in Veracruz and other parts, come to us without much danger from the adversary. I ordered the alguacil mayor, after having conducted the messengers safely, to go to a province called Calco,[13] bordering on this of Aculuacan; for I had proofs that the natives of that province, although belonging to the league of Culua, wished to become vassals of Your Majesty but did not dare, on account of a certain garrison the Culuans had placed near them.

The said captain left, taking with him all the Indians of Tascaltecal who had carried our baggage, and others who had come with us and had obtained some plunder in the war. The latter marched some distance ahead, as the Captain believed that, if the Spaniards brought up the rear, the enemy would not dare to attack them; but the adversaries in the lake towns and along the coast, as soon as they saw them, attacked the rear of the Tascaltecans and captured, plundered, and even killed some of them. When the captain arrived with the horsemen and foot soldiers, he attacked them vigorously with lances, and killed many; those who escaped retreated to the water and the other towns near by. The Indians of Tascaltecal went back to their country with what remained to them, accompanied by the messengers I had sent. All these being placed in safety, Gonzalo de Sandoval continued his road to the province of Calco, which was very near at hand. Early next morning a large number of the enemy came out to attack him, and, both having formed on the field, our men opened the attack; the horsemen routed two squadrons in such wise that the others quickly abandoned the field, and our forces burned and killed amongst them.

This being accomplished, and that road cleared, the people of Calco came out to receive the Spaniards, all rejoicing together greatly. The chiefs said they wished to come and speak with me, so they left and came to sleep at Tesaico, where some of them appeared before me with two of the sons of the lord of Calco. They gave me about three hundred dollars of gold in pieces and told me how their father had died, and that, at the time of his death, he had told them that the greatest grief he took with him was not to see me before he died, for he had been expecting me a long time; and he had commanded them to come and see me as soon as I should come to this province, and to look upon me as their father. As soon as they had known of my coming to the city of Tesaico, they said that they had wished to come immediately to see me, but, out of fear of the Culuans, they had not dared; nor would they now have dared to come had the captain whom I had sent not arrived in their country; they added that, when they returned to it, I must give them many other Spaniards to conduct them in safety. They also told me that I well knew that never, either in war or otherwise, had they been against me, and that I also well knew that, when the Culuans were attacking our quarters in Temixtitan and the Spaniards whom I had left there while I went to meet Narváez in Cempoal, there were two Spaniards in their country in charge of certain maize which I had sent them to collect; they had escorted these men to the province of Guaxocingo, for they knew that the people there were our friends, so that the Culuans might not kill them as they did all who were outside the quarters in Temixtitan. They told me this and other things, weeping, and I thanked them very much for their good disposition and deeds, promising them that I would always do everything they desired and that they should be well treated. Thus far they have always shown very good will, and have proved very obedient to all that is commanded them on the part of Your Majesty.

These sons of the lord of Calco and those who came with them told me one day that, as they wished to return to their country, they besought me to give them people who would conduct them in safety. Gonzalo de Sandoval, with certain horsemen and foot soldiers, escorted them, with orders after he had left them in their country, to go to the province of Tascaltecal and bring back with him certain Spaniards who were there, and Don Fernando, the brother of Caca-macin, whom I have mentioned before. Four or five days later the alguacil mayor returned with the Spaniards, bringing with him the said Don Fernando. A few days afterwards, I learned that, as he was a brother of the lords of this city, the sovereignty belonged to him, although there existed other brothers. For this reason, and because the province was without a ruler, inasmuch as his brother Guanacacin, the lord of it, had deserted it and gone to Temixtitan, and also because Don Fernando was a very good friend of the Christians, I, in Your Majesty's name, caused him to be acknowledged as ruler. The inhabitants of this city, although at that time there were very few left in it, elected him, and thenceforward obeyed him; many others who were absent, or who had fled, began to return to the city and province of Aculuacan, and they obeyed and served the said Don Fernando; and thenceforward the city began to be rebuilt and well populated.

Two days after this was done, the lords of Coatinchan and Guaxuta came, and told me they had positive information that all the power of Culua would come against me and the Spaniards, for the whole country was full of foes; and that they could not decide whether they should bring their wives and children where I was or if they should take them to the mountains; for they were very much afraid. I told them not to be at all afraid, but to stay in their homes without making any change, adding that I desired nothing so much as to meet the Culuans on the battle field. I advised them to be prepared, and to place their watchmen and scouts over all the country, and, as soon as they saw or learned that the adversaries were advancing, to let me know. So they went away well admonished as to what I had commanded them. That night I prepared all our force, and placed many watchmen and scouts everywhere that was needful; and we never slept the whole night nor thought of anything but this. Thus we were expecting them during the whole night, believing what the chiefs of Guaxuta and Coatinchan had told us.

The next day, I learned that some of the enemy were moving about the borders of the lake, hoping to surprise and capture some of the Tascaltecans who were coming and going for the camp service. I also learned that they had confederated with two towns, subject to Tesaico, which are near the water, in order to do us all the mischief they could; and that they had fortified themselves, and prepared barricades, ditches, and other works necessary for their defence. Upon learning this, I took next day twelve horsemen and two hundred foot soldiers and two small field pieces, and went to the place where they were, about a league and a half from the city. On the way, I met certain of the enemy's spies and others who were advancing, so we charged them, capturing and killing some of them, and those who were left escaped to the water; we set fire to a part of those towns and returned to our quarters victorious and much pleased. The next day three chiefs of those towns came to ask pardon for what had passed, beseeching us not to destroy them, and promising me not to receive those of Temixtitan any more in their town. As they were persons of no importance, and vassals of Don Fernando, I pardoned them in Your Majesty's name.

The next day, there came to me certain of those Indians, with broken and bruised heads, telling me that the men of Mexico and Temixtitan had returned to their town, but, not meeting with the reception to which they were accustomed, had ill-treated the inhabitants and taken some of them prisoners, and that, if no defence had been offered, they would have captured everything. They prayed me to be on the alert, in case those of Temixtitan returned, so as to give them help; and with this they departed to their town.

The people whom I had left making the brigantines in the province of Tascaltecal were informed that a ship had arrived at the port of Veracruz, in which had come thirty or forty Spaniards (besides the sailors), eight horses, cross-bows, muskets, and powder. As they did not know how we were progressing with the war, and had no sure way to reach us, they were anxious; and some of the Spaniards were waiting there, for they did not dare to come on, although they desired to bring me such good news. When one of my servants, whom I had left there, learned that some of them wished to try to reach me, he proclaimed, by the public crier, serious penalties for anyone who should leave there until I had sent orders to do so. But one of my lads, realising that nothing in the world would give me so much pleasure as to know of the arrival of that ship and the help it had brought, left by night, although the country was not safe, and came to Tesaico, where we were greatly amazed to see him arrive alive. We were very glad of the news, as we were in extreme need of relief.

The same day, Most Catholic Lord, certain good messengers from Calco arrived here in Tesaico, and told me that, on account of their having come to offer themselves as vassals of Your Majesty, Mexico and Temixtitan were about to attack and destroy them, and were therefore assembled, and had prepared all their neighbours; hence they besought me to help and aid them in such great necessity, for, if I did not do so, they would find themselves in the greatest straits. I assure Your Majesty, as I wrote in my former account, that next to our own hardships and privations, the greatest uneasiness I felt was caused by not being able to aid and favour the friendly Indians who were molested and harassed by the Culuans for being vassals of Your Majesty. I and my companions would always go to the extent of our possibilities in this, as it seemed to us that in nothing could we further the service of Your Caesarean Majesty more than in favouring and aiding Your vassals. In the emergency in which these Calcans appealed to me, I was unable to do for them what I wished, and I told them I could not, as at this season I had wished to send for the brigantines and had prepared, for this purpose, all the people of the province of Tascaltecal, from whence they had to be brought in pieces, and I was obliged to send horsemen and foot soldiers for them. I told them, however, that as they already knew that the natives of Guajocingo, Churultecal, and Guacachula, were all vassals of Your Majesty and our friends, they should go to them and pray them in my name to give them aid and succour, as they lived very near to their country, and to obtain from them a garrison with whom they might be safe till I could aid them. For the present, I said, I was unable to give them any other assistance.

Although they were not as well satisfied as if I had given them some Spaniards, they thanked me, and begged me to give them a letter of mine to ensure greater success; because between the people of Calco and those two provinces owing to their being of different parties, there had always existed some differences. While occupied in making these arrangements, certain messengers unexpectedly arrived from the said provinces of Guajocingo and Guacachula, who, in the Calcans' presence, told how the chiefs of those provinces had not seen or heard of me since I left the province of Tascaltecal, but, nevertheless, had always kept their watchmen on the hills and mountains which border their country and overlook Mexico and Temixtitan, in order that, if they saw many smokes, which are the signals of war, they might come to help me with their vassals and people; and, as they had recently seen more smoke than ever, they had come to know how I was and if I needed anything, so as to send me some warriors. I thanked them very much, and told them that, by Our Lord's blessing, the Spaniards and myself were well and had always been victorious over the enemy, and that, besides greatly rejoicing in their good will and presence, I rejoiced still more to form an alliance of friendship between them and the Calcans who were present; and I prayed them, as they were both vassals of

Your Majesty, to become good friends and help one another against the Culuans who were wicked and perverse, especially now when the Calcans were in need of aid as the Culuans intended to attack them. Thus they became very good friends and confederates, and, after remaining there two days with me, both departed very happy and satisfied, and rendered one another mutual service.

Three days later, when we knew that the brigantines had been completed and the people who were to bring them were ready, I sent Gonzalo de Sandoval, alguacil mayor, with fifteen horsemen and two hundred foot soldiers to escort them to me. I gave orders to destroy and raze a large town, subject to this of Tesaico, which borders on the confines of the province of Tascaltecal, because its natives had killed five horsemen and forty-five foot soldiers who were coming from Veracruz to Temixtitan when I was besieged there, ignorant at the time that such a great treachery had been practiced against us. When we entered Tesaico this time, we found in their places of worship or mosques of the city the skins of five horses with their hoofs and shoes, as well tanned as they could have been in any part of the world. They had offered these to their idols in token of victory, together with much wearing apparel and other things belonging to the Spaniards. We found the blood of our brothers and companions spilled and sacrificed all about these towers and mosques, a thing which filled us with grief, for all our past tribulations were thus revived. The traitors of that and the other neighbouring towns had placed themselves in ambush on each side of a difficult pass in order to make sure of those Christians when they were descending a slope on foot, leading their horses behind so that they were unable to use them, and to execute upon them the greatest cruelty that has ever been done; for they took them in the midst killing some, while others, whom they captured alive, they brought to Tesaico and sacrificed, tearing out their hearts before the idols. That it happened thus, is proved by the fact that, when the alguacil mayor passed there, certain Spaniards who had accompanied him, found in a house of a village which is between Tesaico and the place where they captured and killed the Christians, a white wall on which the following words were written in charcoal: "Here the unhappy Juan Yuste was kept a prisoner."[14] A thing fit without doubt to break the heart of those who saw it. He was a gentleman, one of the five horsemen. When the alguacil mayor arrived at that town, the natives, conscious of their great guilt, fled, and the horsemen and Spanish foot soldiers and the friendly Indians pursued and killed many and captured many women and children who were declared slaves. However, moved by compassion, he did not kill and destroy all whom he might have, and before he left there he even collected those who survived and restored them to their town, so it is now populated again and repentant of the past.

The alguacil mayor proceeded five or six leagues towards that town of Tascaltecal which is nearest to the borders of Culua, and there he met the Spaniards and the people who were to bring the brigantines. The day after he arrived they left there with the planks and cross timbers, all of which were carried in the most perfect order by eight thousand men; a marvellous sight to see, and it seems to me even to hear of, the bringing of thirteen small ships overland a distance of about eighteen leagues. I assure Your Majesty that from the vanguard to the rear was a distance of two leagues. When they set out, they took eight horsemen and a hundred Spaniards with the van, and more than ten thousand warriors on the flanks, having as captains Yutecad and Teutipil,[15] two chiefs amongst the nobles of the city of Tascaltecal. In the rear-guard, came another hundred odd Spaniards and eight horsemen, and another ten thousand warriors well armed, who had for captain, Chichimecatecle, one of the principal lords of that Province; there were also other captains the latter had brought with him. When they started out, Chichimecatecle escorted the van with the planking, and the other two captains brought up the rear with the joinings; but when they entered the country of Culua the masters of the brigantines ordered the joinings to be taken ahead and the plankings to remain behind; as the latter would cause the most hindrance should any disturbance happen, which would most likely occur in the front. Chichimecatecle, who brought the planking, and until now had led his warriors at the head of the vanguard, took this as an affront, and there was some trouble in pacifying him and making him remain in the rear-guard, because he wished to meet any danger that might present itself. When finally he did agree to this, he nevertheless did not want any Spaniards in the rear-guard, because he was a very brave man and wished to have the honours himself. These captains also brought two thousand Indians carrying provisions. In this order and agreement, they marched three days, and, on the fourth, they entered this city with much rejoicing and noise of kettle-drums when I went out to receive them. As I said above, the people were so spread out that from the entrance of the first until the last had arrived we spent six hours without the line of people being once broken.[16] After they had arrived, and I had thanked the chiefs for the good service they had done us, we assigned them their quarters and provided for them the best we could. They told me they wished to meet the Culuans and that I should see when I commanded it that they and their people were desirous of avenging themselves or dying with us; I told them to rest and that very soon I would give them plenty to do.

When those warriors of Tascaltecal, who were certainly for hereabouts very dashing men, had rested in Tesaico three or four days, I prepared twenty-five horsemen, three hundred foot soldiers, five hundred archers and musketeers, and six small field pieces, and, without telling anyone where we were going, I left the city at nine o'clock in the morning. With me were the captains already named, with more than thirty thousand in their divisions, well organised after their fashion. When it was getting late, we met a body of the enemy's warriors four leagues from the city, and our horsemen broke through them and scattered them and, as the warriors of Tascaltecal were very fleet, they followed, and we killed many of our adversaries; and that night we slept in the field, keeping strict watch.

The next morning, we continued our march, and still I had not given out where I intended to go, because I distrusted some of the people of Tesaico who were with us, for as yet I had no confidence in them, fearing that they might give information to the people of Mexico and Temixtitan of what I intended to do. We arrived at a town called Xaltoca,[17] which is situated in the midst of the lake, and we found around it many trenches full of water and, as these surrounded the town, it was very strong because the horsemen could not enter. Our adversaries yelled a great deal, discharging darts and arrows at us, but the foot soldiers entered, although with some difficulty, and expelled them, and burnt a great part of the town. That night, we slept a league from there, and as day broke we continued our march, meeting the enemy who yelled at us from afar, as they are accustomed to do in war, a thing which is certainly frightful to hear, and, pursuing them, we reached a great and beautiful city, called Guaticlan;[18] finding it deserted, we lodged in it that night.

The next day, we advanced to another city, called Tenainca,[19] where we encountered no resistance, and without halting we went on to another, called Acapuzalco,[20] both of which are on the borders of the lake; but neither did we stop there as I wished very much to reach another city near by, called Tacuba, which is very near to Temixtitan. When we were close to it, we found that there also they had made many trenches filled with water, and that the enemy was on the lookout. As soon as we saw them, we and our friends attacked them briskly, and entered the city, killing some and expelling the other inhabitants from it. As it was already late then, we did nothing else that night, but lodged in a house which was so large that we easily had room for everybody.

At daybreak, our friendly Indians began to pillage and set fire to the whole city except our quarters, and they put such diligence into it that a fourth part was burnt. This was done because, when we were routed the other time in Temixtitan and passed through this city, its inhabitants joined those of Temixtitan and fought us cruelly, killing many Spaniards.

Of the six days we remained in the city of Tacuba, none passed on which we had not some encounters and skirmishes with the enemy. The captains of the Tascaltecans, and some of their men, exchanged many challenges with those of Temixtitan, and they would fight most beautifully one with the other; and many arguments passed between them, with mutual threats and insults, which was undoubtedly a sight to see. During all this time, many of the Indians were killed, without any of our people being injured, though we often entered by the causeways and bridges of the city, where they had so many defences that they resisted us stoutly. Frequently they would pretend to give us a chance to enter, saying: "Come in and enjoy yourselves," and at other times they would say: "Do you think there is now another Moctezuma, so that you can do as you please?" Once, while these speeches were passing, I placed myself, they being on the other side, near one of the bridges they had taken away, and signalled to our people to remain quiet; and they also, when they saw that I wished to speak to them, silenced their people. I then asked them, why they were so foolish as to court destruction? and, if there was amongst them any principal chief, to call him because I wished to speak to him. They answered that the whole multitude of warriors I saw there were chiefs so that I might say whatever I wished. As I did not make answer, they began to insult me. Someone of our men, I do not know who, then called to them that they would die of hunger, for we would not allow them to come out to seek for food; they retorted that they needed none, and that when they did they would eat us and the Tascaltecans. One of them took some loaves of maize bread and threw them towards us saying: "Take it and eat it if you are hungry for we are not"; and immediately they began to yell and attack us.

As my coming to this city of Tacuba had been principally in order to speak with those of Temixtitan, and to learn their intention, and as my being there profited nothing, I decided, at the end of six days, to return to Tesaico and hasten the construction of the brigantines, so as to surround the enemy by water and land. The day we left, we slept in the city of Goatitan, which I have mentioned above, nor did the enemy ever cease pursuing us, though the horsemen would turn against them from time to time, and thus some fell into our hands.

The next day, we set out, and, as our adversaries saw we were leaving, they thought it was from fear, and a great number gathered and began to pursue us. When I saw this, I ordered the foot soldiers to go ahead without stopping, and five horsemen to accompany them, as their rear-guard, while I remained with twenty others. Six of these I ordered to place themselves in ambush in one place, six in another, and five in another, while I, with three more, went to another place; and it was arranged that when the enemy had passed, believing that we were all marching ahead, as soon as they should hear me cry, "Señor Santiago!" they should rush out and attack from behind. When the time came, we appeared, and fell upon them with our spears, and the pursuit lasted in most beautiful style for about two leagues over a plain as smooth as the palms of our hands. Thus many perished at our hands and at those of the friendly Indians; and the others dropped behind and pursued us no further, while we marched on

and overtook our people. That night we slept in a charming town called Aculman, two leagues from Tesaico, for which we left the next day, entering it at
noon, and being very well received by the alguacil mayor whom I had left in
command, and by all the people, who rejoiced at our coming; especially so
because, since the day we left, they had never heard anything of us or what had
happened to us, and they had been anxious for news of us. The day after we
arrived, the chiefs and captains of Tascaltecal, asking my permission, left for
their country very well satisfied to receive a share of the spoils.

Two days after my return to Tesaico, certain Indian messengers came from
the lords of Calco, and told me that they had been commanded to let me know,
on their part, that the people of Mexico and Temixtitan were coming to destroy
them, and asked me, as they had on other occasions, to send them some help. I
immediately arranged to send Gonzalo de Sandoval, with twenty horsemen and
three hundred foot soldiers, whom I charged to make all haste and on arriving to
give all the favour and help possible to those vassals of Your Majesty, our
friends. When he reached Calco, he found awaiting him a great many people,
assembled, not only from that province, but also from Guajocingo and Guacachula; after ordering what was to be done, he left, taking his march towards a
town called Guastepeque,[21] where the Culuans were in garrison and from which
place they did harm to the Calcans. At a town on the road, many of our foes
appeared, but our friends were many and had besides the advantage of the
Spaniards and horsemen; and all united and charged upon them and drove them
from the field, pursuing them with great slaughter. They rested for the night in
that town before Guastepeque and the next day they left. Just as they were
about to reach the town of Guastepeque, the Culuans began to attack the Spaniards, who in a short time routed them, forcing them with great loss out of the
town. The horsemen then dismounted in order to feed their horses and rest
themselves. While thus off their guard, the enemy fell upon the square of the
quarters, screaming and yelling most fiercely, discharging many stones and darts
and arrows. The Spaniards took to their arms, and they and our friends rushed
out against them and expelled them again, pursuing them for more than a
league, and killing many. Very tired, they returned that night to Guastepeque
where they rested for two days.

About this time the alguacil mayor learned that many hostile warriors had
assembled in a town called Acapichtla,[22] so he determined to go thither and see
if they would surrender peaceably upon his demand. This town was very
strongly situated upon a hill where it could not be attacked by the horsemen.
When the Spaniards arrived, the inhabitants, without waiting for anything,
began to attack them, throwing stones on them from the heights; and, although
many of our friends accompanied the alguacil mayor, they dared not attack the

town, seeing its strength, nor engage their adversaries. The alguacil mayor, on seeing this, determined to take the heights of the town by assault or die, and, with the cry of "Señor Santiago!"[23] they began the ascent; and God was pleased to give them such valour that, in spite of the resistance it offered, they took it, but at the cost of many wounded. When the Indians, our friends, followed them, and the enemy recognised their defeat, there was such a slaughter by our people and a throwing of the foe from the heights, that those who were present affirmed that a small river near the town was so dyed with blood that for more than an hour they could not drink, although on account of the heat they were very much in want of water. Having concluded this, and leaving the two towns in peace, though well chastised for their refusal at the beginning, the alguacil mayor returned to Tesaico with all his people, and Your Catholic Majesty may believe that this was a most signal victory, where the Spaniards showed very remarkable valour.

When the people of Mexico and Temixtitan learned that the Spaniards and Calcans had done them such damage, they determined to send certain captains with a large force against them.[24] As soon as the Calcans learned this, they sent to beseech me to send them some aid with all haste, and I again promptly sent the alguacil mayor, with foot soldiers and horsemen; but when he arrived the Culuans and the Calcans had already met in the field and both had fought very stoutly. God was pleased, however, that the Calcans should triumph, and they killed many of their adversaries, and captured some forty of them, amongst whom was a Mexican captain and two other chiefs whom the Calcans delivered to the alguacil mayor to be brought to me. He sent me some of them and others he kept because, for the greater security of the Calcans he, with all the people, remained in one of their towns on the frontier of Mexico. Later, when there seemed to him no further need for his remaining, he returned to Tesaico and brought with him the other prisoners who had remained in his hands. Meanwhile we had many other encounters and skirmishes with the natives of Culua, which to avoid prolixity I do not specify.

As the road between Veracruz and this city of Tesaico was safe for travelling to and fro, the people of that city had news of us every day and we of them, which before was not possible. They sent me by a messenger some crossbows and muskets and powder which pleased us greatly; and two days after, they sent me another messenger by whom they made known that three ships[25] had arrived at the port bringing many people and horses, whom they would immediately send on to me,—aid which God miraculously sent us in proportion to our need.

I have always sought, Most Powerful Lord, to win the people of Temixtitan to our friendship by every way and means I could; on the one hand because I did not wish them to provoke their own destruction, and on the other in order to rest from the hardships of all the past wars; but principally because I knew it would conduce to Your Majesty's service. Whenever I could lay hold of anyone from the city, I would send him back to it, admonishing and requiring the inhabitants to come to terms of peace.

On Holy Wednesday, which was the twenty-seventh of March of the year 1521, I had brought before me those chiefs of Temixtitan who had been taken by the Calcans. I asked if any of them would go to the city and speak on my part to the lords of it, and ask them to stop fighting and give themselves as vassals of Your Majesty as they had before done; for I did not wish to destroy them but to be their friends. Although they took it badly, fearing they would be killed for bringing that message, two of the prisoners determined to go, and asked me for a letter, for, though they did not understand what was in it, they knew that amongst us it was customary, and that by taking it the people of the city would give them credence. I explained also through the interpreters what I wrote in the letter, which was what I had told them. So they left, and I ordered five horsemen to accompany them till they were in safety.

On Holy Saturday, the Calcans and some of their allies and friends sent to tell me that the Mexicans were marching against them, and they showed me on a large white cloth a drawing of all the towns which were to march, and the roads by which they were coming; and they besought me at all costs to send them help. I answered them that within four or five days I would send it, but if meanwhile they found themselves in straits they should let me know and I would aid them. On the third day of the Feast of the Resurrection, they came back to beg me to send help as quickly as possible as the enemy was advancing steadily. I told them I would and announced that for the following Friday twenty-five horsemen and three hundred foot-soldiers should be ready.

The Thursday before, certain messengers came to Tesaico from the provinces of Tazapan, Mascalcingo, and Nautan,[26] and from other cities in their neighbourhood, telling me that they came to give themselves as vassals of Your Majesty and to be our friends, as they had never killed any Spaniards nor rebelled against Your Majesty's service. They brought me certain pieces of cotton cloth for which I thanked them, and promised them that if they were good, they would receive good treatment; so they went away very well content.

The Friday following, which was the fifth of April of the said year 1521, I left this city of Tesaico, with the thirty horsemen and three hundred footmen who had been equipped, leaving in it twenty other horsemen and three hundred footmen under the command of Gonzalo de Sandoval, the alguacil mayor. More than twenty thousand men of Tesaico went with me, and we marched in good order and slept in a town in Calco, called Talmanalco,[27] where we were well received and quartered. Since the Calcans became our friends, they have kept a strong fort and garrison there, for it is on the Culuan frontier. We arrived at Calco the next day at nine o'clock but did not stop, except to tell the chiefs of my intention to make a tour round the lakes, as I believed that after accomplishing this march, which was important, the thirteen brigantines would be found complete and ready to be launched. After speaking to the Calcans, I left at vespers that day, and reached one of their towns where more than forty thousand friendly warriors joined us, and there we slept that night. As the natives of the town told me that the Culuans were expecting me in the field, I ordered that at a quarter before daybreak everybody should be on foot and ready.

After hearing mass, we began our march, I taking the vanguard with twenty horsemen, and leaving ten for the rear-guard; and in this order we crossed some very steep sierras. At two o'clock in the afternoon, we arrived at a very steep hillock on the top of which there were many women and children, while its slopes were covered with warriors who at once began yelling loudly, sending up smoke signals, discharging their slings, and throwing stones and darts, so that in approaching them we sustained much injury. Although we saw they did not dare to wait for us on the field, it appeared to me that, even though our road led us elsewhere, it was cowardly to go on without giving them a lesson, lest also our friends should suspect we did it out of cowardice; and I began, therefore, to reconnoiter about the hillock. It was about a league in circumference and certainly was so strong that it seemed madness to assail it; but although I might have laid siege to it and obliged them to give themselves up from sheer want, I could not spare the time to do this. Being thus perplexed, I determined to assault its slopes at the places I had examined, and gave orders to Cristobal Corral, lieutenant of sixty foot soldiers whom I had always in my company, to attack them with his infantry and ascend its steepest sides with certain musketeers and archers to follow him; and to Rodriguez de Villafuerte and to Francisco Verdugo that they with their men and certain archers and musketeers should mount on another side; and to the captains Pedro Dircio and Andres de Monjaraz to assault it from another side with some few archers and musketeers; and that upon hearing a musket-shot all should resolve to mount, winning either victory or death.

Immediately on the discharge of the musket, they began the ascent, and won two slopes of the hillock from the adversaries, but were unable to get any higher because, such were the steepness and ruggedness of the rock that they could not sustain themselves neither with feet nor hands. The Indians with their hands hurled many rocks from above, and these in rolling broke into pieces which scattered, doing infinite damage; and the attack of our enemies was so fierce that they killed two Spaniards and wounded more than twenty, stopping our advance. Seeing that it was impossible to do more, and that such great numbers

of foes were gathering to help those on the hillock that the country was covered
with them, I ordered the captains to retreat; and, having descended, the horsemen charged those on the plain and drove them from the field, killing them with
their lances during a pursuit which lasted for an hour and a half.

The people being many, the horsemen scattered from one part to another, and
after having again assembled some told me that about a league further on they
had seen another hillock with many people on it, but that it was not so strong;
that on the plains near it were many people; and that there were to be found
there two things which we did not find on this other, one was water and the
other less strength in the position, so we might without danger capture the
people. Although I much regretted not having obtained the victory, we left and
slept that night near the other hillock, where we endured much hardship and
privation; neither did we find any water, nor all that day had we or the horses
drunk any; thus we passed that night hearing a great noise of kettle-drums,
trumpets, and yells from our enemies.

As soon as day dawned, certain captains and myself began to examine the hill,
which seemed to us almost as strong as the other; but it had two high points on
its summit which were easier to mount and which were defended by many warriors. My captains and I with other *hidalgos* who were there took our shields
and went on foot towards it (for the horses had been taken to be watered about
a league off), only for the purpose of seeing its strength and where it might be
attacked; when the people saw us, although we said nothing to them, they followed us. When we reached the foot of the hillock, the men on the peaks, believing I intended to attack those in the centre, abandoned their positions to come
to their help. Seeing this blunder, and that by taking the peaks they would be at
a great disadvantage, I very quietly ordered a captain to mount quickly with his
people and capture the steepest points which they had abandoned; and he succeeded. I, with the rest of my force, began to mount the hillock where most of
the enemy was gathered; and it pleased God that I should capture the slope
and that we should reach a height almost equal to that whence they fought,
which result had appeared almost impossible without infinite danger. One of
the captains had already planted his banner on the highest point, and from there
he began to discharge muskets and cross-bows at the enemy, and they, seeing
the injury they sustained, and that the battle was lost, made signs of surrender,
laying down their arms. As my policy is always to convince these people that I
do not wish to injure them, no matter how blameworthy they may be, especially
when they are willing to become vassals of Your Majesty; and as they are intelligent and understand this very well, I ordered the fighting to cease, and when
they came to speak to me I received them very well. Observing how well they
were treated, they made this known to those on the other hillock, who although

they were victorious, decided to give themselves as vassals to Your Majesty, and came to me asking pardon for the past.

I remained two days in this town near the hill, from where I sent the wounded to Tesaico. Starting again, I arrived at ten o'clock in the morning at Guastepeque, which I have already mentioned, where we lodged in the chief's house, situated in the most refreshing gardens ever seen. These gardens have a circuit of two leagues, and in their midst flows a very beautiful rivulet, and at intervals of two cross-bow shots are kiosks and very gay flower beds, and an infinite number of different fruit trees, many herbs, and fragrant flowers; certainly it is an admirable thing to see the charm and grandeur of this place. We reposed that day here, where the natives provided us all the pleasure and service they could. The next day we left, and at eight o'clock in the morning we arrived at a great town called Yautepeque, where many hostile warriors were awaiting us. When we first arrived, it seemed that they wanted to make us some sign of peace, either out of fear or to deceive us, but immediately afterward, without any further cause, they fled, abandoning their town. As I did not care to delay there, I pursued them with my thirty horsemen for about two leagues till I got them to another town called Gilutepeque,[28] where we killed many of them. We found the people in this town off their guard, because we got there ahead of their scouts, so some were killed, and many women and children were taken, and the rest fled. I remained there two days, believing the chief would give himself as vassal to Your Majesty, but as he never came I ordered fire to be set to the town when I departed. Before I left it, there came certain persons of the former town, called Yautepeque, praying me to pardon them and offering to give themselves as vassals to Your Majesty. I received them willingly because they had already been well chastised.

On the same day I left, I came at nine o'clock in the morning within sight of a well-fortified town, called Coadnabaced,[29] within which was a large force of warriors. The town was so strong, and surrounded by so many hills and ravines some sixty feet in depth, that no horseman could enter it except by two ways, which were then unknown to us; and even to reach them we would have been obliged to make a circuit of about a league and a half. An entrance also could be effected by wooden bridges had they not removed them. The place was so secure and protected, that even had we been ten times as many they could have held it notwithstanding. Upon our approach, they discharged many darts, arrows, and stones at us; but while they were skirmishing with us in this manner, an Indian of Tascaltecal crossed unobserved by a very dangerous pass, and when the enemy suddenly saw him they believed the Spaniards were entering the same way, and thus in a panic they fled with the Indian behind them. Three or four lads, servants of mine, and two from another company, when they saw the Indian cross, followed him, and also reached the other side. I led the horse-men along the sierra to find an entrance to the town, while the enemy in-cessantly discharged darts and arrows at us; for between them and us there was only a narrow ravine. While they were occupied in fighting with us, they had not seen the five Spaniards, so our men took them suddenly from behind, stabbing and slashing at them, taking them completely by surprise, for they did not know that their own people had abandoned the pass by which the Spaniards and the Indians had crossed; so they became so frightened that they lost courage to fight, and the Spaniards killed them, till, perceiving how they had been tricked, they began to fly. Our foot soldiers were already in the town, and began to set fire to it while the enemy abandoned it; and thus escaping the latter reached the sierra although many of them perished, for the horsemen pursued and killed many.

After we discovered how to enter the town, which was about mid-day, we lodged ourselves in some houses in a garden, though we found the place almost all burnt. It was quite late when the chief and other notables, seeing they could not defend themselves in spite of their strong town, and fearing we might pur-sue and kill them in the hilly ground, decided to come and offer themselves as vassals of Your Majesty; I received them as such, and they promised that hence-forth they would always be our friends. These Indians and the others who came to give themselves as vassals of Your Majesty, after we had burnt and destroyed their houses and property, told us that the reason they were so tardy in seeking our friendship was because they thought that they would make good their fault by first allowing us to injure them, believing that this done we would not after-wards be so angry with them. We slept that night in the town, and the next morning marched through deserted and waterless pine forests, passing through a defile, suffering much from fatigue and want of water, so that some Indians who accompanied us perished from thirst. We stopped that night at some farms, seven leagues from the town.

At daybreak we resumed our march and came in sight of a large city, called Suchimilco,[30] which is built on the fresh-water lake. As the Indians were notified of our coming, they had digged many ditches and canals and removed the bridges at all the entrances to the town, which is three or four leagues from Temixtitan. Within, there were many brave-looking people determined to de-fend themselves to the death. As soon as we arrived there and had collected all our people, disposing them in good order and discipline, I dismounted and ad-vanced with certain foot soldiers towards a ditch which had been made, and on the other side of which were infinite warriors. When the fighting began at the ditch, the archers and musketeers did them much damage, so they abandoned it and the Spaniards threw themselves into the water and passed over to dry land.

After half an hour's fighting, we captured the greater part of the city, and the defenders retired in their canoes on the waterways. They fought until nightfall, when some of them sued for peace, but others continued fighting; and so many times did they make overtures without fulfilling them, that finally we discovered they did this from two motives, first that they might carry off their property while we were discussing peace, and secondly to gain time until help should reach them from Mexico and Temixtitan. They killed two Spaniards who had got separated from the others to plunder and found themselves in their extremity beyond reach of assistance.

In the evening, the enemy was debating how to manage that we should not escape alive from their city, and a great number decided to attack us where we had entered; on seeing them advance so rapidly we were surprised to observe their strategy and agility. Six horsemen and myself, who were readier than the others charged amongst them and frightened by the horses they fled, we following them through the city, killing many, though we found ourselves in a great conflict because they were so daring that many of them ventured to face the horsemen with their swords and shields. While we were pell-mell amongst them and in a great confusion, the horse I rode fell through sheer fatigue, and as some of the adversaries saw me on foot they rushed upon me. While I defended myself against them with my lance, an Indian of Tascaltecal,[31] when he saw me in danger, rushed to help me, and he and a servant of mine who joined him helped me to raise the horse. In the midst of this, the Spaniards came up, and the enemy all deserted the field, and I with the other horsemen returned to the city, for we were very weary. Although it was almost night and time for rest, I commanded that all the raised bridges over the water should be filled up with stones and adobes, so that the horses could go and come from the city without obstacle; nor did I leave there till all those difficult crossings had been repaired. We passed that night using great vigilance and giving close attention to the watches.

The next day, all the natives of Mexico and Temixtitan who already knew we were in Suchimilco planned an attack with great force by water and land, so as to surround us; for they believed we could not again escape from their hands. I mounted one of the towers of their idols to see how they would approach and where they would attack us, that I might give all necessary orders. After I had completed our preparations, there appeared on the water a large fleet of canoes which I believe exceeded two thousand; and in them there came more than twelve thousand warriors, in addition to whom there arrived such a multitude of people by land that they covered the whole country. Their captains came at their head, carrying our captured swords in their hands, and naming their provinces, crying, *"Mexico! Mexico! Temixtitan! Temixtitan!"* and shouting insults at us, and threatening to kill us with the swords they had taken from us before in the city of Temixtitan. After I had settled where each captain was to be placed, and as on the mainland there was a great multitude of the enemy, I advanced to attack them with twenty horsemen, and five hundred men of Tascaltecal divided into three companies. I ordered them, as soon as they had scattered the enemy, to collect at the foot of a hill about a half a league from there, where many of the foe had also assembled. When we separated, each division pursued the enemy on its respective side, and, after having routed them and killed many with our swords, we retired to the foot of the hill; there I ordered certain foot soldiers, my servants, who had served me and were very agile, to try to mount the steepest part of the hill. I with the horsemen would then circle round behind, where it was more level, and we would take them in the middle. Thus it happened that, when the enemy saw the Spaniards climbing the hill, they turned, believing they could retreat at their ease, but instead they encountered us, who were about fifteen horsemen; and we fell upon them, as did likewise the warriors of Tascaltecal, so that in a very short time more than five hundred of them perished, and all the others escaped and fled towards the mountains. Six other horsemen planned to go up a very broad and level road, using their lances on the enemy. Half a league from Suchimilco they came upon a squadron of very dashing troops coming to help their countrymen, and routed them, killing some with their lances. When all the horsemen had assembled, we returned about ten o'clock to Suchimilco, finding at the entrance many Spaniards awaiting our return to know what had happened to us; and they told me they had been in great straits and had done their utmost to drive out the enemy, of whom a great number had perished. They gave me two of our swords they had retaken from them, and told me that the bowmen were out of arrows and could get no more. While hearing this, before we dismounted, a great body of the enemy appeared on a very broad causeway, yelling wildly, and promptly we fell upon them, driving them into the water which bordered the causeway on each side; thus we routed them, and, collecting our people, we returned very tired to the city, which I burned entirely except for the part where we lodged. Thus we stopped in the city three days, incessantly fighting, and finally we left having burnt and razed it to the ground. Certainly it was a sight worth beholding, as it had many towers of their idols built of stone and mortar; but, in order not to enlarge, I do not specify many other notable things concerning the city.

The day I left, I went out to a square, which is on the mainland adjoining the city, where the natives held their markets, and I gave orders to ten horsemen to go ahead, and to another ten to march in the middle with the foot soldiers, while I took another ten in the rear; and when the people of Suchimilco saw us leaving, believing it was from fear of them, they attacked our rear, setting up fierce yells. Thereupon the ten horsemen and I returned and fell on them, pursuing them till we drove them into the water; after which they did not bother us any more, and we continued our march. At ten o'clock in the morning we arrived in the city of Cuyoacan two leagues from Suchimilco, as well as from the cities of Temixtitan, Culuacan, Uchilubuzco,[32] Iztapalapa, Cuitaguaca, and Mizqueque, all of which are situated on the water, the furthest being about a league and a half distant. We found it deserted, and lodged in the house of the chief, where we remained two days.

Since I was to lay siege to the great city of Temixtitan as soon as the brigantines were finished, I wished first to see the port of the city and the entrances and exits, and where the Spaniards might attack or be attacked. The day after we arrived, therefore, I took five horsemen and two hundred foot soldiers and went, by a causeway leading into the city of Temixtitan, to the lake which was very near, where we saw an infinite number of canoes on the water with countless warriors in them. We reached a barricade they had erected across the causeway, and the foot soldiers began to attack it; although it was very strong and a stout resistance was offered and ten Spaniards were wounded, we finally won it, killing many of the enemy, although the archers and musketeers exhausted their arrows and powder. From this place, we saw how the causeway led directly through the water until it entered the city of Temixtitan, a full league and a half distant, and that likewise on the other, which goes to Iztapalapa, there were crowds of innumerable people. When I had considered all that it was necessary to observe, for it was likely that a garrison of horsemen and foot soldiers would have to be established here in this city, I ordered our people to retire, and we returned to the town, burning their houses and the towers of their idols.

We departed next day from this city to go to Tacuba, which is two leagues from here, where we arrived at nine o'clock in the morning, using our lances in one place and another along the way, for the enemy came from off the lake to attack and jeer at the Indians who carried our baggage; finding themselves worsted, however, they let us proceed in peace. I have already said that my principal purpose was to make a circuit of all the lakes, in order to reconnoitre and inspect the country better, and also to give help to our friends, hence I did not care to stop in Tacuba. The people of Temixtitan, who were so near there that the city extends almost to the mainland of Tacuba, seeing that we went on, recovered much confidence and with great daring attacked the centre of our baggage-train; but as the horsemen were well stationed and the ground was all level thereabouts, we had great advantage over them, without risking any danger ourselves. As we were galloping from one side to the other, two of the several youths, my servants, who usually followed me, did not do so, but chanced to go aside where they were captured by the enemy, who, we believe, put them to a very cruel death, as was their custom. God knows how grieved I was by it, both because they were Christians, and also because they were brave men who had served Your Majesty well in this war. After leaving this city, we continued our march through other neighbouring towns, and rejoined our people, where I learned how the Indians had captured those youths. To avenge their death, and because the enemy followed us with the greatest insolence in the world, I, with twenty horsemen, concealed myself behind some houses, and, as the Indians saw the other ten with the people and baggage going ahead, they followed them fearlessly by another very broad and level road; thus, when we saw that they had passed somewhat, I shouted in the name of the Apostle Santiago and we fell upon them furiously. Before they could reach the canals near there, we killed more than a hundred splendid chiefs; after which they did not care to follow us any further. This day we slept two leagues beyond, in the city of Coatinchan, tired out and wet, as it had rained a great deal that afternoon; and we found it deserted. We set out the next day, using our lances from time to time on some Indians who came to yell at us, and we slept at a town, called Gilotepeque,[33] finding it also deserted. The next day, we went at twelve o'clock to a city, called Aculman,[34] belonging to the lordship of the city of Tesaico, where we slept that night and were well received by the Spaniards, who rejoiced at our coming as if it were their salvation; because after I had left them they had heard nothing of me till the day we arrived. They had suffered various alarms in the city, and the inhabitants had been daily saying to them that the men of Mexico and Temixtitan would fall on them while I was absent. Thus, with God's help, this expedition was concluded, and it was a very great enterprise in which Your Majesty received great service, for many reasons, as I shall hereafter state.

When I came for the first time to the city of Temixtitan, Very Powerful and Invincible Lord, I ordered, as I made known to Your Majesty in my other relation, that certain plantations should be established for Your Majesty in two or three of the most desirable provinces. I sent two Spaniards to one of them, called Chinantla,[35] which is not subject to the Culuans; in the others, which were, the Culuans killed those who were at the plantations when they made war on me in Temixtitan, and took everything they had, which was a very considerable sum according to the estimates of this country. During almost a year I could learn nothing about the Spaniards who settled in Chinantla, nor, while all those provinces were in revolt, could they hear any thing from us. The natives of Chinantla, being vassals of Your Majesty and enemies of the Culuans, told those Christians that the Culuans had made fierce war upon us, and, as they believed few or none of us had come out alive, they would not allow the Spaniards to leave the country; and thus these two stayed there. One of them, who was a youth and a soldier, they made their captain, and at this time he went out with them to fight their enemies, over whom he and they were victorious most of the time. When it pleased God they should afterwards return, and reorganise, and obtain some victories over the enemy who had routed and expelled us from Temixtitan, the people of Chinantla told those Christians that they knew there were Spaniards in the province of Tepeaca, and that, if they wished to learn the truth, they would risk sending two Indians who, although they had to pass through much hostile country, could travel at night and off the highway till they reached Tepeaca. The better man of the two Spaniards sent a letter by those two Indians, the tenor of which was as follows: "Noble Sirs, I have written Your Worships two or three letters, but I do not know if they have reached you or not as they have had no answer, so I doubt whether this will obtain one. I make it known to you, Sirs, that all the natives of this country of Culua are up in arms and have attacked us many times; but always (praise be to Our Lord for it) we have been victorious. We have also had daily war with the natives of Tuxtepeque, for they are allies of Culua. Those who have remained in the service of Their Highnesses as their vassals are seven towns of Tenez; and Nicolas and I have always stopped in Chinantla, which is the capital. I would like very much to know where the captain is, in order to write to him and make known what has happened here. If perchance you can write me where he is, and will send twenty or thirty Spaniards, I would go thither with two of the chiefs from here who wish to see and speak with the captain. It would be well for them to come now because it is the harvest time for cacao, and the Culuans hinder it by making war. May the Lord guard the noble persons of Your Worships, according to your desire. From Chinantla, I know not what date of the month of April, of the year 1521. At the service of Your Worships, Hernando de Barrientos."

When the two Indians arrived with this letter in the province of Tepeaca, the captain, whom I had left there with certain Spaniards, sent it immediately to me at Tesaico; and we all rejoiced greatly at receiving it, because, though we had always confided in the friendship of Chinantla, sometimes the thought occurred to us that they might confederate with Culua and kill the two Spaniards. I immediately wrote, giving them an account of what had happened, and telling them to have hope, for, although they were surrounded on every side by enemies, by God's pleasure, they would very soon find themselves free and able to come and go in safety.

After having made the circuit of the lakes, during which I gathered much important information for laying siege to Temixtitan by land and water, I stopped in Tesaico, strengthening myself as best I could with people and arms, hastening to get the brigantines finished and making a canal to take them to the lake; which canal was begun immediately after the planks and joinings of the brigantines had been brought, and extended from one side of our camp to the lake. From the place where the brigantines were being joined there was quite a half a league's distance to the lake. More than eight thousand natives of Acolhuacan and Tesaico were employed daily for fifty days; for the channel of the canal was more than twelve feet deep and as many in width, all staked and walled. Thus, the water which flows through it would by its own force carry them to the lake, so that we could take the smaller vessels without danger, and with little labour to the water. It certainly was a very great work, worthy of admiration.

As soon as the brigantines were finished and put in the canal on the twenty-eighth of April[36] of the said year, I made a review of all my people and found eighty-six horsemen, a hundred and eighteen bowmen and musketeers, seven hundred and odd foot soldiers with swords and shields, three heavy iron guns, fifteen small bronze field pieces and ten cwt. of powder. Having finished the review, I charged and recommended all the Spaniards to obey and comply with the ordinances which I had made respecting the conduct of the war, and to be merry, and keep up their courage inasmuch as they saw how Our Lord was leading us to victory over our enemies; for they well knew that when we entered Tesaico we had brought only forty horsemen, but that God had helped us even more than we had thought, for a ship had arrived with horses, men, and arms, as they had seen; and I said principally that the fact that we were fighting to promote the spread of our faith and for the reduction to Your Majesty's service of so many revolted provinces, should fill them with courage and zeal to conquer or die. They all answered, demonstrating a willingness and desire for this; and we passed the day of the review in great rejoicing, longing to see ourselves already engaged in the siege and to bring this war to an end, on which the peace or further disturbance of these parts so much depended.

The next day, I sent messengers to the provinces of Tascaltecal, Guajucingo, and Churultecal, to let them know that the brigantines were ready, and that I and all of my people were about to surround the great city of Temixtitan. Therefore I begged them, since they were notified by me and had already prepared their people, that as many of them as possible and as well armed as they could be, should set out and join me here in Tesaico, where I would wait ten days for them, and that they should by no means exceed that time, because it would disarrange everything that had been planned. When the messengers arrived, the people of those provinces were already prepared and eager to meet the Culuans: those from Guajucingo and Churultecal came to Calco as I had ordered, for the siege was to be begun near that place. The captains of Tascaltecal arrived in Tesaico with very brilliant and well-armed forces, five or six days before the Feast of the Holy Ghost, which was the time I had designated to them. When I learned that day of their approach, I went out to meet them with great rejoicing, and they came so gladly and so well disciplined that things could not have been better. According to the account the captains made, there were more than fifty thousand warriors, who were well received by us and given quarters.

The second day after the Feast, I ordered all the foot soldiers and horsemen to assemble in the square of the city of Tesaico, that I might divide them and assign them to the captains, who were to lead them in three divisions to be stationed in three cities which are around Temixtitan. I made Pedro de Alvarado[37] captain of one division, assigning him thirty horsemen, eighteen archers and musketeers, and one hundred and fifty foot soldiers with swords and shields, and more than twenty-five thousand warriors of Tascaltecal; these were to make their headquarters in Tacuba. I made Cristobal de Olid captain of another division, to whom I assigned thirty horsemen, eighteen archers and musketeers, and a hundred and sixty foot-soldiers with swords and shields, and more than twenty thousand warriors of our allies; these were to make their headquarters in Cuyoacan. Of the third division, I made Gonzalo de Sandoval, alguacil mayor, captain, assigning him twenty-four horsemen, four musketeers, fifteen archers, and a hundred and fifty foot soldiers with swords and shields, fifty of whom were chosen among those I had brought in my company, and more than thirty thousand men of the people of Guajucingo, Churultecal, and Calco. This division was to go to the city of Iztapalapa for the purpose of destroying it, and afterwards to advance over a causeway in the lake, protected by the brigantines, in order to join with the garrison at Cuyoacan, so that after I entered the lake with the brigantines, the alguacil mayor might fix his headquarters wherever it seemed to him most convenient. For the thirteen brigantines with which I was to enter the lake, I left three hundred men, almost all of whom were sailors[38] and well drilled, so that in each brigantine were twenty-five Spaniards; and each small vessel had a captain, a pilot, and six archers and musketeers.

According to the foregoing order the captains, who were to command the forces in the cities of Tacuba and Cuyoacan, after receiving instructions as to what they were to do, left Tesaico on the tenth of May, and slept in a fine town, called Aculman, two and a half leagues from there. The same day, I learned that some dispute had arisen between the captains about the quarters, and, to settle this and re-establish peace, I immediately sent a person who reproved and pacified them.[39] On the morning of the next day, they left there, and passed the night in another town, called Gilotepeque, which they found deserted, as it was within the enemy's country. The next day, they continued their march according to their instructions, and slept in a city, called Guatitlan, which I have before mentioned to Your Majesty, and which they also found deserted. The same day they passed through two other cities and towns, where they likewise found no people. At the hour of vespers, they entered Tacuba, which they also found deserted, and made their quarters in the houses of the chief, which are very beautiful and large. Although it was already late the warriors of Tascaltecal made an inspection of the entrance of two causeways leading to the city of Temixtitan and fought bravely for two or three hours with the people of the city until night separated them, when they returned safely to Tacuba.

The next morning, the two captains agreed, as I had commanded them, to cut off the aqueducts which supplied Temixtitan with fresh water. One of them went with twenty horsemen and some archers and musketeers to the source of the water, about a quarter of a league from there, and broke the pipes, which were of wood and mortar and stone, fighting valiantly with those of the city who defended the spring by land and water. At last he routed them and accomplished his purpose, cutting off the fresh water from the city—a very politic stratagem. The same day, the captains repaired certain dangerous passes, bridges, and aqueducts, in the neighbourhood of the lake, so that the horsemen might the more easily gallop from one part to another. This delayed them three or four days, during which they had many skirmishes with those of the city, wherein some Spaniards were wounded, many of the enemy killed, and many bridges and dikes captured. There was much bandying of words, and many challenges between those of the city and the warriors of Tascaltecal, things very remarkable and worthy of notice.

The captain, Cristobal de Olid, departed with the people who were to be garrisoned in Cuyoacan, two leagues from Tacuba, and the captain, Pedro de Alvarado, stayed with his people in garrison at Tacuba, where he had skirmishes daily with the Indians. The same day that Cristobal de Olid left for Cuyoacan, he and his men arrived at ten o'clock in the morning and lodged in the houses of its chief, finding the city deserted. The next morning, with about twenty horsemen, some archers, and some six or seven thousand warriors of Tascaltecal they went to take a look at the causeway leading to Temixtitan; and they found the enemy well prepared, the causeway broken up, and many barricades erected. They engaged the enemy, and the archers wounded and killed some of their number. This was repeated for six or seven days, on each of which there were many encounters and skirmishes. One night, at midnight, certain watchmen of the city gave their cry near our quarters and the Spanish watchman cried "To arms!" whereupon our men sallied forth, but none of the enemy were to be found, for the cry which had alarmed them had been given very far from headquarters. As our people were distributed in so many places, the garrisons longed, as for their salvation, for my arrival with the brigantines and they continued hopeful those few days until I arrived, as I shall hereafter relate. During those six days, they would meet from both headquarters daily as they were near each other, and the horsemen scoured the country killing many of the enemy with their lances and bringing into the headquarters from the mountains great quantities of maize, of which bread is made, the principal food of these parts, and much superior to that of the Islands.

In the preceding chapters, I stated that I remained in Tesaico with three hundred men and the thirteen brigantines. As soon as I knew the divisions were in the places assigned for their camps, I could embark and take a look at the city and do some damage to the canoes. Although I very much wished to go by land, to give directions in the camps, the captains were persons who could be trusted with what they had in hand, while the affair of the brigantines was a matter of great importance, requiring stern discipline and attention, so I determined to embark in them, because we calculated to have the greatest risk and adventure by water. The principal persons of my company, however, required me in due form to go with the garrisons, as they believed that they were to undertake the most dangerous part. The day after the Feast of Corpus Christi, Friday, at dawn, I ordered Gonzalo de Sandoval, alguacil mayor, to go with his people directly to the city of Iztapalapa, about six short leagues from there; shortly after mid-day they arrived there, and began to burn it, and to fight with its people, who, when they saw the great force of the alguacil mayor, for more than thirty-five or forty thousand of our allies had gone with him, retreated to their canoes. The alguacil mayor, with all the people accompanying him, lodged in that town, and remained there that day awaiting my orders and what might happen to me.

Immediately after I had despatched the alguacil mayor, I embarked in the brigantines, and we started with sails and oars; and while the alguacil mayor was fighting and burning the city of Iztapalapa, we came in sight of a very large and strong hill[40] near that city, all surrounded by water, where, from the towns around about the lake as well as from Temixtitan, many people had collected, for they well knew that our first encounter would be with those of Iztapalapa, and they were there for their own defence and also to attack us if possible. When they saw the fleet coming, they began to shout and make great smoke signals so that all the cities of the lake might know and be prepared. Although my intention was to attack that part of Iztapalapa which is on the water, we retraced our course to that hill or knoll and I leaped on it with a hundred and fifty men; it was very steep and high and it was with much difficulty that we began to ascend it. We stormed their trenches on the top, and pitched into them in such wise that not one of them escaped, except the women and children. In this fight they wounded twenty-five Spaniards, but it was a beautiful victory.

As the people of Iztapalapa had made smoke signals from some towers of their idols which stand on a very high hill near the city, Temixtitan and the other cities on the water knew that I had already entered the lake with the brigantines, and they quickly assembled a very great fleet of canoes to attack us, and to discover what sort of things the brigantines were; and from what we could judge the canoes exceeded five hundred in number. When I saw that their course was straight towards us, I, and the people who had disembarked on that great hill, re-embarked in great haste, and I ordered the captains of the brigantines not to move at all, so that the canoes believing that from fear of them we did not dare to move out towards them might decide to attack us. Thus they directed their fleet against us with great impetus; but at about two arrow-shots' distance they stopped and remained still. I strongly desired that the first encounter with them should be a great victory and inspire them with a dread of the brigantines, which held the key of the whole war, for both the Mexicans and we were exposed to the greatest damage on the water. It pleased Our Lord that, while we were observing one another, a very favourable land wind sprang up, enabling us to attack them; so I immediately ordered the captains to break through the fleet of canoes and pursue them till they took refuge in Temixtitan. As the wind was very good, we bore down in the midst of them, though they fled as fast as they could, and destroyed an infinite number of canoes and killed and drowned many of the enemy, the greatest sight to be seen in the world. We followed them in this pursuit fully three long leagues, until we shut them up amidst the houses of the city; and thus it pleased Our Lord to give us the best and greatest victory which we could have asked or desired.

The garrison of Cuyoacan could see better than that of Tacuba the movements of the brigantines, and when they beheld all the thirteen sails on the water, favoured by such good weather, knocking the enemy's canoes to pieces, they afterwards assured me it was the one thing in the world which gave them the most pleasure and that they most wished for. As I have said, they and those at Tacuba strongly wished me to come there, and with good reason, for both garrisons were in the midst of such multitudes of enemies; but Our Lord miraculously inspired them and diminished the enemy's courage so that they were unable to decide to attack our camp, but had they done so, they would have done great harm to the Spaniards, although they were always well prepared and determined to conquer or die, like men cut off from all succour save what they hoped from God. When the garrison of Cuyoacan saw us pursuing the canoes, most of the horsemen and foot soldiers took the road towards the city of Temixtitan, and fought very stoutly with the Indians who were on the causeway. They captured the trenches which had been made, and passed over many abandoned bridges, on foot and on horseback under cover of the brigantines which sailed near the causeway. Our allies of Tascaltecal and the Spaniards pursued the enemy, some of whom they killed and others they forced to seek refuge in the water on the other side of the causeway from where the brigantines approached. Thus victoriously they advanced a long league on the causeway until they reached the place where I stopped with the brigantines, as I shall hereafter relate.

We continued chasing the canoes with the brigantines for nearly three leagues. Those which escaped us took refuge amongst the houses of the city, and, as it was already vespers, I ordered the brigantines to retire, and we arrived with them at the causeway. Here I determined to land with thirty men and capture two small towers[41] of their idols, which were surrounded by a low wall of stone and mortar; and, when we landed, they fought us very stoutly to defend them, but finally after much danger and trouble we captured them. I immediately landed and mounted three heavy iron field pieces which I had brought. As about half a league of that causeway between that point and the city was crowded with the enemy, and on both sides of the causeway the water was covered with canoes full of warriors, I ordered one of the field pieces to be aimed and fired, which raked the causeway, and did much execution amongst the enemy. Owing to the carelessness of the gunner, all our powder was set fire to when he fired, although it was little. I presently sent a brigantine to Iztapalapa, some two leagues distant, where the alguacil mayor was, to bring all the powder he had.

Although, at the beginning, it was my intention on embarking in the brigantines to go to Cuyoacan and plan to do as much damage as possible, as soon as I had landed on the causeway that day and had captured those two towers, I determined to establish my headquarters there, and to keep the brigantines near the towers. I also ordered the force at Cuyoacan and some fifty of the alguacil mayor's soldiers to come there next day. Having determined these measures, we passed the night with caution, for we were in much danger, as all the people of the city gathered there on the causeway and on the water. At midnight a great multitude of people arrived in canoes and began to attack our camp by the causeway: certainly they threw us into great fear and alarm, especially as it was at night and they never attack at such an hour nor had they ever been seen to fight at night except when they were very sure of victory. As we were well prepared, we fought with them, using the small field pieces from the brigantines, each of which carried one, and the archers and musketeers did their part. Thus they dared not advance further, nor did they arrive near enough to do us any injury; so they left off attacking us for the remainder of the night.

Next morning at daybreak, there arrived at my camp on the causeway, fifteen archers and musketeers, fifty men armed with swords and shields, and seven or eight horsemen from the garrison at Cuyoacan. When they got there, those of the city were fighting with us from canoes and on the causeway, and the multitude was such that on land and water we could see nothing but people, who shouted and yelled so that it seemed the world was sinking. We fought with them, advancing on the causeway and capturing a bridge which they had removed, and a barricade they had made at its entrance. We did them such damage with the field pieces and the horsemen, that we almost shut them up amidst the first houses of the city. As many canoes were collected on the other side of the causeway where the brigantines could not pass, doing us much harm with the arrows and darts they discharged at us on the causeway, I ordered an opening to be made near our camp, and sent four brigantines through from the other side, which as soon as they passed through, shut up all the canoes amongst the houses of the city, so that they did not dare in any way to come out into the open. On the other side of the causeway, the other eight brigantines fought with the canoes and shut them up amongst the houses, following in amongst them, where, until then, they had not ventured to go, because there were so many shallows and stakes which prevented them. When they found canals where the brigantines could enter with safety, they fought with the people in the canoes and captured some of them, and burned many of the houses in the outskirts. We spent all that day in fighting in the aforesaid manner.

The following day, the alguacil mayor departed from Iztapalapa with his people, Spaniards as well as our allies, for Cuyoacan whence there is a causeway about a league and a half in length to the mainland. After making about a quarter of a league, the alguacil mayor reached a small city [Mexicaltzingo] which is also on the water, in many parts of which it was possible to ride on horseback; the inhabitants began fighting with him, but he routed them, killing many, and burning and destroying the entire city. When I learned that the Indians had made a great breach in the causeway, which the people could not easily cross, I sent two brigantines to help them, and these were used as bridges for the foot soldiers to cross over. When they had crossed, they went to camp at Cuyoacan, and the alguacil mayor with ten horsemen took the causeway road to our camp. Upon his arrival he found us fighting, so he and his men joined in and began to fight with the people on the causeway with whom we were engaged. When the alguacil mayor began to fight, the enemy pierced his foot with a dart, but, although he and some others were wounded that day, we did such harm amongst them with the large field pieces and cross-bows and muskets, that neither those in the canoes, nor those on the causeway, dared come near us, but showed more fear and less pride than they had formerly exhibited. Thus we remained six days, having daily combat with them, and the brigantines set fire to all the houses they could in the outskirts of the city, for they discovered canals by which they could enter the outskirts and environs, and penetrated to the heart of it.

This produced a very desirable effect, as they put a stop to the movements of the canoes, none of which dared to come within a quarter of a league of our camp. The next day, Pedro de Alvarado, captain of the garrison at Tacuba, reported to me that the people of Temixtitan came in and out as they pleased by a highway which leads to some towns on the mainland, and by another small one which joins it, and he believed that should they find themselves hard pressed, they would escape by that way. Although I desired their departure more than they themselves did, as we could more easily overcome them on the mainland than in the big fortress they had on the water, nevertheless in order to completely shut them in so that they could not profit by anything from the mainland, I ordered the alguacil mayor (although he was wounded), to go and plant his camp at a little village at the end of one of the two causeways. He left with twenty-three horsemen, a hundred foot soldiers, eighteen archers and musketeers, leaving me fifty other soldiers for my company; and, when he arrived the next day, he planted his camp where I had commanded him. Thenceforward the city of Temixtitan was surrounded on all sides wherever they could reach the mainland by the causeways.

I had, Very Powerful Lord, two hundred Spanish foot soldiers in the camp on the causeway, amongst whom were twenty-five archers and musketeers, besides the people on the brigantines, who were more than two hundred and fifty. As we had the enemy completely invested and had many friendly warriors, I determined to penetrate into the city as far as possible by the causeway, while the brigantines should cover our rear on the one side and the other. I ordered some horsemen and foot soldiers of the division in Cuyoacan to repair to my camp and enter with us, and ten horsemen to remain at the entrance of the causeway, protecting our rear. It seemed best that some force should remain in Cuyoacan, because the natives of Suchimilco, Culuacan, Iztapalapa, Chilobusco, Mexicalcingo, Cuitaguacad, and Mizquique, which are all on the water, were rebellious and in favour of those of the city, and should they wish to take us on our rear, we would be protected by those ten or twelve horsemen I ordered to guard the causeway, while many more remained in Cuyoacan with more than ten thousand Indian allies. I likewise ordered the alguacil mayor and Pedro de Alvarado to attack, from their positions, that same day, for I wished on my part to gain as much of the city as was possible.

Thus, I left the camp early in the morning, and advanced on foot along the causeway. We speedily found the enemy, defending a breach in the road, one lance-length in width and as much in depth, where they had built an earthwork; both our attack and their defence were very stubborn. Finally we took it, and advanced further by the causeway, until we reached the entrance of the city, where stood a tower of their idols, at the foot of which was a broad, high bridge, crossing a very wide street of water defended by another strong earthwork. As we reached this place, they began to attack us, but as the brigantines were on

both sides of the causeway, we took it without loss, which would have been
impossible without their aid. As soon as they began to abandon the earthwork,
our men landed from the brigantines, and we crossed the water, as did those of
Tascaltecal, Guajocingo, Calco, and Tesaico, who were more than eighty thousand men. While we filled up that broken bridge with stones and adobes, the
Spaniards captured another earthwork in the principal street, which is the
broadest one in the city, but, there being no water there, it was very easily captured. They followed in pursuit of the enemy the whole length of the street until
the latter reached another bridge which had been raised, with the exception of
one broad beam by which they crossed. After the enemy had safely crossed to
where they were protected by the water, they quickly removed it. They had
thrown up on the other side of the bridge another great breastwork of earth and
adobes. When we arrived there, we could not pass without throwing ourselves
into the water, and this was very dangerous, as the enemy fought very valiantly,
and on both sides of the street there was an infinite number of them fighting
very stoutly from the roofs; but when some archers and musketeers arrived and
we fired with two field pieces up the street, we did them much damage. As soon
as we saw this, certain Spaniards threw themselves into the water and crossed
to the other side, which it required two hours to accomplish. When the enemy
saw them cross, they abandoned the breastwork and the roofs, and took to flight
through the street, and thus all our people passed over.

I immediately ordered that bridge filled up and the breastwork destroyed,
and meanwhile the Spaniards continued the pursuit along the street and our
Indian allies followed for about two bow-shots distance until they reached another bridge which is near the square and the principal buildings of the city.
They had not removed this bridge nor did they have an earthwork, for they
never thought we would gain what we did that day, nor did even we expect to
accomplish half as much. A field piece was placed at the entrance of the square,
and did the enemy much damage, for they were so numerous that they completely filled the space. The Spaniards, seeing there was no water there, which
was the usual danger, determined to penetrate into the square, and, when those
of the city saw this determination carried out, and beheld the great multitude of
our allies, (although they were not afraid of them without us) they fled, and the
Spaniards and our allies pursued them till they shut them up in the court of their
idols, which is surrounded by a wall of stone and mortar. As will have been seen
from another description of this, it has as great a circumference as a town of
four hundred households; it was however quickly abandoned by them, and the
Spaniards and our allies captured it, remaining in it and on the towers for a long
while. When the inhabitants of the city discovered there were no horsemen,
they turned against the Spaniards and expelled them by force from the towers

and the court and enclosure, during which our men found themselves in much hardship and danger; as they came in more than a retreat[42] they turned under the arches of the courtyard. But the enemy attacking them very stoutly, they abandoned this position and retired to the square, whence they were expelled by force and driven into the street, so that the field piece there had to be abandoned. The Spaniards, being unable to withstand the force of the enemy, had to retreat exposed to great danger, in the midst of which it pleased God that three horsemen should advance into the square; when the enemy saw them they believed there were more, and took to flight; and the horsemen killed some of them and recaptured the court and enclosure I mentioned above. In the principal and highest tower, which has a hundred and some steps to the top, ten or twelve of the principal Indians of the city fortified themselves, but four or five Spaniards forced their way up and overpowered and killed all of them in spite of their stout defence.[43] Five or six horsemen afterwards concerted with others and laid an ambush in which they killed more than thirty of the enemy.

As it was now late, I ordered our people to collect and retire, and, while doing so, such a multitude of the enemy pressed on them, that, had it not been for the horsemen, the Spaniards could not possibly have escaped without injury. But, as I had had all the difficult passes in the street and causeway, where danger was anticipated, well filled in with adobes by the time of retiring, the horsemen could easily move about, so they turned against the enemy, who were harassing our rear-guard four or five times in the length of the street, killing some of them with their lances. Although the enemy saw they sustained damage, the dogs rushed on so furiously that we could not check them nor would they stop following us. The whole day would have been spent in this manner, had they not already taken many terraces giving on to the street, and the horsemen were from this cause in much danger. Thus we hastened forward along the causeway to our camp without losing a single Spaniard, although we had some wounded; and we set fire to most of the best houses in that street, so that when we entered again they could not injure us from the roofs. The alguacil mayor and Pedro de Alvarado fought very stoutly this day from their positions, and at the time of the combats we were a league and a half from one another; the population of the city is so extended that perhaps I even diminish the distance between us. Our allies who were with them were infinite and fought very well, retiring that day without sustaining any loss.[44]

In the meantime, Don Fernando, Lord of Tesaico and the province of Aculuacan, of whom I have heretofore made relation to Your Majesty, succeeded in winning over all the natives of his city and province to our friendship, who till now were not so steadfast in it as they afterwards became. Many chiefs and the brothers of Don Fernando daily joined him, determined to declare for us and to fight against those of Mexico and Temixtitan. As Don Fernando was still a youth and professed great love for the Spaniards, recognising the favour, which, in the name of Your Majesty, had been extended to him in the gift of so great a lordship, though there were others whose rights to it preceded his, he worked his utmost to induce his vassals to come and fight against those of the city, and expose themselves to the same danger and hardship as we ourselves. He spoke with his brothers, six or seven in number, all well disposed, beseeching them to bring all the people of their lordships to help me. He sent one of them, called Istrisuchil, who is twenty-three or twenty-four years of age, very brave, beloved and feared of all, as captain, who arrived at the camp on the causeway with more than thirty thousand warriors, very well supplied in their fashion, and another twenty thousand joined the other two camps.[45] I received them gladly, thanking them for their good disposition and conduct. Your Caesarian Majesty may well judge how valuable was this help and friendship from Don Fernando, and how those of Temixtitan felt it, to see those whom they considered their vassals, friends, relatives, and even fathers, brothers, and sons, marching against them.

Fighting went on in the city for two days, as I have said above. As soon as these people came to our help, the natives of Suchimilco, which is on the lake, and some Otomí[46] tribes who are a mountain people, more numerous than those of Suchimilco, and who were slaves of Moctezuma, came to offer themselves as vassals of Your Majesty, begging me to pardon their tardiness. I received them very well, and was pleased at their coming, for they constituted the only danger to our camp in Cuyoacan.

From the camp on the causeway we had, with the help of the brigantines, burned many houses in the outskirts of the city, and not a canoe dared venture there. I deemed it sufficient for our safety to keep seven brigantines about our camp, and I therefore decided to send three to each of the other camps of the alguacil mayor and Pedro de Alvarado, instructing the captains that, as supplies of fresh water, fruits, maize, and other provisions came from the mainland on those sides, they should cruise about both day and night, taking turns, and moreover that they should back up our people when we planned an assault to force an entrance into the city. The allotment of these six brigantines to the two other camps was a very necessary and profitable measure, for every day and night they captured many canoes and prisoners.

These measures being decided, and the people above mentioned having come peaceably to our help, I told them I had determined to enter and fight in the city two days hence, that therefore they should all assemble, by that time, well prepared and furnished for war; for by this I would recognise whether they were our true friends; and they promised to be ready. The next day, I had the people prepared and equipped, and I wrote to the camps and two brigantines what I had determined and what they should do.

After having heard mass next morning, and having instructed the captains as to what they should do, I left our quarters with fifteen or twenty horsemen and three hundred Spaniards and all our allies, who were an infinite number, and, advancing along the causeway, we found the enemy already waiting for us, three bow-shots from the camp, yelling fearfully. During the three preceding days there had been no fighting with them so they had undone all we had accomplished in filling up the breaches in the causeway, making them very much stronger and more dangerous to capture than before. The brigantines accompanied us on both sides of the causeway, for they could approach very near, and do much damage with field pieces, muskets, and crossbows. Discovering this, our men landed and captured the breast-works and bridge; we crossed to the other side and pursued the enemy, who immediately fortified themselves in the other breast-works and bridges they had prepared, which, although with greater trouble and danger than before, we also captured, expelling them from the street and square where the great houses of the city stand. I ordered that no Spaniard should leave there while I and our allies were filling the breaks in the causeway with stones and adobes, which was such a labour, that although ten thousand Indians helped us, it was already the hour of vespers when we had finished making repairs; during all which time the Spaniards and our allies were constantly fighting and skirmishing and preparing ambushes, in which many of the enemy perished. I rode with the horsemen through the city for a while, and in the streets where there is no water, we killed with our lances all whom we could catch, thus holding them at a distance, nor did they dare to come on dry ground. Seeing that they were so rebellious and showed such determination to defend themselves to the death, I inferred two things: first that we should recover little or none of the treasures they had taken from us, and the other, that they gave occasion and forced us to totally destroy them. This last reason caused me the greater grief, for it weighed on my soul and made me reflect on what means I might employ to frighten them, so that they should realise their error and the injury they would sustain from us; and I kept on burning and destroying the towers of their idols and their houses. In order to make them feel it the more, I this day ordered fire to be set to the great houses in the square, where the Spaniards and I had first been quartered when they expelled us from the city. They were so extensive that a prince with more than six hundred persons of his household and retinue could be lodged in them. Some others close to them, though somewhat smaller, were also very splendid and fine, and Moctezuma kept all kinds of birds in them. Although it grieved me much, I determined, as it grieved them even more, to burn these edifices. This seemed to cause the enemies immense sorrow, as well as to their allies in the cities about the lake, for none of them ever thought our force would be sufficient to penetrate so far into the city; and they were greatly dismayed. After setting fire to those houses, I collected our people, as it was already late, in order to return to our camp, and, when those of the city saw we were retiring, an infinite number of them charged us and fell upon us furiously, attacking our rear-guard. As the whole street was available to the horsemen, we turned on them, lancing many every time; nevertheless they would not keep away from our rear, yelling all the time. On this day, they felt and showed great dismay, especially when they saw us in their city, burning and destroying it, and the natives of Tesaico, Calco, Suchimilco, and the Otomí fighting against them, each shouting the name of his province; and in another quarter those of Tascaltecal, all showing them their countrymen cut in pieces, telling them they would sup off them that night and breakfast off them next morning, as in fact they did. We returned to our camp to rest, for we had laboured much during that day, and my seven brigantines had entered that day into the city by the water streets and burned a greater part of it. The captains of the other camps and the six brigantines fought very well that day, and about what happened to them I might dilate a great deal, but to avoid prolixity, omit doing so, and limit myself to saying that after the victory they retired to their camp without suffering any loss.

Early in the morning of the following day, after having heard mass, I returned to the city with all the people in the same order, so as not to give the enemy time to excavate the bridges and rebuild the barricades; but notwithstanding that we were very early, two of the three water streets, which crossed the street leading from this camp to the large houses of the square, had been re-established as during the preceding days and were very difficult to capture; so much so that the combat lasted from eight o'clock in the morning till one o'clock in the afternoon, during which we used up almost all the arrows, ammunition, and musket balls, which the archers and musketeers had with them. Your Majesty may well believe that our danger each time we captured these bridges was unequalled, because to take them, the Spaniards were obliged to swim across to the other side, which many could not do, because the enemy awaited them with knife and lance thrusts to prevent their landing. But as they no longer had roofs on the other side from whence to injure us, and we used our crossbows from this side on them (for we were the throw of a horseshoe from each other), the Spaniards daily gathered new courage and were determined to cross, for they saw my determination, and sink or swim, the thing must be done. It may seem to Your Majesty, that after having gone through such danger to gain these bridges and barricades, that we were negligent in not holding them after having won them, so as not to be obliged every day to again go over so much danger and trouble,

which unquestionably were very great, and certainly it must appear thus to
those who were absent. But Your Majesty should know that this could in no
wise be done, because two things were required to do it, either that the camp
should be transferred from where it was to the square enclosure of the towers
of the idols, or that a guard should be placed at the bridges during the night;
and neither one nor the other could be done without great danger, nor was there
possibility of it, because placing the camp in the city we should have had to
sustain a thousand contests day and night and at every hour, and they would
have fought us and given us intolerable labour, attacking us on every side, they
being so many and we so few. As for placing people to guard the bridges by
night, the Spaniards were so weary after fighting all day, that it was impossible
to do this, and hence we were obliged to retake them every day when we entered the city. That day, as we were delayed in retaking those bridges and
refilling them, no time was left for anything else, except that by another principal street leading to the city of Tacuba, two other bridges were captured and
filled up, and many good houses in this street were burned; thus the afternoon
came on and with it the hour for retiring, which was always accompanied by
little less danger than taking the bridges, for seeing that we were in retreat,
those of the city would recover as much courage as if they had won the greatest
victory in the world, and we were flying from them. To retire it was necessary
that the bridges should be well filled up and made level with the ground of the
streets, so that the horsemen might freely gallop from one place to another; and
as they pursued so eagerly we sometimes feigned in the retreat to be flying, and
then the horsemen would turn on them and we would always capture twelve or
thirteen of the bravest, and with these manoeuvres and some ambushes we constantly laid for them, they would always get the worst of it. Certainly it was an
admirable thing to see, for, although the injury and damage, with which they
were threatened from us at the hour of our retreat, was notorious, they would
nevertheless follow us until they saw us out of the city. With this we returned
to our camp, and the captains of the other camps reported to me that they had
done very well that day, and had killed many people by water and land.

The captain Pedro de Alvarado who was in Tacuba, wrote to me that he
had captured two or three bridges, for he was on the causeway which leads
from the market of Temixtitan to Tacuba, and the three brigantines I had given
him could reach a landing place on the same causeway, and he had not been
exposed to as much danger as on the preceding days, and where he was there
were more bridges and breaks in the causeway, although there were fewer roofs
than in the other directions.

During all this time the natives of Iztapalapa, Oichilobuzco, Culuacan, Mez-
quique, and Cuitaguaca, which as I have said are on the fresh-water lake, would

never seek peace, nor had we all this time sustained any injury from them; and as the Calcans were very loyal vassals of Your Majesty, and saw that we had enough to do with those of the great city, they joined with other towns on the borders of the lake, to do all the damage they could to those towns on the water. Seeing we were daily victorious over those of Temixtitan, and on account of the injury they were sustaining and might sustain from our friends, these rebellious natives determined to come; and they arrived in our camp and besought me to pardon them the past, and to order the Calcans and their other neighbours to do them no further injury.[47] I told them I was pleased with this and harboured no anger against any except those of the city; and that we might believe their friendship sincere, I prayed them, that inasmuch as I was determined not to raise the siege till I had taken the city by peace or war, and as they had many canoes capable of aiding me, they should prepare everything they could with as many warriors as were in their towns, to henceforward aid us on the water. I also prayed them that inasmuch as the Spaniards had few and miserable huts, and it was the rainy season, to build us as many houses in the camp as they could, and to bring adobes and beams from the houses of the city which were nearest to the camp. They answered that the canoes and warriors were prepared every day, and they served me so well in building the houses, that, between the two towers on the one side and the other of the causeway where I was lodged, they built so many that from the first house to the last, there was a distance of three or four bow-shots. Your Majesty may see how broad is this causeway, which crosses the deepest part of the lake, from the fact that between these houses, built on both sides, there was ample room to go and come on foot and horseback. There were constantly in the camp, between Spaniards and Indian servants, more than two thousand persons. All the warriors, our friends, were lodged in Cuyoacan, a league and a half from the camp; and the people of these towns likewise supplied us with provisions, of which we stood in great need; especially with fish and cherries, of which there is such a quantity about here, that, during the five or six months of the year they last, they are sufficient for double the inhabitants of the country.

As we on our side had entered the city two or three days successively, besides three or four before, and had always been victorious against the enemy and had killed an infinite number, with our field-pieces, crossbows, and muskets, we thought that any hour they would move to propose peace, which we desired as our own salvation; but nothing availed to bring them to this determination. To reduce them to greater straits, and to see if they could be forced to make peace, I decided to enter the city each day in three or four divisions. I therefore ordered all the people of the cities situated on the water, to come in their canoes, so that day there were in our camp more than a hundred thousand men, our friends. And I ordered the four brigantines, with half the canoes (as many as fifteen hundred) to go on one side, and the other three, with as many more canoes, to go on another, and overrun the greater part of the city and burn and do all the damage they could. I entered by the principal street and found it all free up to the large houses of the square, none of the bridges having been opened. I advanced to the street which leads to Tacuba, where there were six or seven bridges. From there, I ordered a captain to enter another street, with sixty or seventy men and six horsemen to protect their rear, and with them went more than ten or twelve thousand Indians, our friends; and I ordered another captain to do the same in another street; and I, with the remaining people, advanced on the street to Tacuba. We captured three bridges which we filled up, and, because it was already late, left the others for another day, when it could be better done, for I wished to occupy that street so that the people of Pedro de Alvarado's camp might communicate with ours, and go from one camp to the other, and the brigantines the same. That day was one of great victory, both on water as well as land; and some plunder was obtained from the city. In the camps of the alguacil mayor and Pedro de Alvarado there was also great victory.

The next day, I again entered the city in the same order as before, and God gave us such a triumph that, in the parts where I penetrated, there seemed to be no resistance at all, and the enemy retired so rapidly that it appeared we had captured three-fourths of the city. The division of Pedro de Alvarado also attacked them briskly, and, undoubtedly on that day and the day before, I was positive they would sue for peace, in favour of which, with or without victory, I made every demonstration I could. Nevertheless, we saw no signs of peace in them, and we retired that day to our camp, very gladly, although we were grieved to our very hearts to see their determination to die. In these past days, Pedro de Alvarado had captured many bridges, and, in order to hold and defend them, he placed a guard of foot soldiers and horsemen on them throughout the night, while the remainder of his people returned to camp, three-quarters of a league from there. As this labour was unendurable, he determined to move his camp to the end of the causeway leading to the market place of Temixtitan, which has a square much larger than that of Salamanca, all surrounded by arcades, to reach which it was necessary to capture only two or three more bridges, but as they were very broad and dangerous, he was occupied in it some days, during which he fought constantly, and obtained victory. And that day of which I spoke in the past chapter, when he saw the enemies waver, and that where I was engaged they gave continual and stout combats, he got such a taste of victory with the bridges and barricades he had captured, that he determined to pass them, and capture a bridge where they had destroyed the causeway for more than sixty paces, and where the water had entered to a depth of about nine feet; and as the attack was made the same day and the brigantines helped so much, he crossed the water and captured the bridge and pursued the enemy who fled. Pedro de Alvarado hastened to have that pass filled so that the horsemen might cross, and also because I had daily admonished him by writing and by word of mouth not to gain a palm of ground without having the exit and entrance for the horsemen absolutely assured, as they in reality sustained the war. When the enemy saw there were only forty or fifty Spaniards and some of our friends on the other side, and that the horsemen could not cross, they turned on them so quickly that they drove them back and into the water, where they captured three or four Spaniards alive, who were immediately sacrificed; and they killed some of our friends.[48]

Finally Pedro de Alvarado retired to his camp, and when I arrived in ours that day and learned what had happened, it caused me the greatest grief in the world, as this was an event to encourage the enemy, and they might think that we would not again dare to enter. The reason why Pedro de Alvarado wished to take the bad pass, was, as I say, because he had overcome a great part of the Indians' force, and they showed some weakness, and chiefly because his people importuned him to capture the market-place; for, having gained that, almost the entire city would be taken, as all the forces and hopes of the Indians centered there: and, as Alvarado's men saw that I stoutly continued to combat the Indians, they feared that I might capture the market place before they did, and as they were nearer to it than we, they held it as a point of honour to take it first. For this reason the said Pedro de Alvarado was much importuned, and the same happened to me in our camp, for all the Spaniards eagerly besought me to enter by one of the three streets leading to the market-place, for we found little resistance, and that once captured we would have less hardship. I alleged every possible reason for not doing it, although I concealed the real cause, which was the inconvenience and dangers which presented themselves to me; for in order to reach the market-place, there were infinite roofs and bridges and broken causeways, so that each house by which we had to pass, was converted into an island surrounded by water.

When I learned, that afternoon upon reaching the camp, of Pedro de Alvarado's disaster, I determined to go to his camp the next morning, to rebuke him for what had happened, and to see what had been accomplished, and where he had moved his camp, and to advise him as to his security, and for the attack on the enemy. I was undoubtedly astonished, when I reached his camp, to see how far towards the middle of the city it was, and the bad places and bridges he had taken, so that I no longer blamed him so much as he had seemed to deserve; having talked with him, therefore, about what he should do, I returned that day to our camp.

This finished, I effected several entries into the city at the usual points, and the brigantines and canoes fought in two places, and I in four others within the city, and we always obtained the victory, and many of the adversaries were killed because numberless people daily returned in our favour. I hesitated to penetrate farther into the city, on the one hand that our enemies might reconsider their determination and stubbornness, and on the other because our entrance could not be effected without great danger, as they were very united, strong, and desperate unto death. As the Spaniards observed such delay, and that for more than twenty days they had never ceased fighting, they importuned me, in such manner as I have heretofore stated, to enter and take the market-place, because, having gained that, the enemy would have little space left to them from which to defend themselves, and, if they did not surrender, they would die from hunger and thirst, having no water to drink save the salt water of the lake. When I excused myself, the treasurer of Your Majesty told me that the entire camp insisted upon it, and that I ought to do it. I answered him and other persons who were in favour of this plan, that their object and wish were excellent, and that I desired to do it more than anybody else, but that I refrained for the reason his importunity forced me to say; which was that, although he and others approved of it, there might be others who, on account of the great danger would not. And finally, they forced me so much that I agreed to do what I could, after first consulting the people of the other camps.

The next day I conferred with some of the principal persons of our camp, and we agreed to notify the alguacil mayor and Pedro de Alvarado that we would enter the city on the following day, and make an effort to reach the market-place, and I wrote to them what they were to do on the Tacuba side, and, besides writing, I sent two of my servants to explain the whole business, that they might be better informed. The course they were to follow was this: The alguacil mayor was to come, with ten horsemen, one hundred foot soldiers, and fifteen musketeers, to Pedro de Alvarado's camp, leaving in his own camp ten other horsemen, with whom he should arrange that they were to lie in ambush behind some houses at the hour of the next day's battle; and that he should remove all his baggage as though he were breaking up his camp, so that when the enemy came in pursuit, those in ambush would fall upon their rear. The said alguacil mayor with his three brigantines and the three of Pedro de Alvarado were to take that bad pass, where Pedro de Alvarado had been routed, filling it up quickly, and in marching forward they were not to advance one step without having first filled it up and repaired it; and, if they could advance to the market-place without any great risk or danger, they were to make every effort to do so, as I would do the same; and they were to note well that, although I sent to say this, I did not oblige them to advance a single step which might expose them to any defeat or mishap, and that I communicated this to them because I knew them, and that they would put their face to what I ordered them, even though they knew that by it they might lose their lives. My two servants went to the camp and met the said alguacil mayor and Pedro de Alvarado there to whom they stated the case as we had agreed here in our camp. As they had to fight in one place only, and I in many, I had asked them to send me seventy or eighty foot soldiers who would enter with me next day; these came with my two servants and all slept that night in my camp according to the orders which I had sent them.

This order given, the next day, after having heard mass, the seven brigantines with more than three hundred canoes of our friends, left our camp, and I, with twenty-five horsemen, my people, and the seventy men from the camp of Tacuba, began our march and entered the city, where I divided them in this manner: From the point we had already reached, three streets led to the market-place, which the Indians called Tianguizco,[49] and into the principal one, leading to the said market-place, I told Your Majesty's treasurer and accountant [Julian de Alderete] to enter, with seventy men and more than fifteen or twenty thousand of our friends, and that in his rear he should take seven horsemen; and that as they captured the bridges and barricades they should be filled up; and they took a dozen men with picks in addition to our friends, who were most useful for the purpose of filling up the bridges. Two other streets lead from the streets of Tacuba to the market-place and are narrower, having more causeways, bridges, and water streets, and I ordered two captains to enter by the broadest of them, with eighty men and more than ten thousand Indians, our friends, and, at the mouth of that street of Tacuba, I placed two heavy field pieces with eight horsemen to guard them. With eight other horsemen and one hundred foot soldiers, amongst whom were more than twenty-five archers and musketeers, and with an infinite number of our friends, I pursued my road, penetrating by the other narrow street as far as possible.

I halted the horsemen at the entrance of it, and ordered them on no account to advance from there, nor to follow after me unless I first ordered them to do so. I then dismounted and we arrived at a barricade they had made at the end of a bridge, which we took with a small field piece, the archers and musketeers advancing by a causeway, which the enemy had broken at two or three different places. Besides these three combats we waged, our friends who entered by the roofs and other places were so numerous that it did not seem that anything could resist us. When the Spaniards took those two bridges, the barricades, and the causeway, our friends advanced by the street without taking any spoils, while I remained with about twenty Spaniards on a small island. I observed that certain of our friends were engaged with the enemy, who sometimes would repel them, driving them into the water, but with our assistance they would turn again upon them. Besides this we took care that from certain cross streets those of the city should not sally out to take at their backs the Spaniards, who were advancing along the street.

They sent to tell me at this time that they had advanced much and were not very far from the market-place, and in any case they wished to push on because they already heard the combat which the alguacil mayor and Pedro de Alvarado were waging on their side. I sent orders that they should on no account advance a step without leaving the bridges well filled up, so that, if they needed to retreat, the water would be no obstacle or embarrassment, for therein lay the danger; and they returned to tell me that all they had gained were well repaired and I might go myself and see if it was so. Dreading that they might go astray, and commit blunders respecting the filling up of the ditches, I went thither, and found that they had passed over a ditch in the street which was ten paces broad, with water flowing through it ten feet in depth, and that in passing they had thrown wood and maize and reed grass into it; as they had passed few at a time and with care, the wood and maize had not sunk, and they, in the joy of victory, were going ahead so recklessly that they believed the work had been very thoroughly done. The moment I reached that wretched bridge, I saw the Spaniards and many of our friends returning in full flight, and the enemy like dogs setting on them; and, seeing the impending mishap, I began to cry, Stop! Stop! but when I arrived at the water I found it full of Spaniards and Indians as though not one straw had been put into it. The enemy charged so furiously, killing amongst the Spaniards, that they threw themselves into the water with them, and their canoes came by the water streets and captured the Spaniards alive. As the affair came about so suddenly, and I saw the people being killed, I determined to remain there and die fighting; and the most that I and my men could do was to lend our hands to some unlucky Spaniards who were drowning and help them out; and some came out wounded and others half drowned and others without weapons. I sent them on ahead. Such was the number of the enemy that they surrounded me and some other ten or fifteen who had remained with me.

Being entirely occupied in helping those who were drowning, I had not observed or thought of my own danger, and already certain Indians had grasped me and would have carried me away had it not been for a captain of fifty whom I always had with me, and another youth of my company, who, after God, gave me my life, and, in giving it me, as a valiant man he there lost his own. Meanwhile, the Spaniards who had been routed were retreating by the causeway, and as it was small, and narrow, and on a level with the water which those dogs had intentionally prepared in this manner, and as many of our own friends, who had also been routed, were also going by it, the road was so encumbered, and there was such a delay in advancing, that the enemy had time to come up from both sides and take and kill as many as they chose. And that captain who was with me, called Antonio de Quiñones, said to me, "Let us go away from here and save yourself, as you know that without you none of us can escape"; but seeing that he could not prevail upon me to go, he grasped me by the arms, to force me to retire. Although I would have rejoiced more in death than in life, by the importunity of that and of my other companions, we began to withdraw, fighting with our swords and bucklers against the enemy, who surrounded us. At this moment a servant of mine rode up on horseback and cleared a little space, but immediately a lance thrown from a low roof struck him in the throat, and overthrew him.

In the midst of this great conflict, waiting for the people to pass that small causeway and reach safety while we held back the enemy, a servant of mine arrived with a horse for me to mount, because such was the quantity of mud on that small causeway, brought there by those who fell in and climbed out of the water, that no one could keep his feet, especially on account of the jostling of one another in trying to save themselves. I mounted, but not to fight, because it was impossible on horseback; for, could it have been done, those eight horse-men whom I had left on a small island at the beginning of the causeway would have been there, but they could not do other than go back by it, and even the return was so perilous that two mares mounted by my servants fell from the causeway into the water, one of whom the Indians killed and the other some of our soldiers saved. Another young servant of mine called Cristobal de Guzman mounted a horse, which was given to him at the small island to bring to me to save me, and he and the horse were killed by the enemy before they reached me; his death filled the whole camp with such sadness that the sorrow of those who knew him is still fresh to-day. Finally it pleased God that, after all our troubles, those who were left should reach the street of Tacuba, which is very broad, and, having collected the people, I, with my horsemen, stopped in the rear where the enemy were charging with such triumph and pride that it seemed that they would leave nobody alive. Retiring as best I could, I sent word to the treasurer and accountant to retreat to the square in good order. I sent the same order to the other two captains who had entered by the street leading to the market, both of whom had fought valiantly and captured many barricades and bridges which they completely filled up, from which cause they were able to retreat without injury. Before the treasurer and accountant retired from the breastwork where they were fighting, those of the city had already

thrown two or three heads of Christians at them, although then they did not
know whether they came from Pedro de Alvarado's camp or from ours. And we
all gathered in the square, so many of the enemy charging on us from every
side that we had enough to do to keep them off, and even in places where before
this rout they would never have dared to come, they killed three horsemen
and ten soldiers. Immediately after, in one of the towers of their idols which
was near the square, they offered many perfumes and incense of gums which
they use in this country, very much like *anime*, offering them up to their idols
in sign of victory; and even if we had wanted to stop this it could not be done,
as almost all the people were already hastening towards the camp. In this rout,
the adversary killed thirty-five or forty Spaniards and more than one thousand
Indians, our friends, and wounded more than twenty Christians; and I came
out wounded in one leg. A small field piece was lost and many crossbows,
muskets, and arms.[50]

Immediately after obtaining this victory, the defenders of the city, in order
to frighten the alguacil mayor and Pedro de Alvarado, took all the living and
dead Spaniards whom they had captured, to Tlaltelulco, which is the market,
and, in some lofty towers there, they stripped them and sacrificed them, opening their breasts and taking out their hearts to offer them to the idols. This
the Spaniards in Pedro de Alvarado's camp could see from where they were
fighting, and in the naked white bodies which they saw sacrificed they recognised that they were Christians; and, although they were saddened and dismayed by this, they retreated into their camp, having fought very well that day
and arrived almost to the market-place which would have been won that day
if God, on account of our sins, had not permitted so great a misfortune. We returned to our camp sadly, somewhat earlier than we were accustomed to on
other days; also because we heard the brigantines were lost as the Mexicans
had fallen on our rear with the canoes, though it pleased God that this should
not be true. The brigantines and canoes of our friends had indeed found themselves in tight straits; so much so that a brigantine was almost lost, and the
captain and the master were both wounded, the captain dying within eight
days.

That day, and the following night, the people of the city rejoiced greatly with
trumpets and kettle-drums so that it seemed the very world was sinking, and
they opened all the streets and bridges over the water, as they had them before,
and lighted fires, and placed night watchmen at a distance of two bow-shots
from our camp; for, as we were all so disordered, and wounded, and without
arms, we needed to rest and recuperate ourselves. Meanwhile the enemy had
time to send their messengers to many provinces subject to them, telling them
how they had obtained a great victory and killed many Christians, and that

they would soon finish all of us, and that by no means would they sue for peace with us; and the proofs they carried were the heads of the two horses and some of those Christians they had killed, carrying them about, and showing them wherever it seemed useful, which confirmed the rebels more than ever in their stubbornness. However, lest they should become too proud and divine our weakness, some Spaniards on foot and on horseback, with many of our friends, would go into the city to fight every day, albeit they never could gain more than some of the bridges of the next street before reaching the square.

Two days after our rout, which was already known in all the neighbourhood, the natives of a town called Cuarnaguacar [Cuernavaca], who had been subject to the city but had given themselves for our friends, came to the camp and told me that the people of Marinalco,[51] their neighbours did them much injury and destroyed their fields, and that they also had joined with the large province of Cuisco,[52] and intended to attack them and kill them because they had given themselves as vassals of Your Majesty, and our friends; once the people of Cuarnaguacar were destroyed, their enemies would then come against us. Although what had passed was still so recent, and we were rather needing to receive than to give help, since they asked it of me with such urgency, I determined to give it to them, although I encountered much opposition, and it was said that in taking people from our camp I was destroying myself. I dispatched eighty foot soldiers and ten horsemen under Captain Andres de Tapia with those who had come to ask our aid, charging him earnestly to do whatever was required for Your Majesty's service and for our security; as he saw the need in which we were, he should spend not more than ten days in going and coming. He left, and reached a small town between Marinalco and Coadnoacad,[53] where he found the enemy expecting him; and he, with the people of Coadnoacad and those he had with him, began his battle on the field, and our forces fought so well that they routed the enemy, pursuing them until they reached Marinalco, which is situated on a very high hill where the horsemen could not approach. Seeing this, they destroyed that part which is in the plain, and returned to our camp within the ten days. In the upper part of this town of Marinalco, there are many fountains of excellent water, a very refreshing thing.

While this captain was absent, some Spaniards on foot and on horseback entered with our friends into the city as far as the large houses which are on the square, to fight, as I have already said; they could not advance further because the enemy had opened the water street which is at the entrance of the square and is very broad and deep; and, on the other side, there was a very large and strong entrenchment, where they fought with one another until night separated them.

A chief of the province of Tascaltecal, called Chichimecatecle, of whom I have heretofore written that he had bought the timbers that had been prepared in that province for the brigantines, had resided with his people, since the beginning of the war, in the camp of Pedro de Alvarado; and when he saw, after the preceding rout, that the Spaniards did not fight as before, he determined to make an entrance with only his own people. Leaving four hundred of his bowmen at a dangerous broken bridge he had taken (which had never before happened without our aid), he and his people advanced with great shouts, cheering and naming their province and lord. They fought very bravely that day and there were many wounded and dead on both sides; and those of the city believed that they had trapped them because it is their custom, when their adversaries retire, to follow them with much persistence, although it be without chance of victory, believing that in crossing the water, where it sometimes happens there is a certain danger, they may take revenge on them. To forestall this danger and to provide help, Chichimecatecle had left four hundred bowmen at the water pass, and, while his men were retiring, those of the city suddenly charged them, and the warriors of Tascaltecal threw themselves into the water, and, under the protection of the bowmen, they crossed, leaving the enemy greatly surprised at the resistance they encountered, and at the daring which Chichimecatecle had displayed.

Two days after the Spaniards had returned from fighting in Marinalco, as Your Majesty will have seen in the chapter before the last, there arrived at our camp, ten Indians of the Otomí who had been slaves to the inhabitants of the city, and, as I have said, had given themselves as vassals of Your Majesty, coming every day to help in fighting; and they told me that the lords of the province of Matalcingo, who are their neighbours, made war upon them, and destroyed their land, burned a town, captured some of the people and were destroying everything they could, intending to come to our camps and attack us, so that those of the city could sally forth and overcome us. We gave credit to most of this, because, each time, for a few days past, that we had entered to fight, the Culuans had threatened us, with the people of this province of Matalcingo, which, though we had not much information, we well knew was large and twenty-five leagues distant from our camp. In the complaint these Otomís made of their neighbours, they gave us to understand that they wanted help, and, although they asked it at a very needy time, confiding in the help of God, and in order to break the wings of those of the city who daily threatened us with these people and hoped for aid, which could only come from them, I determined to send Gonzalo de Sandoval, alguacil mayor, with eighteen horsemen and one hundred foot-soldiers, amongst whom there was only one bowman: he departed with them and the Otomí, our friends; and God knows the danger which attended all who went as well as all who were left. But, as it was necessary to show more courage and valour than ever, and to die fighting, we hid our weakness from friends as well as from foes, and many and many times the Spaniards declared they hoped it might please God to leave them their lives and to see them victorious over the city, even though no other profits should come to them neither in it, nor in any other part of the country; by which the risk and extreme need in which we found ourselves and our lives may be judged.

The alguacil mayor left that day, and slept in a town of the Otomí which is on the frontier of Marinalco, and, the following day, he started very early, arriving at some small hamlets of the said Otomí, which he found deserted, and a good part of them burnt. Advancing more on to the plain, he found near a river bank many warriors who, having just finished burning another town, retreated when they saw him. On the road, were found many loads of maize and roasted children which they had brought as provisions and which they left behind them when they discovered the Spaniards coming. After crossing a river a little ahead of them in the plain, the enemy began to recover, and the alguacil mayor charged on them with the horsemen and put them to confusion; and they fled on the road straight towards their town of Matalcingo, about three leagues from there, the pursuit lasting until the horsemen had shut them all up in the town. There they awaited the Spaniards and our allies who were killing those who had been stopped and left behind by the horsemen. More than two thousand of the enemy perished in this pursuit. When those on foot and our friends, who were more than sixty thousand, overtook the horsemen, they began to rush towards the town where the enemy made a stand, while the women and children, goods, and chattels, were safe in a fort situated on a very elevated hill near that place. But as our force fell on them suddenly, they forced the warriors also to retire to the fort on that elevation, which was very steep and strong. They burned and sacked the town in a very short time, but the alguacil mayor did not attack the fort, as it was late and also because his men were very tired for they had fought during the entire day. The enemy spent that night in yelling and in making an uproar with their kettle-drums and trumpets.

The next day, in the early morning, the alguacil mayor led all the people to scale the enemy's fort, though fearful of finding himself in difficulties from their resistance. On arriving, however, they found none of the adversaries, and certain of our Indian friends, descending from the elevation, said that there was nobody there and that all the enemy had left at daybreak. In the midst of this, they discovered on all the surrounding plains, a great number of people, who were Otomí, and the horsemen, believing that they were enemies, galloped towards them and lanced at three or four of them; and as the language of the

Otomí is different from that of Culua they did not understand them, except that they threw away their arms and came towards the Spaniards, who even after that lanced three or four. But they understood well enough that this had happened from our men not recognising them. As the enemy did not wait, the Spaniards determined to return to another of their towns which was also hostile; but, seeing such a force come against them, the inhabitants came out peaceably. The alguacil mayor spoke kindly to the chief of that town, and told him that he already knew that I would receive with good will all who came to offer themselves as vassals of Your Majesty although they might be very culpable; that he besought him to speak with those of Matalcingo so that they might come to me of their own choice; he agreed to do this and also to bring those of Marinalco to peace. Thus victorious the alguacil mayor returned to his camp.

On that day, some Spaniards fought in the city, and the citizens had sent word to ask our interpreter to come, because they desired to discuss peace, which, as it appeared, they wished only on the condition that we should all leave the country. They did this with the object of resting some days and of furnishing themselves with necessaries, although we never overcame their disposition to fight. While engaged in these parleys with the interpreter, our people were very near the enemy with only a broken-down bridge between them, and an old man amongst them in full sight of all very slowly drew from his provision bag certain things which he ate, so as to give us to understand that they were not in want, for we had told them that they would starve to death; and at this our friends assured the Spaniards that the peace was all a pretence and that they wished to fight. That day, however, no other fighting took place, because the chiefs told the interpreter to call me.

Four days after the alguacil mayor had returned from the province of Matalcingo, the chief of it and those of Marinalco and the province of Quiscon, which is large and important and had also rebelled, came to our camp and asked pardon for the past, offering to serve well; and thus they did and have done until now. While the alguacil mayor was away in Matalcingo, those of the city determined to come at night and fall on the camp of Alvarado. A quarter before dawn, they made the attack, and, when the watchmen on horseback and foot perceived them, they called "To Arms," and those who were ready charged on them. When the enemy perceived the horsemen, they threw themselves into the water; in the meantime our people came up and fought them for three hours. When we in the camp heard one of the field pieces firing, fearing they might be routed, we ordered the people to arm themselves and enter the city, so as to thus draw off the attack from Alvarado. As the Indians found the Spaniards so courageous, they decided to return to the city, where we continued to fight during the day.

By this time, those who had been wounded in our rout were already recovered, and the ship had arrived at Villa Rica, belonging to Juan Ponce de Leon,[54] who had formerly been routed in the country or island of Florida. They sent me certain powder and crossbows, of which we stood in very extreme need; and now, thanks to God, all about here there is not a province which is not in our favour. Seeing that the people of the city were so rebellious, and displayed such determination to die as no race had ever shown, I knew not what means to adopt to relieve our dangers and hardships, and to avoid utterly destroying them and their city, which was the most beautiful thing in the world. It was useless to tell them that we would not raise our camps, or that the brigantines would not cease to make war on them, or that we had destroyed those of Matalcingo and Marinalco, and that nowhere in the country was anyone left to help them, or that they could not obtain maize, nor wheat, nor fruit, nor water, nor any provisions from anywhere. The more I spoke of these things, the less sign of yielding did we see in them; rather we found them more courageous than ever, both in their fighting and their scheming. Seeing that things went on in this way, and that already more than forty-five days had been spent in this siege, I determined to take means towards our security and to further straiten the enemy. This latter consisted in our gaining the streets of the city and demolishing all the houses on both sides, so that henceforward we would not go one step ahead without levelling everything, so that which was water should be made into dry land, no matter how much time it took. I called the lords and chiefs of our allies and told them what I had determined, so that they might have their workmen bring their spades and *coas*, which are certain poles which they use, similar to the Spanish hoe. They answered me that they would do this with the best good will, and that it was a very good decision at which they rejoiced greatly, because they perceived that in this way the city would be destroyed, which was what they desired more than anything else in the world.

Three or four days passed in concerting this plan; the people of the city easily divined that we were planning some mischief against them, and they also, as it afterwards appeared, were arranging what they could for their defence, as we likewise conjectured. Having concerted with our friends that we would attack them by land and water, the next morning, after having heard mass, we took the road to the city, and when we reached the water pass and barricade near the great houses of the square, intending to attack them, the people of the city asked us to be quiet as they wished to sue for peace. I ordered my people to cease fighting, and told them that the lord of the city should come there to speak to me, and arrange the conditions of the peace. After telling me that they had already gone to call him, they detained me for more than an hour, but in truth they did not want peace, as they themselves immediately showed, for, while we were quiet, they began to throw adobes and darts and stones at us. When I saw this, I attacked the barricades and captured them, and on entering the square we found it strewn with large stones to impede the horses moving over it; for generally it is these which do the most fighting. We also found a street barricaded with dry stones, and another filled with stones, so that the horses could not pass through them. During the rest of that day, we filled up the water street which leads out from the square, so that the Indians never opened it again, and thenceforward we began, little by little to destroy the houses and to shut up, and fill up completely, all we had gained on the water. As we were accompanied all day by more than one hundred and fifty thousand warriors, a good deal was accomplished; and thus we returned that day to our camp, and the brigantines and canoes of our friends, after doing much damage to the city returned to rest. The next day we again entered the city in the same order, as far as the enclosure and large court where the towers of the idols are. I ordered the captains to do nothing else but fill up the water streets and level the dangerous passes we had captured; and as for our friends, some of them should level and burn the houses and others should fight in the customary places, while the horsemen should guard the rear of all. I ascended the highest tower that the Indians might recognise me, for I also knew that they would be much vexed to see me mounted on the tower; and from there I encouraged our friends and gave aid wherever it was necessary, while they were incessantly fighting. Sometimes it was the adversaries who retreated, and sometimes our allies whom three or four horsemen aided and inspired with infinite courage to turn against the enemy.

In this wise and order, we entered the city on the five or six following days, and always at the hour of retreat we would put our allies ahead and post a number of Spaniards in ambush in some of the houses, the horsemen remaining behind and feigning to retreat hastily, so as to bring them out of the square. With these and the ambushes of the foot soldiers we would kill some of them every afternoon with our lances. On one of these days there were seven or eight horsemen in the square, hoping the enemy would come out, but, as they saw that they did not appear, they feigned to retreat, and the enemy, fearing that they would be caught at the corner, as had sometimes happened, stationed themselves by some walls and roofs in an infinite number. As the horsemen, who were eight or nine, charged towards them, the Indians held the entrance of the street from above so that they could not pursue those of the enemy who passed through it; so they were obliged to retire. The enemy, elated by having forced us to retreat, charged very lustily, and were so well on their guard that without themselves being injured they forced the horsemen to retreat, and wounded two horses. This prompted me to arrange a good ambush, as I will

recount hereafter to Your Majesty. The afternoon of that day, we returned to
our camp, leaving everything we had gained assured and levelled, and the people of the city very boastful because they believed that we had retired out of
fear. That afternoon, I called the alguacil mayor by messenger to come to our
camp before daybreak with fifteen of his own and Pedro de Alvarado's horsemen.

The alguacil mayor arrived the following morning at the camp with fifteen
horsemen, and I obtained another twenty-five from those at Cuyoacan, so that
there were forty in all. I ordered ten of them to join in the morning with our
force, and in conjunction with the brigantines to go in the same order as heretofore to attack the enemy and to destroy and capture everything possible;
when the time for them to retire came, I would start with the other thirty
horsemen. When the larger part of the city was demolished they should in the
mêlée drive the enemy into their entrenchments and water streets, keeping them
there until the hour of retiring, when I and the other thirty horsemen would
secretly form an ambuscade in the large houses in the square. The Spaniards
did as I ordered, and at one o'clock after mid-day I set out with the thirty
horsemen, and stationed them in those houses while I went to the city and
mounted the high tower as I habitually did. While I was there, some Spaniards
opened a sepulchre and found in it more than fifteen hundred *castellanos* worth
of articles in gold. At the hour of returning, I ordered that they should begin
to withdraw in a compact body, and that from the first moment of leaving the
square the horsemen should feign an attack, behaving as though they hardly
dared to make it, choosing the time when they saw a great number of people
in and about the whole square. The men posted in ambush longed for the hour
to arrive, because they much desired to act their part well, and were already
tired of waiting. I then joined them, as the infantry and horsemen began retiring through the square, accompanied by the Indians our friends, who understood all about the ambush. The enemy rushed out, yelling as if they had gained
the greatest victory in the whole world, and the nine horsemen feigned to
charge them across the square, and then suddenly to fall back; and, when they
had done this twice, the enemy acquired such fury that they pressed up to the
very croups of the horses and were thus decoyed towards the end of the street
where the ambush was laid. When we saw the Spaniards had passed ahead of
us, and heard the shot of a gun fired which was the signal agreed upon, we
knew that the time to sally forth had arrived; and, with the cry of "Señor
Santiago!" we suddenly fell upon them, and rushed forward into the square
with our lances, overthrowing and stopping many, which latter our friends,
who joined in the pursuit, were able to capture. In this ambush more than five
hundred, all of the bravest and most valiant of their principal men were killed,

and, that night, our allies supped well, because they cut up all those whom they had killed and captured to eat. Such was the fright and wonder of the enemy at seeing themselves suddenly routed that there was no more shouting the whole afternoon, nor did they dare to show their heads in the streets, nor on the roofs, except where they were entirely protected and safe. About nightfall, the people of the city sent certain slaves to see if we had retired, or what we were doing. As they appeared in the street, some ten or twelve horsemen charged and pursued them, so that none of them escaped.

Such was the consternation of the enemy from this, our victory, that during the rest of the war they never again dared to enter the square when we were retiring, even if only one horseman was there; nor did they ever dare to come out against an Indian or foot soldier, fearing that another ambush might spring up beneath their feet. The victory God was pleased to give us that day was one of the principal causes why the city was taken sooner, for the natives were dismayed by it and our friends doubly encouraged; so we returned to our camp, intending to hasten on the war, and, until we finished it, not to let a single day pass without entering the city. We suffered no loss that day, except that, during the ambush, some of the horsemen collided with each other, and one was thrown from his mare, which galloped directly towards the enemy who wounded her severely with arrows, and she, seeing the ill-treatment she got, returned to us; and that night she died. Although we grieved exceedingly at it, for the horses and mares gave life to us, our grief was less than had she died in the hands of our enemies, as we feared would happen; had such been the case, their satisfaction would have outweighed their grief for those we had killed. The brigantines and canoes of our friends made great havoc that day in the city without suffering any loss.

We already knew that the Indians of the city were much discouraged, and two poor creatures, who came out by night to our camp because they were starving, told us that during the night they came to hunt amongst the houses and search in those parts we had already captured, looking for herbs and wood and roots to eat. Since we had already filled up many of the water streets, and repaired many of the bad places, I determined to enter the city before daybreak, and do all the damage I could. The brigantines left before dawn and I with twelve horsemen and some foot soldiers and our friends, came in suddenly, having first placed spies, who, at daybreak made signs to us in our ambush to come and charge on a vast number of people. But they were of the most miserable class who had come out to search for something to eat, most of them being unarmed, and women and boys. We did much damage amongst them all over the city, wherever we were able to move about, so that between prisoners and killed they exceeded more than eight hundred, and the brigantines also captured people in canoes who were fishing, making great havoc amongst them. As the captains and chiefs of the city saw us moving about at an unaccustomed hour, they became as frightened as by the recent ambush, and none dared to come and fight with us, so we returned to our camp well satisfied with great spoils and food for our friends.

The next morning, we entered the city, and, as our friends had observed the systematic order we followed in the destruction of it, the multitude which daily came with us was beyond all reckoning. We finished taking the whole street of Tacuba that day and filling up the bad places in it, so that the people from Pedro de Alvarado's camp could communicate with us through the city. We won two other bridges on the principal street leading to the market-place, filling them up, and we burned the houses of the lord of the city, who was a youth of eighteen, called Guatimucin, being the second ruler since the death of Moctezuma; and the Indians had many strong places amongst these houses, as they were large and solid and surrounded by water. Two other bridges were also captured in other streets which run near the one leading to the market, and many passes were filled up, so that three of the four quarters of the city were already ours, and the Indians could only retreat to the strongest part of it which comprised the houses furthest out in the water.

The following day, which was the feast of the Apostle Santiago [July 25th], we entered the city in the same order as before, following the large street to the market-place and capturing a broad water street where the enemy was well fortified. We were delayed there for some time; and it was dangerous capturing it, nor were we able to fill it up in the whole of the day (as it was very broad), so that the horsemen could cross to the other side. The Indians, seeing we were all on foot, and that the horsemen had not passed over, attacked us with some fresh troops, many of them very splendid; but, as we turned upon them with our many archers, they retreated towards their barricades and forts, badly wounded with arrows. Besides this, all the Spanish foot soldiers carried their pikes, which I had ordered made after our rout, and which were very useful. Nothing was heard all day on each side of the principal street but the burning and destroying of the houses, which was certainly pitiful to see, but as nothing else could avail we were obliged to follow those tactics. When the people of the city saw such ruin, they encouraged themselves by telling our friends to go on burning and destroying as it was they who would have to rebuild the city in any case, because if they [the Mexicans] were victorious they would make them do it, and if not they would have to rebuild it for us; and it pleased God that this last should turn out to be true, for they are indeed the ones who have to do this work.[55]

Very early on the morning of the next day, we entered the city in the customary order, and, arriving at the water street which we had filled up the day before, found it in the same state we had left it; and, advancing about two bow-shots, we captured two large ditches of water, which had been cut in the same street, and arrived at the small tower of their idols, in which we found certain heads of Christians whom they had killed; a sight which filled us with much commiseration. And from that tower, the street in which we were, led straight to the causeway of Sandoval's camp, and, on the left side, another street in which water no longer flowed, led to the market; they still held only one against us, nor could we pass it that day, though we fought the Indians stoutly. God, Our Lord, gave us victory every day, and the worst always fell on them. It was late that day when we returned to our camp.

The next day, while preparing to return to the city about nine o'clock in the morning, we observed from our camp that smoke was rising from the two highest towers which were in Tatelulco, or the market-place of the city. This we could not understand, for it seemed something more than the incensing which the Indians usually made to their idols, so we suspected that Pedro de Alvarado's men had arrived there, and, although this was the fact, we could not believe it. Pedro de Alvarado's men certainly behaved very valiantly, for there were many bridges and barricades to capture and the greater part of the enemy always came to defend them; but as he saw that on our side we were hedging the enemy in, he did everything he could to enter the market-place, because their whole strength was centered there. However, he could arrive only within sight of it, and capture those towers and many others which adjoin the same market-place, forming an enclosure almost like that of many of the towers in the city; the horsemen had hard work and were forced to retreat with their horses wounded, and thus Pedro de Alvarado and his people returned to his camp. We could not, that day, capture a bridge and water street which still remained to be taken in order to reach the market-place, without filling up and levelling all the bad places, and on retiring they pressed us very hard, although at their cost.

We again entered the city on the morning of the following day, and, encountering no obstacle before reaching the market-place, except a water course and its barricade near the small tower of which I have spoken, we attacked it, and the standard bearer and two or three other Spaniards threw themselves into the water, so the defenders immediately abandoned the pass, which we filled and made passable for the horsemen. While we were repairing it, Pedro de Alvarado arrived by the same street with four horsemen, to our mutual satisfaction, for this was the way to speedily finish the war. Pedro de Alvarado left a file of guards in the rear, not only for the purpose of preserving what had been won, but also for his protection, and, as the pass was quickly repaired, I, with some horsemen, went to view the market-place, and ordered that the others should not advance beyond that pass. Afterwards we reconnoitred the square for a short time, inspecting its arcades whose roofs were full of the enemy. As the square was very large, and they saw the horsemen moving about there, they did not dare to attack. I ascended that large tower which adjoins the market-place, in which, and in others also, we found the heads of the Christians whom they had killed and offered to their idols, as well as those of the Indians of Tascaltecal, our friends between whom and the Mexicans there was a very ancient and cruel feud. I saw from that tower that we had without doubt captured seven-eighths of the city, and, seeing that such a number of the enemy could not possibly hold out in such straits, chiefly because those houses left them were so small and each built over the water, and above all because of the great famine prevailing amongst them, for we found the gnawed roots and bark of trees in the streets, I determined to suspend fighting for a day and devise some measure to save this multitude of people from perishing. The harm done them caused me such compassion and distress that I continually importuned them with offers of peace, but they answered that in no wise would they surrender and that only one man being left he would die fighting, and that of all they possessed we could never obtain anything for they would burn it and throw it into the water whence it would never more appear. Not wishing to return evil for evil, I dissembled, and refrained from fighting.

As very little powder was left to us, we had in the last fifteen days discussed somewhat about making a catapult;[56] and, though there was no first-class master-workman who knew how to do it, some carpenters offered to make a small one. Although I always believed that we would not succeed in this work, I consented that they should make it, and, in those days when we had the Indians cornered, they finished it and took it to the market-place to station it on a sort of square theatre which stands in the middle, and which is built of stone and mortar and is about fourteen feet in height, and about thirty paces long from one corner to the other; when they celebrated their plays and festivals, the performers placed themselves on this where all the people in the market both above and below the arcades could see them. After the catapult was brought there, three or four days were occupied in placing it, and the Indians our friends threatened those of the city with it, telling them that with this engine we would kill them all. Although no other result was obtained (as indeed there was none) except the fright it caused, from which we thought the enemy would surrender, it would have been sufficient; the deception was a double one because neither the carpenters fulfilled their design nor did the defenders of the city (although they were much frightened) take any step to surrender, while

I disguised the failure of the catapult by pretending that moved by compassion, we forbore to kill them all.

The next day, after placing the catapult, we returned to the city, and, as three or four days had passed without any fighting, we found the streets by which we passed full of women and children and other miserable people, who came out so emaciated and thin, that it was the greatest pity in the world to behold them, so I ordered our friends not to hurt them. But, none of the warriors appeared where any harm could reach them, though we saw them on the tops of their roofs, covered with the blankets they wear, and without weapons. I had them required that day to make peace, but their replies were inconclusive. As they occupied us most of the day with this, I sent them word that I intended to attack them and that they should withdraw all their people, otherwise I would permit our friends to kill them. They said they desired peace, and I answered them that I did not see amongst them their lord with whom I must treat, but when he came for that purpose I would give him a safe conduct and we would discuss peace. Seeing it was all mockery, and that they were prepared to fight with us, I ordered Pedro de Alvarado, after having admonished them many times and in order to reduce them to extreme necessity, to enter with all his people through a large quarter which the enemy held, and in which there were more than one thousand houses; and I, with those of our camp, came on foot from another side, because we could not avail ourselves of the horsemen. The fight between us and our enemies was very stubborn, but finally we won that whole quarter, and, such was the slaughter committed upon our enemies, that between killed and wounded there were more than twelve thousand.

Our allies handled the enemy most cruelly, for they would in no wise spare any life, although they were reproved and punished by us.

We returned next day to the city, and I ordered that no fighting should take place nor any harm be done to the enemy, who, when they saw such a multitude of people, and their own vassals and subjects, arrayed against them, and saw their extreme necessity, which left them not even a place to stand, save upon the bodies of their own dead, moved by the desire to escape such a great misfortune, asked us why we did not put an end to them; then suddenly they said to call me as they wished to speak to me. All the Spaniards wished that this war might finally end, and, pitying such misery, they rejoiced, believing that the Indians wanted peace; so they came gladly to call and importune me to come to a barricade where certain chiefs wished to speak to me. I knew that little profit would come of my going, but I determined at all events to go, although I knew their not surrendering all depended on the sovereign and some three or four other chiefs of the city, for the others, dead or alive, all desired to be out of it. And when I arrived at the barricade, they told me that, as they held me to be the son of the sun, and as the sun in such brief period as a day and a night, made the circuit of the entire world, I ought likewise to finish killing them speedily and save them from so much suffering, because they wished to die and go to heaven to their Ochilobus,[57] who was awaiting to give them rest; this being the idol which they hold in the greatest reverence. I said many things in reply to persuade them to surrender, and nothing availed with them, although they perceived in us greater wishes and offers for peace than had ever been shown to any other vanquished, for with the help of Our Lord we were the victors.

Having reduced the enemy to the last extremity, as may be gathered from what has been said, and in order to win them from their evil intention, which was their determination to die, I spoke to one of their noble chiefs, the uncle of Don Fernando, lord of Tesaico, who had been captured fighting in the city, and whom we held prisoner. Although badly wounded I asked him if he wished to return to the city, and he answered me, "yes," and, when we entered it the next day, I sent him, with certain Spaniards, who delivered him to the people of the city; and, to their chief, I had spoken exclusively in order that he might talk to the sovereign and the other chiefs about peace, and he promised to do everything that was possible. The people of the city received him with much deference as a nobleman, and, when they took him before Quatamucin, their sovereign, and he began to speak of peace, it is said they immediately ordered him to be killed and sacrificed, and the answer we were awaiting they gave us with great yells, saying that they wanted nothing but death. They began to discharge arrows and stones at us, and fought us very stoutly, so much so that they killed a horse with a dagger which one of them had taken from one of our friends; but finally they paid dearly for it, because many of them perished, and thus we returned that day to our camp.

The next day, we again entered into the city, and our adversaries were so reduced that an infinite number of our friends ventured to remain there during the night; having come in sight of the enemy we did not care to fight with them, but only moved about in their city, because every hour and every moment we believed that they would come to surrender. In order to persuade them, I rode near one of the barricades and called certain chiefs, who were behind them, whom I already knew, and said to them that since they saw that everything was lost, and recognised that, if I wished, none of them would escape why was it that Quatamucin their lord did not come to speak with me; that I promised to do him no harm, and if he and they wished for peace they would be well received and well treated by me. I gave them other reasons, with which I provoked them to many tears; and, weeping, they replied that they well recognised their error and perdition, and that they would go and speak to their lord and return speedily with the answer, asking me not to go away from there. So they went away, returning within a short space to tell me that, inasmuch as it was already late their lord had not come, but that at noon on the following day he would certainly come to speak with me in the market-place; so we returned to our camp. I ordered that on the next day that high square platform which stood in the middle of the market-place should be prepared for the lords and princes of the city, and that they should likewise prepare a repast for them; and this was done accordingly.

We went into the city early the next morning, and I ordered the people to be prepared in case the inhabitants intended to perpetrate any treachery, so that we might not be surprised; I also cautioned Pedro de Alvarado who was there. When we reached the market-place, I sent word to Quatamucin, telling him that I was waiting for him, but, it appeared he had determined not to come, but sent five of his nobles or chief lords of the city whose names, as it is not worth while, I do not give here. They came and told me that their lord had sent them to pray me to pardon him if he did not come, that he was greatly afraid to appear before me, and also that he was ill and that they had come hither to hear my commands, which they would obey; although the sovereign did not appear we rejoiced a great deal that these chiefs had come, as it seemed to us that here was now a way to reach a speedy end of the whole business. I received them with a show of gladness, and immediately ordered meat and drink to be given them, in partaking of which they showed their craving and need for it. When they had eaten, I told them to speak to their lord to persuade him not to be afraid, for I promised him that no annoyance would be offered him if he appeared before me, nor would he be detained, but that, without his presence, no good understanding could be reached, nor agreement made. I ordered some refreshments to be taken to him, and they promised me to do all that was in their power; and thus they departed. Two hours afterwards, they returned, and brought me some fine mantles of cotton, such as they use, and they told me that Quatamucin their lord would by no means come, and that he refused to discuss it. I again repeated to them that I did not know why he mistrusted me, inasmuch as he saw that to them whom I knew to be the principal promoters of the war, and who had sustained it, I nevertheless extended good treatment, allowing them to come and go in security without being in any way annoyed, and I besought them to speak again to him, and to urge his coming because it was for his advantage. They answered me that they would do so, and bring me the answer the next day; and thus they left and we also withdrew to our camp.

The next day, those chiefs came to our camp very early in the morning and asked me to come to the square of the market of the city, because their sovereign wished to speak to me. Believing it was true, I mounted my horse and awaited him where it had been agreed, for more than three or four hours, but he never chose to appear before me. As I saw the mockery, and it had already become late, and that neither the other messengers nor the lord came, I sent for the Indians, our friends, who had been left at the entrance of the city almost a league from where we were, whom I had ordered not to advance beyond there because the people of the city had asked me that, whilst treating for peace none of them should be inside it. Neither they nor those of Pedro de Alvarado's camp delayed in coming, and, when they arrived, we attacked some of the barricades and water streets which they held, no other strong force being left them, and we charged amongst them ourselves, as well as our friends, according as we pleased. Before leaving the camp, I had ordered that Gonzalo de Sandoval should proceed with the brigantines to the place where the Indians had fortified themselves in the houses, thus holding them surrounded, but not attacking them until he should observe that we began to fight; in such manner that, holding them thus surrounded, they had no place to go except amongst the dead, and on the roofs which were left them. For this cause, they neither had, nor procured, arrows, nor darts, nor stones, with which to hurt us. Our friends accompanied us, armed with swords and shields, and such was the slaughter done that day on water and on land, that with prisoners taken they numbered in all more than forty thousand men; and such were the shrieks and the weeping of the women and children that there was none whose heart did not break; and we had more trouble in preventing our allies from killing and inflicting tortures than we had in fighting with the Indians, for no such inhuman cruelty as the natives of these parts practice was ever seen amongst any people. Our allies obtained very great plunder, which we could not prevent, because we were about nine hundred Spaniards, and they more than one hundred and fifty thousand men, and no attention or diligence was sufficient to prevent them from robbing, although we did everything possible to stop it. One of the reasons why I refused to go to extremes in those previous days was that, by taking them by assault, they would probably throw what they had into the lake, and if they did not do so our allies would steal everything they found; and, for this reason, I feared that but a small part of the great wealth existing in the city, as shown by what I had before obtained for Your Highness, would be secured for Your Majesty. As it was already late, and we could no longer endure the stench of the dead which had lain for many days in those streets (the most pestilential thing in the world), we returned to our camps.

That afternoon, I arranged that, as on the next day following we should again enter the city, three large field pieces should be prepared which we would take to the city, because, as I feared that the enemy were so compact that they could not turn round, the Spaniards in charging might be crushed by mere numbers, and therefore I wanted to do them some damage with the field pieces in order to force them out towards us. I ordered the alguacil mayor likewise to be prepared to enter, the next day, with the brigantines, through the canals of a large lake extending amongst some houses where the canoes of the city were all gathered; and there were already so few houses left where they might shelter that the lord of the city, with certain of the chiefs, had placed himself in a canoe, not knowing what to do with themselves. Thus we planned our entrance on the morning of the following day.

When day had dawned, I had our whole force prepared, and the large field pieces brought out; and I had, the day before, ordered Pedro de Alvarado to await me in the square of the market-place, and not to begin fighting until I arrived. All being assembled, and the brigantines ready for action, behind the houses on the water, where the enemy were gathered, I ordered that, on hearing a musket-shot, the land force should enter the small part which was still to be captured, and force the enemy towards the water where the brigantines would be awaiting them; and I cautioned them particularly to look after Quatamucin, and to endeavour to take him alive, because then the war would stop. I mounted the top of a roof, and, before the fight began, I spoke with some of the chiefs of the city whom I knew, and asked them why their lord did not come, seeing that they were in such straits, and I said they ought not to be the cause of all perishing; and told them to call him, saying that nobody need be afraid; and it seemed that two of those chiefs went to call him. After a short time, they returned with one of the highest chiefs of all of them, who was called Ciguacoacin,[58] captain and governor of them all, whose counsel was followed in everything concerning the war. I showed a very good disposition towards him, so that he might be reassured and have no fears, and finally he told me that the sovereign would in no way appear before me, and that he rather preferred to die where he was, and that he himself was much grieved at this decision but that I could do as I pleased. Recognising by this his determination, I told him to return to his own people, and that he and they might prepare themselves, as I was determined to attack them, and finish destroying them; and so it happened. More than five hours had passed in these parleyings, and the inhabitants of the city were all treading on the dead, others in the water were swimming, and others drowning themselves in the large lake where the canoes were collected. Such was the plight in which they were, that no understanding could conceive how they could endure it; and an infinite number of men, women, and children kept coming towards us, who, in their haste, pushed one another back into the water and were drowned amidst the multitude of dead. It appears they had perished to the number of more than fifty thousand, from the salt water which they drank, or from starvation, and pestilence. All these bodies, (in order that we should not understand their extremity), were neither thrown into the water lest the brigantines might come across them, nor were they thrown outside their boundary, lest we should see them about the city; and thus, in the streets they occupied, were found heaps of dead, so that nobody could step without trampling them. As the people of the city came towards us, I ordered Spaniards to be stationed in all the streets, to prevent our allies from killing those unhappy creatures, who were beyond number; and I also ordered the captains of our allies not to allow in any way those fugitives to be killed, but, as they were so many, it was not possible to prevent it that day, so more than fifteen thousand persons were massacred. Meanwhile, some of the chiefs and warriors of the city were brought to bay on some roofs and in the water, where they could no longer stop, or hide from us all their disasters and their weakness which had become very apparent; and, seeing that the afternoon was coming on us, and that they would not surrender, I had two large field pieces directed against them to see whether they would surrender then, because they would suffer greater damage by our giving permission to our friends to attack them, than by those two field pieces, which caused some destruction. As this also brought no result, I ordered the signal of the musket to be fired, whereupon the corner they still held was immediately taken, and those who were in it were forced into the water, and others who had not fought surrendered. The brigantines swiftly entered that lake, and broke into the midst of the fleet of canoes, and the warriors no longer ventured to fight.

It pleased God that the captain of a brigantine, called García Holguín, overtook a canoe in which there were some distinguished people, and, as he had two or three cross-bowmen in the prow of the brigantine, and was crossing in the front of the canoe, they signalled to him not to shoot because their sovereign was there. The canoe was quickly captured, and they took Quatamucin,[59] and the lord of Tacuba, and the other chiefs who were with him; and the said captain, García Holguín,[60] immediately brought the said sovereign of the city and the other chief prisoners to the terrace where I was, which was near the lake. When I invited them to sit down, not wishing to show any rigour, he approached me and said to me in his language that he had done all that on his part he was bound to do to defend himself and his people, until he was reduced to that state, and that I might now do with him as I chose; and placing his hand on a dagger which I wore he bade me stab him with it and kill him. I encouraged him, and told him not to be afraid; and this lord having been made prisoner, the war immediately ceased, which God Our Lord was pleased to bring to its end on this day, the Feast of San Hipólito, which was the 13th of August in the year 1521. So that from the day when we laid the siege to the city, which was the

30th of May of the said year, until it was taken, seventy-five days passed, in which Your Majesty may perceive the hardships, dangers, and cruelties, which these, your vassals, suffered, and in which they so exposed themselves that their deeds will bear testimony of them. In all these seventy-five days of the siege, none passed without more or less fighting.

On the day of the imprisonment of Quatamucin, and of the capture of the city, we returned to camp, having gathered the spoils found that day, and given thanks to Our Lord for the signal mercy and the much wished for victory He had granted us. I remained in the camp for three or four days, and afterwards we came to the city of Cuyoacan where I have remained until now, providing for the good order and government and pacification of these parts. Having collected the gold and other things, we had them melted, with the approbation of Your Majesty's officials, and what was melted amounted to one hundred and thirty thousand *castellanos,* of which one fifth was given to the treasury of Your Majesty, besides one fifth of other duties belonging to Your Majesty, such as slaves and other things, as will be more extensively seen from the account of all belonging to Your Majesty, which will go signed with our names. The remaining gold was distributed amongst myself and the Spaniards, according to the conduct, service, and quality of each. Besides the said gold, there were certain made pieces, and jewels of gold, of which the best was given to the treasurer of Your Majesty.

Amongst the plunder which was obtained from the said city, many bucklers of gold were found; plumes, and feather work, and things so marvellous that they cannot be described in writing, nor can they be comprehended without being seen. And being such as they are, it seemed to me they should not be divided but should all be placed at the disposition of Your Majesty, for which purpose I assembled all the Spaniards, and besought them to approve of all these things being sent to Your Majesty, and that the shares belonging to them and me should be placed at Your Majesty's disposition, which they rejoiced in doing with much good will. They and I send them for Your Majesty's acceptance by the procurators whom the council of this New Spain has deputed.

As the city of Temixtitan was so important, and so renowned throughout these parts, it seems it came to the knowledge of the lord of a very great province, seventy leagues distant from Temixtitan, called Michoacan,[61] how we had destroyed and desolated it, and, considering the strength and grandeur of the said city, it seemed to the lord of that province that, inasmuch as it could not defend itself, there was nothing which could resist us. So, from fear or whatever cause he chose, he sent certain messengers, who, through the interpreters of his language, told me on his part, that their lord had learned that we were vassals of a great ruler, and that, with my approval, he and his people desired to become vassals and have friendship with us. I answered that it was true that we were all of us the vassals of that great ruler, who was Your Majesty, and that we would make war upon those who refused likewise to be so, and that their lord and they had done very well. As I had received news some short time since of the South Sea, I also inquired of them whether it could be reached through their country; and as they answered me affirmatively, I prayed them to take with them two Spaniards, whom I would give them, so that I might inform Your Majesty about that sea and their province. They replied that they were glad to do so with much good will, but that, to reach the sea, they would have to pass through the country of a great lord, with whom they were at war, and for this reason they could not now reach the sea. The messengers from Michoacan remained here with me three or four days, and I made the horsemen skirmish for them, in order that they might describe it, and, having given them certain jewels, they and the two Spaniards set out for the said province of Michoacan.

As I said in the foregoing chapter, Most Powerful Lord, I had obtained a short time ago information of another sea to the south, and had learned that, in two or three different directions, it was twelve or fourteen days' journey from here. I was very much concerned because it seemed to me that in discovering it a great and signal service would be rendered to Your Majesty, especially as all who have any knowledge or experience of the navigation in the Indies have held it to be certain that, with the discovery of the South Sea in these parts, many islands rich in gold, pearls, precious stones, spices, and other unknown and admirable things would be discovered: and this has been and is affirmed by persons of learning and experience in the science of cosmography. With this desire, and wishing to render Your Majesty this most singular and admirable service, I dispatched four Spaniards, two through certain provinces, and the other two through certain others; and, having first informed myself of the routes they were to take, and giving them guides from amongst our friends, they departed. I ordered them not to stop until they had reached the sea, and, upon discovering it, to take actual and corporeal possession of it in the name of Your Majesty.

The first travelled about one hundred and thirty leagues through many beauful and fair provinces without encountering any hindrance, and arrived at the sea, and took possession of it, in sign of which they placed crosses on the coast of it. Some days afterwards, they returned with an account of the said discovery, and informed me very minutely of everything, bringing me some of the natives of the said sea [coast] and also very good samples from the gold mines, which they found in some of those provinces through which they passed; I send these, with the other samples of gold, to Your Majesty. The other two Spaniards were somewhat longer, because they travelled about one hundred and fifty leagues through other parts until they reached the sea, of which they likewise took possession. They brought me a full description of the coast, and, with them, came some natives of it. I received them and the others graciously, and they, having been informed of Your Majesty's great power, and given some presents, returned very contented to their country.

In the other account, Most Catholic Lord, I told Your Majesty, how, when these Indians routed and expelled me from the city of Temixtitan the first time, all the provinces subject to the city rebelled against the service of Your Majesty, and made war upon us; and, by this account, Your Majesty may see how we reduced to Your Royal service almost all the provinces which had rebelled. Certain provinces on the coast of the North Sea at ten, fifteen, and thirty leagues' distance from the said city of Temixtitan, had revolted and rebelled, and their natives had treacherously killed certainly more than one hundred Spaniards who had thought themselves safe. I could not possibly proceed against them before the conclusion of the war, so, after I had dispatched those Spaniards who had first discovered the South Sea, I determined to send Gonzalo de Sandoval, alguacil mayor, with thirty-five horsemen, two hundred Spaniards, some of our allies, and some of the chiefs and natives of Temixtitan, to this province, which we called Tatactetelco and Tuxtepeque and Guatuxco and Aulicaba; and, having been instructed how to conduct this expedition, he began his preparations for it.

At this season, the lieutenant, whom I had left in the town of La Segura de la Frontera, in the province of Tepeaca, came to this city of Cuyoacan, and informed me how some of the natives of that province and other neighbouring ones, vassals of Your Majesty, were troubled by the natives of the provinces of Guaxacaque [Oaxaca] who made war on them because they were our friends, and, besides it being necessary to correct this evil, it was well to secure that province of Guaxacaque, because it was on the road to the South Sea, and to pacify it would be very advantageous as well for the aforesaid as for other reasons, which I will hereafter state to Your Majesty. The said lieutenant told me that he had privately received information respecting that province, and that we could subjugate it with a small force, because, while I was in the camp against Temixtitan, he had gone there, as those of Tepeaca had urged him to make war upon the natives of it, but, not having taken more than twenty or thirty Spaniards they had forced him to return, less leisurely than he would have wished. Having heard his relation I gave him twelve horsemen and eight Spaniards, and the said alguacil mayor and the lieutenant left the city of Guaxacaque on the 15th October, 1521.

When they reached the province of Tepeaca, they there made their review, and each departed on his conquest. The alguacil mayor wrote to me five days later that he had arrived at the province of Guatuxco, and that, although he had much apprehension that he would find himself in straits with the enemy as they were very skilful in war and had many forces in the country, it had pleased Our Lord that he should be received peaceably; and that, although he had not reached the other provinces he felt sure that all the natives of them would offer themselves as vassals of Your Majesty. Fifteen days later, other letters of his arrived in which he reported to me that he had advanced, and that the whole of the country was already at peace, and that it seemed to him it would be well to settle in the most accessible parts and thus make sure of it, as we had already discussed many times before, and for me to decide what should be done in the matter. I wrote, thanking him very much for what he had done on his expedition in the service of Your Majesty, telling him that all he reported about settling was approved by me, and I sent him word to establish a town of Spaniards in the province of Tuxtepeque, and to call at Medellin,[62] I sent the appointment of alcaldes and municipal officials, all of whom I charged to look after Your Majesty's service and the good treatment of the natives. The Lieutenant of Segura de la Frontera departed with his people for the province of Guaxaca with many friendly warriors from that neighbourhood, and, although the natives of that province set themselves to resist, and fought two or three times very stoutly against him, they finally surrendered peacefully without sustaining any damage; he wrote very minutely respecting all this, informing me that the country was very good, and rich in mines, and he sent me a very remarkable sample of gold from it, which I also forward to Your Majesty; and he remained in the said province awaiting my commands.

Having taken measures for the accomplishment of these two conquests, and having heard of the good success of them, and seeing how I had already peopled three towns with Spaniards and that a number of them still remained with me in this city, I debated where to establish another town within the circuit of the lakes; for it was needed for the greater security and peace of all these parts. Considering also that the city of Temixtitan, which was a thing so renowned and had made itself so important and memorable, it seemed to us that it was well to rebuild it, for it was all destroyed. I distributed the lots to those who offered themselves as householders, and I appointed the alcaldes and municipal officers in the name of Your Majesty, as is customary in your kingdoms; and, while the houses were being built, we agreed to continue living in this city of Cuyoacan, where we are at present. In the four or five months since the rebuilding of the said city of Temixtitan was begun it is already very beautiful, and Your Majesty may believe that each day it will become nobler, so that as it was before the head and mistress of all these provinces, so it will be henceforward; it is being and will be so built that the Spaniards will be perfectly strong and safe, and supreme lords of the natives, secure from any fear of being assailed by them.

In the meantime, the chief of the province of Tecoantepeque, which is near the South Sea where the two Spaniards discovered it, sent me certain notables by whom he offered himself as vassal of Your Majesty, and made me a present of certain jewels, pieces of gold, and feather work, all of which was delivered to the treasurer of Your Majesty; I thanked the messengers for what they told me on behalf of their chief, and I gave them certain presents which they took and returned very happy.

At this season, those two Spaniards returned from the province of Michoacan, whence the messengers had come from that chief, and told me that the South Sea could be reached by that way, except that it had to be done through the country of a chief who was his enemy. A brother of the chief of Michoacan came with the two Spaniards, and other chiefs and servants with him, exceeding two thousand persons, whom I received, showing great love towards them; and they gave me on the part of the chief of the said province, who is called Calcucin, a present for Your Majesty of shields of gold, weighing [*word missing*] marks, and many other things which were delivered to Your Majesty's treasurer. To show them our customs, and let them report to their chief, I had all the horsemen ride to the square, where they manoeuvred and skirmished, the foot soldiers marching in file, and the musketeers firing their muskets and firing with the artillery against the tower. The chiefs were all dreadfully frightened to see the effect it made, and to see the horses manoeuvring; then I had them taken to see the destruction and desolation of the city of Temixtitan, and they were astonished on beholding it and its strength and its fortress, situated as it was in the water. After four or five days, I gave them for their chief many such things as they esteemed, and others for themselves, so they departed very happy and satisfied.

I have heretofore made relation to Your Majesty about the river of Pánuco, which is fifty or sixty leagues down the coast from the city of Veracruz, where the ships of Francisco de Garay had gone two or three times and received a good deal of hurt from the natives of the said river on account of the little tact which the captains who had been sent there had shown in the traffic they attempted to establish with the Indians. Afterwards, when I perceived that on the whole coast of the South Sea there was a lack of harbours, and that none was equal to the harbour of that river, and also because those natives, after coming to me to offer themselves as vassals of Your Majesty, are making war against the vassals of Your Majesty, our friends, I felt it very necessary to send a captain there with a force to pacify all that province, and, if the country was a likely one for settlement, to establish a town on that river, so that the entire neighbourhood might be assured. Although we were few and scattered in three or four places, from which reason there was some opposition to taking more people from here, nevertheless, both in order to help our friends, and because, after the taking of the city of Temixtitan, ships had arrived bringing some people and horses, I prepared twenty-five horsemen and one hundred and fifty foot soldiers to go with their captain to the said river.

While engaged in dispatching this captain, they wrote to me from Veracruz that a ship had arrived in its port, in which there came Cristobal de Tapia,[63] inspector of the foundries in the island of Hispaniola. I received a letter from him the next day afterwards, in which he made known to me that his coming to this country was for the purpose of taking charge of its government by order of Your Majesty; for this purpose he said he had brought the royal provisions, but would in no wise present them until we met, which he desired should happen immediately. As his animals had been fatigued at sea, he had not begun his journey and he prayed me to give orders how we might see each other, either by his coming hither or my going to the sea-coast. Immediately I received his letter, I answered it, saying that I rejoiced at his arrival, and that nobody could have come provided with Your Majesty's orders for holding the government of these parts whom I would receive with more satisfaction, not only on account of our mutual acquaintance, but also as fellow neighbours and early settlers in the island of Hispaniola.

Since the pacification of these parts was not so complete as it should be, and any novelty would disquiet the natives, I besought Fray Pedro Melgarejo de Urrea, commissary of the Cruzada,[64] (who accompanied us in all our hardships and well knew the state of things here, making himself so useful in Your Majesty's service that we had availed ourselves of his devotion and advice), to go and see the said Tapia, and to examine the warrants of Your Majesty; and, since he knew better than anyone else what was profitable to your royal service in these parts, to come to some agreement with the said Tapia as to what was most advantageous, for I conceived that he would not exceed them in any way. I besought him thus in the presence of Your Majesty's treasurer, who also charged him in the same sense. He departed for the city of Veracruz where the said Tapia was staying; and to insure that, in the city or wherever the Inspector might come, he would be well served and accommodated, I sent two or three notable persons with the said Father. After they left, I awaited his answer.

Meanwhile I was preparing for my departure, giving orders about some things necessary to Your Majesty's service, and for the pacification and quieting of these parts. Some ten or twelve days afterwards the justice and Municipal Council of Veracruz wrote to me that the said Tapia had presented the provisions he brought from Your Majesty and your governors in your royal name, and that they had been received with all due reverence, but as for executing them, they had answered that as most of the Municipal Council were here with me, aiding in the siege of the city, they would report to them, and all would do and comply with what was most profitable to Your Majesty's service and the good of the country. The said Tapia was somewhat displeased by this reply, and had even attempted something scandalous. As this grieved me somewhat, I replied, praying and charging them very much to look chiefly to Your Majesty's service, endeavouring to satisfy the said Tapia and not to give occasion for any tumult as I was about starting to see him, ready to comply with what Your Majesty had ordered and was most suitable to your service. Being on the very eve of starting on my journey, and the captain and people, whom I intended to send to the river Pánuco, having been detained here, where it was necessary, while I was away for this city to remain well guarded, the Procurators of this New Spain requested me with many protestations not to leave, because, as this entire province of Mexico and Temixtitan had only recently been pacified, it would be disturbed by my absence, and much injury would be done to the service of Your Majesty and to the tranquillity of the country; they gave many other causes and reasons for their said requirement that I should not leave this city at that present time, and they told me they would go themselves to the city of Veracruz where the said Tapia was staying, with power of attorney from the councillors, and would see the warrants of Your Majesty and do all that was suitable to Your Royal service. As this seemed to us expedient, the said procurators left, and I wrote to the said Tapia letting him know what was happening, and that I was sending my power of attorney to Gonzalo de Sandoval, alguacil mayor, and to Diego de Soto and Diego Valdenebro, who were there in the town of Veracruz, in order that in my name, they together with the municipal councillors and procurators of their municipal councils, might take measures to do what was suitable to Your Majesty's service and for the good of the country; for they have been and are persons who would do so. They met Tapia, who was already on the road, accompanied by Fray Pedro, and required him to return to the city of Cempoal, and there Tapia presented Your Majesty's provisions which were received by all, with the submission due to Your Majesty. As for executing them, they appealed that to the presence of Your Majesty, because such was advantageous to your royal service for the causes and reasons apparent in their same petition, and as will appear more fully from what passed; all of which the procurators who came from this New Spain carried, signed by a public notary. After exchanging other decrees and requirements between the said inspector and the procurators, he embarked in his ship as he was required to do, because, after publishing that he had come to be governor and captain of these parts his presence had caused some disquietude, and the people of Mexico and

Temixtitan had plotted that the natives here should rebel and work a great treason, which, if it had been carried out would have been worse than the past. The plan was, that certain Indians who were in Mexico, agreeing with the natives of this province which the alguacil mayor had gone to pacify, should come to me in all haste, telling me that twenty ships had arrived on the coast with a great many people, and that, as they had not come on land, they could not be good people, and that I should come there and see what was the matter, they having prepared themselves, and going with me as warriors; and, to make me believe this, they brought me a drawing of the ships on paper. As they brought me this news secretly, I immediately divined that their intention was mischievous, and its purpose was to get me out of this province, for the chiefs of it had known all these past days that I had been prepared to march, but seeing that I remained quiet they devised this plan. I dissembled with them, and afterwards captured some who had invented the plot.

The coming of the said Tapia and his want of experience of the country and its people caused a great deal of confusion, and his remaining here would have done much harm, had not God remedied it, and he would have done better service to Your Majesty, if when he was in the island of Hispaniola he had refrained from coming, without first consulting Your Majesty, and making known the condition of things in these parts. For he had learned from the ships I had sent to the said island for help, and knew clearly that the scandal it was hoped to create by the coming of the armada of Pánfilo de Narváez had been remedied, principally by what the governors and royal council of Your Majesty had provided; and more still, for the said Tapia had been required many times by the Admiral and the judges and officials of Your Majesty who reside in the said island of Hispaniola not to interfere in these parts without Your Majesty first being informed of everything that had happened, and hence they forbade his coming under certain penalties; but by scheming and looking more to his private interest than to Your Majesty's service he obtained the revocation of the prohibition. I relate all this to Your Majesty, because, when the said Tapia left, the procurators and myself did not send a report, for he would not have been a good carrier of our letters, and also that Your Majesty may see and believe that, in not having received the said Tapia, Your Majesty had been well served, as will be more fully proven as often as may be necessary.

In a chapter before this, I made known to Your Majesty that the captain, whom I had sent to conquer the province of Guaxaca, was waiting there for my commands, and, as he was needed, and was judge and lieutenant in the town of Segura de la Frontera, I wrote to him to give the eighty men and ten horsemen whom he had to Pedro de Alvarado. The latter I had sent to subjugate the province of Tututepeque, forty leagues beyond Guaxaca near the South Sea, where they did much damage to, and made war against, those who had given themselves as Your Majesty's vassals, and to those of the province of Tututepeque, because they had allowed us to come through their country to discover the South Sea. Pedro de Alvarado left this said city the last of January of this present year, and, with the people he took from here, and with those he got in the province of Guaxaca, he united forty horsemen, two hundred foot soldiers, aided by forty archers and musketeers, and two small field pieces. Twenty days later, I received letters from the said Pedro de Alvarado, saying that he was on the road towards the province of Tututepeque, and he told me that he had captured certain native spies, and obtained information from them; for they had told him that the lord of Tututepeque and his people were expecting him on the field and he was determined to do in that journey all he possibly could to pacify that province, and besides the Spaniards had collected many and good warriors.

While waiting to hear the end of all this business, I received letters on the 4th of the month of March of the same year from the said Pedro de Alvarado in which he reported to me that he had entered that province, and that three or four towns of it had set themselves to resist him, but had not persevered in it, and that he had entered the town and city of Tututepeque, and had been well received as far as appearances went; and that the chief had asked him to lodge there in some of his great houses, which were thatched with straw, but that, inasmuch as the place was not very suitable for the horsemen, he had not accepted, but had come down to a part of the city which was more level; that he had also done this because he had learned that the chief had planned to kill him and all of them, by setting fire at midnight to the houses where the Spaniards were lodged.

When God had disclosed this baseness, he had feigned ignorance and, as if accidentally, had carried the chief and his son with him and had decided to keep them in his power as prisoners; they had given him twenty-five thousand *castellanos* and from what the vassals of that chief had told him, he believed there were great treasures. The whole of the province was as pacified as possible, and they carried on their markets and commerce as before. The country was very rich in gold mines, for in his presence they had taken out a sample which was sent to me. Three days before, he had been to the sea, and taken possession of it for Your Majesty, where, in his presence, they had taken out a sample of pearls which he likewise sent to me, and which I sent to Your Majesty, together with the sample from the gold mines.

As God, Our Lord, had well guided this business, and fulfilled my desire to serve Your Majesty on this South Sea, being as it is of such importance, I have provided with so much diligence that, in one of the three places where I discovered the sea, two medium-sized caravels and two brigantines are being built:

the caravels for the purpose of discovering, and the brigantines to follow the coast. For this purpose, I sent, under a reliable person, forty Spaniards, amongst whom go ship-masters, ship-carpenters, wood-sawyers, blacksmiths, and sea-men; and I have sent to the city for nails, sails, and other things necessary for the said ships, and all possible haste will be used to finish and launch them. Your Majesty may believe that it will be a great thing to accomplish this, and the greatest service since the Indies have been discovered will be thus rendered to Your Majesty.

While I was in the city of Tesaico, before we laid siege to Temixtitan, prepar-ing and furnishing ourselves with the necessities for the said siege, and en-tirely unaware of what certain persons were plotting, one of the conspirators warned me that certain friends of Diego Velázquez, who were in my com-pany, had treasonably plotted to kill me, and that amongst them they had elected a captain, an alcalde, and alguacil mayor, and other officials. My in-former begged that I should thwart this by all means, for, besides the scandal which would follow, respecting my person, it was clear that not a Spaniard would escape, for, seeing us turned against one another not only would we find the enemy against us, but even those whom we regarded as friends would join in and finish with all of us. I thanked Our Lord, because in the discovery of this treachery lay the remedy. We immediately seized the principal offender, who spontaneously confessed that he had designed and planned, with many persons whom he betrayed in his confession, to assault and kill us, and to take the Government of the country for Diego Velázquez, and that it was true he had designed to appoint captains and alcaldes, and that he himself was to be the alguacil mayor, and that he was to seize and kill me. Many persons were in-volved in this, whom he had placed on a list which was found in his lodgings (although torn in pieces), together with the names of persons with whom he had spoken of the said affair; he had not only contemplated this in Tesaico, but he had also communicated it, and spoken of it during the war against the prov-ince of Tepeaca. After hearing the confession of this man, who was called An-tonio de Villafaña, a native of Zamora, and as he reiterated it, the judge and myself condemned him to death, which was executed on his person.[65] Although we found others inculpated in this offence, I dissembled with them, treating them as friends, because the case being mine, although more properly it might be said to be that of Your Majesty, I was not willing to proceed rigorously against them; this dissimulation has not produced much advantage, because since then some partisans of Diego Velázquez have started many intrigues, and have secretly created many seditions and scandals, in which it has been neces-sary for me to be more on my guard against them than against our enemies. But God, Our Lord, has always conducted everything in such a manner, that, without executing any punishment on them, there has been, and exists, peace and tranquillity; and if from henceforth I should discover anything else it shall be punished as justice dictates.

After the city of Temixtitan was captured, and while we were in Cuyoacan, Don Fernando, the lord of Tesaico died, which much grieved us all because he was a good vassal of Your Majesty and a great friend of the Christians; and with the approval of the chiefs and the notables of that city and of his province the lordship was given in the name of Your Majesty to a younger brother, who was baptised and took the name of Don Carlos,[66] and as far as we know he has followed until now in the footsteps of his brother, and seems much pleased with our habits and conversation.

I made known to Your Majesty in the other account how there was a very high and conical mountain near the provinces of Tascaltecal and Guaxocingo, from which much smoke almost constantly issued, ascending straight like an arrow.[67] As the Indians gave us to understand that it was a very fearful thing to ascend it, and that those who went there perished, I made certain Spaniards undertake it, and examine the summit of the mountain. When they ascended, the smoke came out with such noise that they neither could nor dared to reach its mouth; and afterwards I made some other Spaniards go, who ascended twice, reaching the mouth of the mountain where the smoke comes out, and from one side of the mouth to the other it was two crossbow-shots, for the circumference of it is almost three-quarters of a league, and the depth is so great that they could not see the bottom of it, and they found near the circumference some sulphur, deposited there by the smoke. They heard such a great noise made by the smoke that they made all haste to come down, and before they had descended to the middle of the mountain an infinite number of stones came rolling down, greatly endangering their position; and the Indians held it a very great thing to have dared to go where the Spaniards had gone.

In one of my letters, I told Your Majesty that the natives of these parts were much more capable than those of the other islands, appearing to be as intelligent and as reasonable as is ordinarily considered sufficient; wherefor it appeared wrong to oblige them to serve the Spaniards as those of the other islands do, though without some assistance, the conquerors and settlers of these parts would on the other hand be unable to maintain themselves. In order not to force the Indians to help the Spaniards, it seemed to me that Your Majesty might order that as compensation the latter should receive assistance from the incomes which here belong to Your Majesty for their provisions and sustenance; respecting this Your Majesty may provide what seems profitable to your service, according to the more extensive relation which I have made to Your Majesty. Seeing the many and continual outlays of Your Majesty, and that we ought rather to augment your rents by all possible means than to be an occasion of further expenses, and considering also the long time we have spent in the wars, and the necessities and debts caused thereby, and the delay attendant upon Your Majesty's decision in this case, and above all the many importunities of Your Majesty's officials and of all the Spaniards from which it was impossible to excuse myself, I found myself almost forced to place the chiefs and natives of these parts amongst the Spaniards, to recompense them for the services they have rendered to Your Majesty. Until something else is ordered or this confirmed, the said chiefs and natives serve and give each Spaniard to whom they are allotted the needful for his subsistence. This step was taken with the approbation of intelligent persons, who have had, and have, great experience of the country, for there was nothing else possible not only for the maintenance of the Spaniards but also for the preservation and good treatment of the Indian, as is shown in the more extensive relation which the procurators who now go from this New Spain will make to Your Majesty. The plantations and farms of Your Majesty have been established in the best and most convenient provinces and cities.

Most Catholic Lord, may God Our Lord preserve and augment the life and very royal person and powerful state of Your Caesarean Majesty with increase of much greater Kingdoms and Lordships, as your royal heart may desire. From the City of Cuyoacan of this New Spain of the Ocean Sea on the 15th of May, 1522. Most Powerful Lord, Your Caesarean Majesty's very humble servant and vassal who kisses the royal hands and feet of Your Majesty.

HERNANDO CORTES.

the chronicle
of fray
francisco de aguilar

Cortés' companions-at-arms, each according to the measure of his ambition, engaged in further military conquests or settled down to enjoy the benefits from their land grants. One of the latter was Alonso de Aguilar. During all the campaigns, from the time of the landing at Cozumel, Aguilar distinguished himself for his integrity and quiet valor, and was given such responsible assignments as guarding Moctezuma when that sovereign was imprisoned by Cortés.

After the Conquest, Aguilar received a fair allotment of land and Indians, and the privilege of a *venta*, or hostelry, situated on the highway between Puebla and the port of Veracruz. In a few years he became a man of considerable wealth. Then in 1529, at the age of fifty, he released his Indians and gave up all his possessions to enter the Dominican order.

Abrupt as the decision may have seemed to his old companions, it is apparent from his writing that Aguilar was contemplative by nature, and that he had brooded about the moral aspect of the Conquest. As Fray Francisco de Aguilar he served in the most menial capacity for forty-two years, until his death at the age of ninety-two. By his own testimony, when he was more than eighty "and nearing the end of my lifespan" he was persuaded by his fellow monks to write the story of his participation in the Conquest of Mexico. It is very likely that he dictated his brief history, since he suffered from gout for thirty-five years, and at the end was so crippled that he could not feed himself.

Aguilar's chronicle, which is contained in the following pages, is prefaced by an apology for his inelegant style, and a promise to adhere steadfastly to the truth in narrating the events and circumstances of the Conquest. As a history it is well organized, succinct and, more than any other account, conveys what it felt like to live in perpetual terror of the Indians.

I, Fray Francisco Aguilar, professed member of the Order of Friars Preachers[1] and one of the conquistadors that first came to this land with Hernando Cortés, wrote this on reaching the age of more than eighty years, at the request of certain of the religious who importuned me and said that inasmuch as I was nearing the end of my span of life I should leave them a written account of my participation in the conquest of New Spain, and tell how it was conquered and taken. I herewith give my account as an eyewitness, briefly and in plain words, without circumlocutions; but if perchance the style and manner of telling is not so delightful nor pleasing to the reader as I might wish, may he at least derive satisfaction from the truth concerning this business, which it has been my principal aim to pursue, and to which end I have set down what happened in the order of the expeditions we made in carrying out the conquest of this land.

first jornada [2]

Don Diego Colón, the admiral who discovered Santo Domingo, sent Diego Velázquez, provincial governor and honorable gentleman, to the Island of Cuba, which he explored and settled. Diego Velázquez sent an account of the exploration and settlement to the King Don Fernando and the Queen Doña Isabel, who in consideration of his industry, perspicacity and sacrifice, and the adroitness he had shown in the seizure and settlement of the Island of Cuba, decided in recompense and payment of his service and labors to name him governor of the island, authorizing him also to discover and settle on the mainland.

Therefore, wishing to make use of his authorization, he made up an armada of five ships with two hundred soldiers and a good crew, and as their captain he commissioned Juan de Grijalva, a man who was valorous as a person and noble by blood and lineage. After setting sail and navigating in favorable weather across the sea, this captain found harbor in the land of Yucatan, at a river which later became known as the Grijalva, and on whose shores was a very large and spacious Indian city.

When the captain and his men had anchored the ships and secured them against the winds, they went ashore in an orderly manner. Upon asking the Indians for water and supplies for his men, he was not only refused but given fierce battle in which one of his men was killed. He and his men were forced to take to the ships and return to Cuba, where Governor Diego Velázquez, on seeing the sorry account he had given of himself, took the armada away from him.

second jornada

In view of the foregoing, and to keep the men from dispersing and the ships from becoming a loss, Velázquez summoned Hernando Cortés, an hidalgo and person of good birth who at that time was a municipal judge. He asked him to take charge of the armada, which Cortés quickly accepted, and Diego Velázquez turned it over to him.

Hernando Cortés devoted himself to the undertaking with such ability and industriousness, as the astute man that he was, that in a few days he had obtained funds borrowed from among his friends, and enlisted another two hundred men, and secured a large supply of provisions.

Later Governor Velázquez, regretting his decision, tried to take the armada away from him, and went to the port with some men to carry this out. But the shrewd Hernando Cortés, taking advantage of the lateness of the day and the good weather, raised anchor, hoisted sail and left. Accompanying him were very wellborn persons: Don Pedro de Alvarado; Don Pedro Puerto Carrero, brother of the Count of Medellín; Diego Velázquez, nephew of the governor; Sandoval; Cristóbal de Olid, and other persons of good birth. There were also Venetians, Greeks, Sicilians, Italians, Biscayans, Montanese, Asturians, Portuguese, Andalusians and Estremenians.

third jornada

Once Cortés and his men had boarded and were at sea, all those noble gentlemen gathered and elected Cortés captain in the name of the king and not in the name of Diego Velázquez the governor. Then Cortés named his captains general, who were Pedro de Alvarado and his brother Jorge de Alvarado, and Gonzalo de Sandoval, second captain; also Cristóbal de Olid and Andrés de Tapia, wellborn persons and valorous men.

The armada sailed to the island named Cozumel, which is right off the coast of the mainland. A man appeared on the coast, running and waving a cloth, and a small brigantine picked him up. It was learned that his name was Hernando (sic) de Aguilar, since he was a Christian, and that he and a companion had been saved from an armada that was wrecked there, and had fallen into the hands of Indians.

Farther on, following the coast, Cortés and his men reached the Grijalva River, which they entered. Captain Cortés ordered ashore a hundred crossbowmen, musketeers and foot soldiers, and two armored horses, to resist the advance of the Indians who came ready for war. There were about forty thousand of them, but with our guns going off, the crossbows shooting, and the horses running, many were killed. Since this was all new to the Indian warriors they were frightened and left the battlefield.

Next day the Indians came in peace and gave themselves as vassals of the emperor, bringing provisions and food, at which the Spaniards were extremely pleased. They also brought a present of some mantles and eight slave women, one of whom was named Marina and later called Malinche.[3] She knew the Mexican tongue and understood the language Aguilar had learned during his six or seven years of captivity, and this news pleased everyone in the company.

From there we sailed along the coast looking for a harbor, and in time we reached the port called San Juan de Ulúa, which is also known as Lua, where the captain ordered certain Spaniards to go ashore with him. The natives, on seeing such things as their eyes had never before set on, gave themselves up to the captain and his men. Then they brought a great quantity of supplies and food, and presents of clothing and other things. They also presented a gift of a gold sun on a shield, and a silver moon, as well as certain gold necklaces, all of which were sent to the emperor.

Not far from where we made camp was a province called Quetlaxtla, with more than forty thousand houses, and close to this province were many others with large and powerful cities. From here the king of the land, whose name was Moctezuma, received news of the arrival of the Spaniards, whom they called *teules,* which means gods; for they regarded us as immortal beings. Then this king sent his ambassadors on several occasions with many presents of gold and necklaces for Hernando Cortés and his men.

Hernando Cortés dispatched some of his men by sea and others by land, and those of us who went by land arrived at a town called Cempoala, which was on a broad plain and situated between two rivers; it had many groves and fruit trees, and an abundance of fish. Captain Hernando Cortés and his men were very well received by the inhabitants. They were very good people and good friends of the Spaniards, and remained loyal to them. From Cempoala, which had more than twenty thousand houses, we went on to look for a better harbor [than San Juan de Ulua], in another town by the sea which later was called Veracruz, where the Spaniards were quartered.

As the Spaniards heard so much from the interpreters Marina and Aguilar about the vastness of the country inland, many of the gentlemen and hidalgos were saying they wanted to go back. It was said that some did so out of fear, and others to inform the governor Don Diego Velázquez, which caused a great deal of disturbance. In view of this Hernando Cortés obtained the support of certain Estremenian friends of his; but without telling them what he had decided to do, he called one of the ships' masters who was a close friend and asked him to go aboard secretly that night, after the men had been ordered ashore, and scuttle all the ships. And so the master boarded the ships without anyone seeing him or knowing what he was going to do, and scuttled them, and next morning all the vessels were found sunk except one caravel.

On seeing this the Spaniards were stunned, but in the end they plucked up courage and ignored the matter; but not to the extent of forgetting their resentment, for Juan Escudero and Diego de Ordaz, who were wellborn persons, and another called Umbría, agreed among themselves to take the caravel and inform Don Diego Velázquez of what was happening. When this came to the attention of Captain Hernando Cortés he had them brought before him. On being asked if there was any truth in what was being said of them, they admitted they wanted to go and inform Don Diego Velázquez. Hernando Cortés then ordered them hanged.[4] Juan Escudero, whose rank of hidalgo did not avail him, was hanged on the spot; but Ordaz, a man of good judgment, was defended by all the captains and finally pardoned.

This action and the scuttling of the ships filled all the Spaniards with fear, and a few days later Cortés ordered a town built at the port, and left forty or fifty Spanish settlers under the command of a captain named Escalante, who remained as his lieutenant. This done, he sent Pedro de Alvarado toward Mexico with a hundred and fifty men, and he himself set out with an equal number. They met further on in an uninhabited region, from where they continued the march until reaching some large towns that were subject to Moctezuma, where the people came out in peace and offered the Spaniards provisions. Later Don Hernando Cortés and his men came in sight of a large province that is called Tlaxcala. Here, over seven or eight leagues of plains, they could see many towns and temples of the kind the Indians build, and on these plains they also saw and met countless numbers of warriors who were very well armed in their fashion. They used cotton *ixcahuipiles*,[5] cudgels and swords, and a great many bows and arrows. Many of them carried standards and gold shields, and other insignia which they wore strapped to their backs, giving them an appearance of great ferocity, since they also had their faces stained, and grimaced horribly, giving great leaps and shouts and cries. These put such fear into us that many of the Spaniards asked for confession. However, Captain Hernando Cortés proved himself very spirited and stronghearted, encouraging the soldiers and making them lose some of their fear. In this manner he established good order among the foot soldiers and horsemen, so that they were ready to give battle.

Marching in this order along the road, which was very wide and good, we reached the edge of the thicket, where we found the way barred with intertwined grass ropes. Then Cristóbal de Olid, like a courageous man, went forward with another horseman to attack the warriors. Since the horses were running with their bell straps, and the artillery had begun firing, the Indians, startled by something so new, hesitated for a moment, so that only two Indians were waiting for the horsemen, one on each side of the road. One Indian at a single stroke cut open the whole neck of Cristóbal de Olid's horse, killing the horse. The Indian on the other side slashed at the second horseman and the blow cut through the horse's pastern, whereupon this horse also fell dead.[6]

At the sight of such boldness our army were taken aback; nevertheless they gave pursuit, in the course of which there were many encounters. Surrounded on all sides, the Spaniards defended themselves bravely, and it was in this battle that Hernando Cortés showed great valor, fighting manfully and giving courage to his troops.

The eleven horsemen remaining with the artillery fought their way little by little to a round hill where there was a village, and some Indian temples at the top, and here the captain fortified himself with all the Spaniards. It would seem that this hill had been put there by the Lord for our protection.[7] We were quartered here for two weeks, each day of which we were attacked from all sides by the Indians. But since the hill was round and the country flat, our horses and crossbowmen and musketeers could maneuver, and the artillery could fire, causing many losses among the masses of Indian warriors that teemed all over the countryside.

For food we ate what we could find in the way of maize and squash, for this was cultivated land, and drank stagnant rain water we found in some cisterns, which was a great hardship.

The Indians came from every direction to attack us, either at daybreak or the dawn watch, but they were the ones who suffered casualties, whereas none, no, not one of us was lost, though it seemed a miracle.[8] This battle or war lasted, as I have said, fourteen or fifteen days and nights. The enemy, seeing that none of us had been killed, thought we were immortal gods, and they began coming to our camp with bread and fruit, and although they were armed it appeared later that they came only to observe our arrangements. They presented their gifts to the captain, and without wasting time on words, looked all about them for a means of attacking us.

These Indians came also at night, and the captain told them through the interpreter that if they came at night the horses and soldiers would kill them. He also told them to ask the other Indians why they made war on him, since he did not wish to fight but was merely on his way to see Moctezuma.

Throughout all this, Captain Cortés and the other captains and their men demonstrated great courage, and never for a minute did their spirits flag on seeing themselves surrounded by such multitudes of warriors. Great vigilance was maintained by day and by night, for the enemy attacked from all sides, but the captain and his men resisted them courageously. The Indians now came at midnight or the dawn watch to try to enter our encampment. Furious at such impudence, the sentinels seized and captured them, and the captain, seeing that the Indians were disobedient of his warning, did not kill any of them but had their ears and noses cut off and tied around their necks, and sent them away terrified.

After so many days of assaulting us day and night without killing a single Christian, the Indians withdrew some distance from the hill, and, as though tired, diminished the force of their attacks. Hernando Cortés observed from his quarters that at a distance of a league, more or less, there were smoke signals indicating a large number of warriors. Alert and courageous as he was, and with the Indians beginning to weaken, he decided to go after them one night with six horsemen and about a hundred soldiers, so at midnight of the night agreed on we started marching in utmost silence, and after we had walked a while the horse that Hernando Cortés was riding began to tremble and then fell dazed to the ground. The captain, with invincible courage and without a moment's confusion, kept right on going on foot with the rest of the company. There were some who said to him: "Sire, this seems a bad sign to us; let us return." But he replied: "I consider it a good one. Onward."

A little further on another horse fell in the same way, and when the men tried to persuade the captain to return, he said staunchly: "May it never please God that I turn back. Onward." In this same way all the remaining horses fell, and the captain still encouraged the men to go on and not stop until they reached the Indians and their smoke. An hour or so later the groom who had stayed with the captain's horse brought him up well and sound, and the captain mounted. In this way the other five horses were also brought up perfectly well, which caused great joy among the company.

We reached the place where they had made the smoke signals, which was a large town called Zumpanchinco, and since we came upon it very quietly we caught them all asleep and unaware of our approach. Hernando Cortés ordered us under threat of severe punishment not to touch a single Indian, nor harm a soul, nor take their maize or anything else of theirs. He also ordered us to encircle their sleeping quarters, but only so that they could not escape, and he went inside, where there were many Tlaxcalan warriors sleeping. They awoke at some noise, and when they saw by the early light of dawn that no harm or injury had been done them, they came before the captain at his command and listened to him through the interpreters Malinche and Aguilar. He told them that, as they had seen, he had defended himself against all their people without the loss of any of his companions, but that many of their own men had been killed against his will and through their own fault for obstructing his way. "Therefore you have seen the truth of these things, for we have surprised you alone and asleep, and have not wished to kill or harm you in any way. And so that you may see the truth, go out into your camp and look about, and then return. If there is anything wrong I shall make amends, and all I ask of you is some provisions for my soldiers."[9]

The Indians went outside and looked everywhere, and as they saw that no damage had been done nor any person killed, and that everything was exactly as the captain had said, they gave their grateful thanks. And so, on seeing Cortés' good will and treatment of them, they provided very large quantities of maize and poultry; so much, that there was enough for the entire camp, and the Spaniards satisfied their hunger.

These Indians and their captains then left for the city of Tlaxcala to inform the lords and officials of the good treatment they had been given. The news was received with great pleasure, and they all decided to visit Captain Hernando Cortés and his men at the camp, taking many supplies and baked bread, and the fruits that grow in their land. With these gifts they presented themselves before Hernando Cortés and bade him welcome. They told him also that they had not waged war on him, and apologized for what had happened, blaming the Chichimecs and Otomís, who were their vassals, and giving us to understand that these were a disorderly people who had made war on us without their consent.

The captain thanked them and gave them some strings of beads, which pleased them very much, and they begged him on behalf of the lords and dignitaries of Tlaxcala to go there as their welcome guests, which the captain accepted with pleasure.

The city of Tlaxcala was about five leagues from there, and the way was full of towns and people. It surprised us very much to see it so large and thickly populated. The city must have had as many as a hundred thousand houses, and before we entered it the lords came out with many presents of clothing of the kind they use, and food. They brought a turkey and some bread for each of the horses, and for the hounds, and also for the guns.

It was a very joyous welcome they gave us, and they lodged us comfortably in some beautiful houses and palaces, where each day they fed us turkeys, fowl, and bread and fruit of the land, which were enough for the entire army.

Captain Hernando Cortés made a fine and lofty address, expressing his gratitude for their good will, and explaining that there had come to them a great and very Christian king to befriend and aid them. And after many conversations they had together, the Tlaxcalans said they offered themselves as vassals of His Majesty, and would obey and serve him in everything they could. This was the truth, and I have told nothing but the truth because I am at the end of my days. For they fulfilled their vow, and fulfill it to this day, because in all the strife and military encounters between the Mexicans and the Christians, the Tlaxcalans supported and aided us with all their strength, often risking their very lives for us, as it was clearly demonstrated. For this the Tlaxcalans are highly deserving, and our lord the king has the obligation to hold them in esteem and give them their complete freedom.

We stayed in this city a number of days, resting and taking pause from our past travails.

Moctezuma the lord and emperor of the land, on learning of the fourteen or fifteen days of war with the Tlaxcalans, grew fearful and dismayed to think that the captain was on the way to his great city; so he repeatedly sent ambassadors and dignitaries with presents of gold and necklaces, to entreat the captain not to go to his city because it was situated in the middle of a lake where we and the horses would drown. In addition to arguments of this kind to dissuade us, it seemed that Moctezuma had stationed a great army along the way, although we did not see it but were only informed of it.

When Maxixcatzin, lord of Tlaxcala,[10] and the other nobles realized that our destination was Mexico, they said to the captain: "Do not enter Mexico, Sire, for the lord there is treacherous and will kill you, as he already has resolved to do. Therefore take care, but if you so command we shall give you many troops to accompany you." The captain replied that he was very grateful to them, and that the offer was a great service to the king, but that he wanted only a few people to show him the way. And in this manner certain lords and captains departed with us.

fourth jornada

On leaving the city of Tlaxcala, Captain Hernando Cortés and his army marched toward another city that was called Cholula. It was a large city and an ally of Moctezuma. At that time it had fifty to sixty thousand houses, closely huddled together, and with flat roofs. The city was situated on a wide plain, and a river ran in front of it. We were amazed at the number and grandeur of its temples. This city was constantly in conflict with Tlaxcala, and was so warlike that it did not fear the Tlaxcalans.

In the center of the city was a building made of adobes, all hand laid, looking like a great mountain, at the top of which, it was said, there was a tower or chamber of sacrifices, but this was now abandoned. All the citizens had good houses with solid roofs, and fresh-water wells. Only a few yards in front of the city was a great extension of cultivated fields.

As we entered the city certain priests came to meet us, dressed in their fashion, and burning incense before us, but without saying any kind of ceremony.

On seeing this the Tlaxcalan nobles said to the captain: "Be it known to you, Sire, that this kind of reception is bad, signifying that they are at war and intend to sacrifice or kill you; therefore be at the ready with your Spaniards, and we will help you."

We were quartered in some large temple rooms, and given nothing but jugs of water and some wood, so that it was the Tlaxcalans who supplied the army as best they could. The city was empty of people. This meant that they were either afraid or ready for war. The captain, seeing how badly we were being treated, summoned several of the Indians who brought us water and wood (but nothing else) and told them through the interpreters that he was surprised at them for not providing us with any food, and advised them that he had not come to make war on them or do them any harm, but was on his way straight to Moctezuma in Mexico. He also warned them that if they did not give him the necessary sustenance he would go through the houses looking for it and taking it by force. This he advised them several times, until five days had passed in which nothing was given nor any attention paid to what the captain requested. In view of this the captains and noblemen of our army demanded that Cortés find provisions or make war on the Cholulans, because the army was in want. Cortés asked them to wait a few days to see if the Cholulans offered themselves peaceably. However, he was so importuned by the captains' requisitions to declare war, that he ordered put to death the Indians who brought wood and water; and so they were killed, and there were about two thousand of them more or less. Some of the Spaniards considered this a bad decision, since the matter could very well have been ignored and passed over.

The captain and his men thereupon left this city and headed for Mexico to see Moctezuma. Maxixcatzin, lord of Tlaxcala, and other nobles advised him not to enter Mexico because it was a city surrounded by water, and warned him that its lord was wily, and did not keep his word, and would kill him; in addition they told him that a large army of Moctezuma's was waiting nearby to kill us, and that the captain should therefore consider carefully what he was doing.

But Hernando Cortés, a man of courageous spirit, was still determined to take up the march.

fifth jornada

Once having departed, and in his eagerness to meet Moctezuma, Captain Hernando Cortés hastened the march toward the great city. On the way he encountered ambassadors of Moctezuma, who told him they had come to show him the way and accompany him.[11] The captain received them pleasantly and took them with him.

Toward the end of the day's march the Tlaxcalan nobles again cautioned the captain, because the ambassadors were taking him by a tortuous route over a rocky mountain where hollows and crevices hid an army ready to kill us. They urged him by no means to go that way, but to follow a smooth route that they would show us. The captain decided to spend the night here, and in the morning told Moctezuma's ambassadors he had been informed that the route they were leading him over was not good for his horses, and that he would like to send some Spaniards ahead with them to see it. When they had left he sent Diego de Ordaz and several others to accompany the Tlaxcalan nobles over the route they said was a good one.

The first group came back and reported that the way was very rocky and full of briars, and that the horses could not pass. Then on the following day Ordaz returned[12] saying he was astonished at what he had seen. We asked him what he had seen, and he said he had seen another new world of large cities and towers, and a sea, and in the sea a very large city, which indeed seemed frightening and awesome.

The captain was undaunted by what he had heard, and in good cheer set out with his men, keeping formation as well as possible, and marching short distances at a time from town to town. Along the road and in the towns we were given whatever food we needed; therefore no soldier or other person would dare take anything or commit any abuse without his risking punishment, for in this the captain took great pains to keep his soldiers disciplined. And such was the feeling of comradeship among us that there was no rioting or quarreling, but on the contrary, everything was shared equally and whatever belonged to one belonged to the others.

In this good order we reached the edge of the great lake, and entered a town that, long before our arrival, was so littered with human filth that it was impossible to set foot in it without getting soiled; from which we deduced there was a powerful army of Moctezuma's quartered there to kill us. We proceeded to the next town, called Cuitlahuac, accompanied by Moctezuma's ambassadors. This town was built on the lake, and to reach it we had to go over a causeway barely wide enough for two horsemen, which was intersected by drawbridges.[13] Here we learned that Moctezuma had commanded that we be served large quantities of food in the courtyards and temple rooms, and they had prepared many fowl and ducks, and fruit, and much bread and maize. But if we dismounted here to eat, the Indians could raise the bridges and give us battle, or even if they did not fight us we could all die here, since there was no way out because the lake was so deep; and even if any of us did get out we could be killed by arrows shot from the canoes that swarmed on the water. Therefore Cortés, a brave man and an astute one, made us form ranks and forbade us to touch so much as a drop of water, or lag behind for any reason whatsoever, and with the utmost celerity he marched us out of there so that we could gain the other side while the Indians thought we were still eating.

Once on the other side, we went to spend the night at a large city called Ixtapalapa, which is on the edge of the lake and a league or league and a half from the city of Tenochtitlan Mexico.[14]

We entered Tenochtitlan over a causeway wide enough for three or four or more horsemen to ride comfortably abreast. The causeway was built across the lake and had wooden bridges that could be raised or removed. The water was so full of canoes loaded with people who were watching us that it was frightening to see such multitudes.

As we approached the city we could see great towers and churches of the kind they build, and large palaces and dwellings. There were over one hundred thousand houses in this city, each house built over the water on wooden piles, with nothing but a beam connecting one house to another, so that each one was a fortress in itself.

On nearing the entrance to the city the captain ordered all the soldiers and horsemen to march in order, armored with their cotton *ixcahuipiles*. Then as we advanced we saw two columns of people coming toward us, the length of two or three crossbow shots, and they were all lords and nobles, and people of apparently great authority. They were richly dressed after their fashion, and walked close to the walls of the houses, keeping their eyes lowered sedately, without looking at the Spaniards or any other born creature, and without speaking a word—in complete silence. The rooftops of the houses were brimming over with people. In the center of these two large processions came that great king Moctezuma, in a litter draped with fine cotton mantles. He could be seen by no one, and none of the Indians accompanying him dared glance at the litter, which was borne on the shoulders of the lords. Before him walked a man with a long staff in his hand, representing the greatness of this ruler. At each side, and behind him, walked other great lords.

When Cortés was within a stone's throw of Moctezuma he dismounted unassisted. Moctezuma emerged from his litter and placed necklaces of gold and precious stones about Cortés, and Cortés placed a string of painted beads about Moctezuma's neck. With all courtesy Moctezuma bade him welcome, saying this was the captain's home, and Cortés thanked him for such a kind reception. And so little by little we reached a very extensive courtyard in which were halls and royal palaces large enough to accommodate more than two thousand people, and where the captain and his men were given quarters. They brought us a plentiful amount of fowl, and bread and maize; so much so that the entire army was well provided.

Moctezuma gave his fealty to the emperor in the presence of a scrivener, and it was certified that he would serve His Majesty as his lord. He said word had been handed down from their ancestors that bearded and armed men were to come from where the sun rises, and they were not to be warred against because they would be the lords of the land. They regarded us as immortal men and called us *teules,* which means gods. With these words, and others I shall omit, this great lord left for other halls and palaces of his that covered a very large area enclosed by water.[15]

These palaces were, as I say, large, and a sight to behold. There were many rooms inside, chambers and antechambers and fine halls. There were canopied beds with mattresses made of large mantles, and pillows of leather and tree fiber;[16] good quilts, and admirable white fur robes; also very well made wooden seats, and fine matting. His household service was large, befitting a great prince and lord. This lord enjoyed bathing morning and night, or rather afternoon. His clothing was not touched by anyone's hands, but wrapped in mantles with other cloths and taken to him with great reverence and veneration. At the hour of the bath a gentleman came with jugs of water and emptied them over him, and then Moctezuma took some water in his mouth and also rubbed his fingers in water. Another gentleman stood by with some large very thin towels which he placed over his arms and thighs, and Moctezuma wiped himself with much display, taking the towels without either of the attendants looking him in the face.

Then he entered his hall, at the front of which and to one side was a lord, and on the other his governor who governed the republic. With these he spoke. Also seated about this hall were numerous great nobles, none of whom dared look him in the face; all of them had their eyes lowered and kept absolute silence.

This king and lord Moctezuma was of medium height and slender build, with a large head and somewhat flat nostrils. He was very astute, discerning and prudent, learned and capable, but also harsh and irascible, and very firm in his speech. If any of the soldiers, or anyone else no matter who he was, spoke loudly or disturbed him, that person was immediately sent out. He was very considerate with those of us who were respectful and took off our caps and bowed to him; he gave us presents and jewelry, and dishes of the food that he ate.

His service was very elaborate, in the manner of a powerful prince. Although he was held captive[17] in one of the halls he was always brought a variety of delicacies kept hot on charcoal braziers, of which he ate very little. The hall was filled with rows of cooked fowl, roasted or prepared in other ways; very large and numerous pies of fowl and cock and turkey; quail, pigeons, and other game birds. Moreover they brought him river and sea fish of all kinds, besides all kinds of fruits from the seacoast as well as the highlands. The kinds of bread they brought were greatly varied—kneaded and very tasty, so that the bread of Castile was not even missed. The plates and cups of his dinner service were very clean. He was not served on gold or silver because he was in captivity, but it is likely that he had a great table service of gold and silver, because later during the war I came upon gold plates that were beautifully ornamented. All this that I have told, I saw with my own eyes, for I had charge of guarding him many days. But to describe all the magnificence of this prince would be an endless task.

[Before this] Diego de Ordaz and some of the other captains had climbed to some high rooftops and looked over this large and very strong city, where every house was a fortress with a bridge that could be removed, and where the surrounding lake teemed frighteningly with canoes and people. Realizing our danger, the captains told Hernando Cortés that it would be advisable to keep Moctezuma in one of the halls in which the Spaniards were quartered. The captain replied that it did not seem right to him, especially since Moctezuma had given his fealty. The captains made this requisition several times, but he did not wish to do it.

Then a letter arrived by post from Escalante, who remained as lieutenant of Veracruz, in which he said that the Indians had made war on him and killed one of his men. On learning of this, Captain Cortés told the captains to accompany him with some soldiers to Moctezuma's palace. When they had entered, Captain Cortés courteously begged Moctezuma to go with him to the Spaniards' quarters so that he would not suffer any ill-treatment. Moctezuma refused, replying eloquently and spiritedly that the captain had no reason for taking him as a captive, after he had received us so well and given fealty to the Spanish king.

Then the captain said to him: "You must go with us because you have waged war and ordered it waged against the Christians I left at the seaport." Moctezuma answered sternly and harshly that he had ordered no such thing. He said: "So that you may see that I speak the truth, I wish to send certain captains of mine after them, to bring them as prisoners." Then Captain Cortés said: "I also wish to send three of my soldiers with your men," and he named the three right there, and they were Andrés de Tapia and I, and a third whose name was Valdelamar.

Next morning we left with Moctezuma's ambassadors, and it was eighty leagues more or less to the place where that lord had waged war. On the way we passed large towns and provinces inhabited by many people. When we arrived at the town of our destination, the lord who had made war was seized and brought to Mexico, and killed for his crime.

Then Captain Cortés ordered Moctezuma to go with him to his quarters, and he did so. He was seized because of the great fear the Spaniards had of him, and was taken to some chambers where he moved about freely without any fetters.

sixth jornada

Just as things were in a peaceful state, and we were free of strife and alarm, Narváez arrived in port with about eight hundred men, sent from Cuba by the governor, Don Diego Velázquez, who commissioned him captain of all these men. In the company were many gentlemen of the nobility who were lords of Indians, having received very good grants in the island of Cuba. There were also some from Santo Domingo, who brought good artillery and well-armed crossbowmen and musketeers. It was said that there were one hundred horse, and that the company were quartered in the city of Cempoala, in a courtyard surrounded by the Indian style of churches, where they were being given the best of treatment.

Since they were many, and had so many horse, artillery and ammunition, Captain Narváez and his men had little regard for Captain Hernando Cortés and his company. Scoffing and belittling him, Narváez let loose certain remarks implying that he was going to destroy Cortés and his men and make them his servants. On learning this, Cortés and his men were rightly indignant, for after having been the first to penetrate this land and pacify such a great kingdom, they naturally expected to become lords with vassals and be greatly honored.

Realizing the gravity of this business, Captain Cortés discussed it with his officers and decided to lead an expedition in person with half the army, or one hundred and fifty of us, most of whom were Islanders[18] and used to campaigning. We left Mexico,[19] then, all of us wearing cotton armor, and only the captain riding horseback. We carried long wooden pikes, with which some soldiers could pierce an adobe wall, and we marched on foot, without provisions, but knowing no fear; we had a courageous captain and soldiers who were determined to die for freedom. Sometimes the captain gave us very good talks, leading us to believe that each one of us would be a count or duke and one of the titled; with this he transformed us from lambs to lions, and we went out against that large army without fear or hesitation.

Narváez, the captain commissioned by Governor Diego Velázquez, knew how Cortés was on his way with few men, and could only think that he was coming to surrender. He was inside the courtyard with all the artillery emplaced there, and there was only one entrance to the courtyard.

We marched stealthily toward him, arriving at midnight. Our plan was to wait for the enemy to fire the guns, whereupon we would throw ourselves to the ground[20] and then make a charge for the artillery; once the artillery was taken, the field was ours.

We had seen a spy on the road as we approached, and his name was Carrasco. He was so swift that Hernando Cortés and his horse could not catch him, and he reached his camp crying "Alarm, alarm," whereupon his companions became confused and disordered. We reached the entrance of the courtyard, and before the enemy could fire the guns we all threw ourselves to the ground. Since the artillery was pointed a little high it was unable to injure anyone except one man who was careless in dropping to the ground before the discharge. On the other hand the enemy had been careless about covering the guns, so that the powder had become wet, for it had been drizzling that night. And so we suddenly and forcibly took possession of the artillery and placed it under guard. The rest of the soldiers entered the courtyard and fought anyone they came up against, with their pikes knocking the horsemen off their mounts and forcing them to surrender.

It was such a great action that by sunrise almost all of the enemy had surrendered. But Captain Narváez, as a courageous captain, still defended himself fiercely with broadsword in hand, refusing to give himself up, until one of the soldiers knocked him down with a pike and took out his eye; whereupon Hernando Cortés arrived, and Narváez surrendered to him.

In spite of the boldness and fury of this action, it was God's pleasure that no one was killed. In this manner Captain Narváez was taken captive, then put in irons and kept under custody. Afterward some horsemen who had retreated, and the rest of the gentlemen in Narváez' company, surrendered to Hernando Cortés. He received them with great pleasure, and all of us were pleased because we knew one another. He then gave them particulars of the great city of Mexico and its neighboring cities.

As we were engaged in our pleasures and merrymaking, Botello, an hidalgo from Puerto de Plata, and a native of La Montaña, came to Captain Cortés and said these words: "Sire, do not tarry long, because Pedro de Alvarado the captain you left in the city of Mexico is in great danger. They have waged war on him and killed a man of his, and are scaling his quarters. You must therefore make haste."

Everyone was frightened at how he knew it, and it was said that he had a demon.

seventh jornada

When Moctezuma, lord and king of the land, saw the sudden departure of Captain Hernando Cortés for the port, it is said he ordered war against Don Pedro de Alvarado, who remained in charge as captain, with one hundred and fifty men. Others said that since Moctezuma was held prisoner and was in the care of Pedro de Alvarado, he did not give the order but that it was given by those who wanted to free him. Pedro de Alvarado met with a very hard fight, for as Botello had predicted, the Indians got as far as scaling the fortress walls. But Moctezuma was shrewd and farsighted and when he learned of Captain Cortés' victory over his opponent the fighting ceased.

Meanwhile the captain marched toward Mexico with one and the other army of more than a hundred horsemen and much artillery as well as crossbowmen and musketeers, and in orderly fashion we came within sight of Mexico. Since Hernando Cortés and the few soldiers he had taken with him had achieved a great feat, a more than Herculean one, they were very arrogant, and neglectful of attributing to God the honor He bestowed in granting such a victory. Because of this, and in the wisdom of the Divine Majesty whose secrets are to such a degree profound that it is beyond human capacity to fathom or comprehend them, His Majesty punished us very severely, although it was not His wish to destroy us entirely, as will be seen from what follows.

As we were about to enter Mexico under this momentum, some of our captains and several noblemen conferred, and seeing the city so defensible and surrounded by water, they said to Captain Cortés: "Sire, remain here in Tacuba, or Coyoacan or Texcoco, and send for Pedro de Alvarado and Moctezuma. For if the Indians should rise we can better defend ourselves here in open country and on the mainland than we could on the lake." This advice, which was very good as it turned out, was refused by the captain. He was of too strong a mettle to accept it, and was instead determined to enter the city.

In the morning, on leaving Tacuba we entered in formation along the causeway across the lake, shooting off our cannon and muskets, running the horses and raising a gay clatter. The captain settled himself in his quarters, as did all of us, and in but a short time our high spirits were to turn into grief or tears.

Two days passed in these pleasures and merriment. Then the captain wrote to Escalante, his lieutenant in Veracruz, giving the letter to a seaman named Antón del Río who could make Veracruz on foot in three days. As this courier left the courtyard to start on his mission, he observed that with great stealth and silence the natives of the city were removing the bridges and deepening the canals. Suspecting what this could mean, he was so troubled that he did

not continue his journey but ran back inside the courtyard to tell what he had
seen. Then suddenly such a multitude of well-armed men stormed the yard
where we were that they gave us a terrible fright, and they fought us cruelly
and viciously. However, Captain Hernando Cortés, after having given the order
to resist this great rabble of Indians, defended himself, and we ourselves,
very valorously.

There were some large courtyards paved with stone, and sections of streets
where no canal ran. The horses could run and give battle here but nowhere
else—for everywhere else the avenues were of water—and here we spent about
two weeks in fierce warfare. Whereas we Spaniards had to come out to fight,
the Indians remained safely beyond the canals and on the rooftops of houses;
and the stones they shot with slings, and the arrows and spears were so many
that no one could withstand them, for they shot the spears with such force that
they pierced a horse or a man if these were not armored. Thus the Indians had a
great advantage over us; they fought in safety whereas we were in terrible
danger.

The captain and soldiers strained like lions to get out of this difficulty, and
therefore in many encounters they killed large numbers of Indians but lost few
Spaniards, though many were wounded by the spears, arrows and stones. They
struggled all day to gain a few streets and fortified houses, but it was of little
advantage. When night came they withdrew to the palaces where they were
quartered, giving the Indians the chance to recover the ground lost and to
further widen and deepen the canals. Gathered in their quarters, the Spaniards
found they had many wounded, and here miraculously the Lord intervened,
because there were two Italians who, with spells and a little oil and dirty wool,
cured a wound in three or four days. The one who writes this speaks from experience, for, having been badly wounded, he was soon cured with these spells.

We kept careful watch from the rooftops, which were heavily guarded because we were being attacked from all sides. At sunrise and even before, the
din and shouting of warriors became terrifying, and by day and by night they
did nothing but hurl spears and stones over the walls of our quarters, so that
we did not dare cross the courtyard but kept close to the walls where they could
not reach us. The whole courtyard was littered with spears and stones, and still
with a great effort the captain and his men went out to fight.

This may have lasted thirteen or fourteen days and nights, and God was paid
for our sins because we had no more provisions nor water to drink except for
a fetid pool of the same salt-water that was in the yard. Seeing this, Captain
Hernando Cortés went to speak to Moctezuma to ask him to beg his warriors
and vassals to stop the war. And Moctezuma replied: "Late have you decided,

sire, for they have already elected my brother and made him lord.[21] Nevertheless I shall go as you command."

And so the captain, well shielded with a steel buckler, and Cervantes the Comendador,[22] covered by a leather shield, stayed in front of Moctezuma to protect him, and accompanied by certain hidalgos and soldiers, they climbed to the roof at the front of the courtyard where the house of the viceroy now stands. It happened that the people below, who were countless in number, were all strangers and did not know Moctezuma. They were shouting so loudly that they shook the city, and were sending such a volley of stones, spears, and arrows that the sky seemed to rain stones and spears and arrows and darts. Therefore when Moctezuma showed his face a little to speak—it was eight or nine o'clock in the morning—there came toward him from among the flying stones one which was round as a ball, and it hit him on the forehead as he stood there between the other two, and he fell.

On this same day and hour, Captain Pedro de Alvarado with some well-armed Spaniards encountered several of the Indian nobles and the governor who ruled the land, Moctezuma's uncle. This governor began telling him to cease fighting, and then immediately they bent down and sat on their haunches, obeying him without offering any resistance. And so our efforts were of little avail because on all sides the war was thick and heated, and they had us closed in to kill us. Yet neither the captain nor his soldiers lost courage.

One day Alonso de Avila, captain of the guard of Hernando Cortés, returned to his quarters tired and dispirited. He had a companion, Botello Puerto de Plata—the one who had told the marqués in Cempoala, "Sire, make haste, because Don Pedro de Alvarado is surrounded and they have killed one of his men"—and when he entered he found Botello crying and said these words to him: "Ah sir, is this a time to be crying?" Botello replied: "And do you not think there is every reason to? I tell you that this night not a man of us shall remain alive unless we find some way to escape."

On hearing this, Alonso de Avila went to Hernando Cortés and told him what had happened; but the captain told him not to believe it, that the man must be a witch.[23] So Alonso de Avila reported the matter to Don Pedro de Alvarado and the other captains, who all went together to Captain Hernando Cortés' quarters to talk to him, but he paid little attention to them. However, they got together with several more and held council, and decided to leave that night.

The plan was to use a portable bridge which had been made of a wide beam, over which we were very silently to cross the canals. This was as impossible as climbing to heaven without a ladder, because the city was teeming with such masses of people that there was hardly room for them inside or out, and they were all hungering for the flesh of the miserable Spaniards. Since they already had us closed in and surrounded they paid no attention to us except to prevent our escape, keeping torches and braziers lighted on the rooftops and sentry posts so that we could not get out without being seen, which we could not have indeed, because the light from the fires was so bright that it seemed like the middle of day.

After reaching their decision, the captains went to Hernando Cortés and requested that he leave or else stay behind, because the rest of them had agreed they should get out and let everyone escape who could. Captain Cortés kept his silence, and after conferring with his own men and captains, ordered how the withdrawal was to be accomplished.

Moctezuma, wounded in the head, gave up his soul to his Maker at about the hour of vespers. In the quarters where he was lodged there were other great lords being held with him, and with the approval of the captains Cortés had them killed, leaving not a single one. Later the bodies were removed and thrown in the porticos where the stores are now.[24] Some of their Indians who had not been killed carried them out, and after night fell, at about ten o'clock, a terrifying mob of women appeared carrying torches and flaming braziers. They came for their husbands and relatives who lay dead in the porticos, and they came for Moctezuma, too. And as the women recognized their men (which we could see, by the great amount of light, from the rooftop where we kept watch) they threw themselves upon them with great sorrow and grief, and raised such a wailing and screeching that it made one fearful. This writer, who was on guard duty, said to his companion: "Have you not seen the hell and flood of tears over there? For if you have not seen it, you may witness it from here." In truth, never in all the war and the difficulties I went through was I so afraid as when I saw that awful lamentation.

As night set in, Captain Hernando Cortés and the other captains gave orders for everyone to leave quietly. However, these preparations were not enough nor was it even possible, because of the brightness of the moon and the lighted braziers in the streets and on the rooftops, to leave without being seen. Many of the Christians were wounded, and provision was made for each of the few horses to carry two or three of them, which meant that there were barely enough horses for all of them. While this was going on a windstorm had risen, so that by nine or ten o'clock[25] it was thundering and hailing as if the heavens were bursting. Rather than a natural thing, it seemed truly that God wished to work a miracle to save us, for it was not possible that all of us should be left there that night to die.

We were taking the aforementioned bridge with us to make the crossings, but it broke into pieces from the weight on it. There was no way to cross the remaining five or six canals—which were a good twelve feet wide, and deep full of water—except that our Lord provided us with the Indian men and women who carried our baggage. As these entered the first canal they drowned, and the heap made a bridge for those on horseback to pass over. In this way we kept pushing the loaded bearers ahead of us, reaching the other side over the bodies of the drowned, until we had crossed the rest of the canals. And in the confusion of drowning Indians some Spaniards also were lost.

When we had crossed the canals and silently reached the end of the causeway, an Indian who was on guard there dropped into the canal and climbed to a nearby roof, and began to shout loudly: "O valiant men of Mexico: What are you doing, that these whom we had ready to kill are getting away from us?" And this he said over and over again. During the tempest and hailstorm I have mentioned, the Indian warriors and sentries had come in out of the downpour and gone to sleep; but we Spaniards put up with any hardships to save our lives. As soon as this sentry gave the alarm, they all ran out with their weapons to cut us off, following us with great fury, shooting arrows, spears and stones, and wounding us with their swords. Here many Spaniards fell, some dead and some wounded, and others without any injury who fainted away from fright. And since all of us were fleeing, there was not a man who would lift a hand to help his companion or even his own father, nor a brother his own brother.

It happened that certain Spanish cavaliers and hidalgos, about forty in all, and most of them horsemen and brave men, were carrying out a great amount of baggage. Captain Cortés' aide, who rode with them, also carried a large amount. Since these Spaniards had to go slowly, the Mexicans, who were the bravest of warriors, blocked their way and forced them back to the courtyards, where they fought with them three days and nights. The Spaniards defended themselves valiantly from the tops of the towers; nevertheless, due to hunger and the swarms of people gathered there against them, they were wiped out.

As we were fleeing it was heartbreaking to see our companions dying, and to see how the Indians carried them off to tear them to pieces. The number of Indians pursuing us could have been about five or six thousand, because the rest of the horde of warriors were occupied in looting the baggage that had sunk in the canals. They were even cutting one another's hands off to get a larger amount of the plunder. And so it happened that God miraculously provided that the baggage, and those who carried it, and the forty men who were left behind, saved us from all being killed and torn to pieces.

It took us from midnight to the night of the following day to reach the Tower of Victory, now called Nuestra Señora de los Remedios, which is half a league away, or a league and a half from the point where we left. On the following morning, after review of the troops, we found that more than half of our army had been killed. The rest of us, nearly starved, began the painful march toward Tlaxcala.

The Indians still followed us, but not many of them, because they were gathering to intercept us and wipe us all out. When we came within sight of a hill we saw the fields of Cuautitlan and Otumba[26] filled with warriors, which struck terror into us. Our captain ordered us to halt at the hill, which was a small one, and ordered that whoever had anything to eat should eat. Then, although he was in tears, he drew himself up and exhorted and encouraged us like a brave captain. He mounted his horse, and had the other forty horsemen mount also, and gave his orders to the captains, who were Don Pedro de Alvarado, Gonzalo de Sandoval, Cristóbal de Olid, and others. To Diego de Ordaz he gave command of the foot soldiers, and the horsemen. He assigned them their men and told each to go out to the attack.

Artillery and harquebuses we had none, for all of it had been lost, but the Lord mercifully abated his wrath and looked upon us with favor, because as Cortés battled his way among the Indians, performing marvels in singling out and killing their captains who were distinguishable by their gold shields, and disregarding the common warriors, he was able to reach their captain general and kill him with a thrust of his lance. Before reaching him he fell twice to the ground and found himself back on his horse again without even being aware who had helped him up. The other Spanish captains, on horseback, also performed marvelous feats of valor in order to escape the death that stared them in the face. While this was going on, we foot soldiers under Diego de Ordaz were completely surrounded by Indians, who almost had their hands on us, but when Captain Hernando Cortés killed their captain general they began to retreat and give way to us, so that few of them pursued us. Advancing slowly and painfully in this manner we gradually neared Tlaxcala.[27]

On seeing that we had escaped in this way, the Mexicans sent ambassadors to the lords of Tlaxcala, and to Xicotencatl, their captain general, bearing many presents and gold necklaces, and other valuable jewels, to persuade them to intercept and kill us. But the Lord touched the heart of Maxixcatzin, the principal lord of Tlaxcala, who had helped us before and had told us not to go to Mexico. He summoned the captain general and said to him: "I have been told that you have received gifts from the Mexicans to go and kill the Christians. Then let it be known to you that I with my men intend to help them, and you may do as you wish, but you will have me to contend with."

Therefore, having heard this, Xicotencatl was afraid to carry out his bad intention, and Maxixcatzin, giving proof of acting like a good Christian, came out to receive our captain and his men, who arrived shattered, wounded, dying and exhausted. He spoke to the captain in these words: "Be welcome, sire, for I spoke truthfully when you went to Mexico, and you did not wish to believe me. This is your home, where you may rest and find pleasure after the hardships you have suffered."

He provided a great abundance of fowl and maize, with which the Spaniards satisfied their terrible hunger, and he gave them quarters and everything they needed. Next day he came to see the captain and passed the time with him, and during the conversation said to him: "In this city there are four lords, and I am the highest of them; I am your friend and faithful servant. There is another called Xicotencatl and he is the captain general of the province because he is a most valorous man. He has been persuaded by the Mexicans, with presents of gold, to kill you. Be warned and on the alert, and be assured that I will befriend you in any way that is possible." And so we rested for fifteen or twenty days.

At this time a ship arrived at the port, in which Juan de Burgos was bringing men and supplies, which cheered us greatly, and the men came to join Captain Cortés. It also happened that certain Spaniards reached port from the dispersed armadas of Ayllon and of Garay, who was governor of Jamaica; and with the men from these armadas, and others who came from the Islands, little by little Captain Cortés rebuilt his army and replaced some of the horses. Then he left for the city of Tepeaca, which gave fealty to the Spanish king without offering resistance. From here the captain sent out officers and men to treat for peace and persuade the people to break their alliance with the Mexicans and accept that of the king. Many towns did so, offering themselves peaceably, and they were well treated by the captain and his officers, who would not permit anything taken from them by force but only asked to be given food, which they did willingly. In this manner many provinces and towns were pacified and gave fealty to the king, and others came from far away to offer themselves peaceably.

As Captain Cortés saw that he had an army sufficient to return and make war on the Mexicans, he decided as soon as his captains were together that he would go to Mexico. First he gave orders for the cutting of timber and its transport by bearers to the city of Texcoco, where it would be used to build brigantines to help fight the Mexicans.

At the same time the Mexicans were fortifying their city, laying in supplies as well as mustering brave warriors, whom they were bringing from all the provinces in order to be prepared, knowing very well what preparations the Christians were making. At their main approaches, which were those of Coyoacan, Tacuba, and Tlatelolco, they had deepened the canals and made strong barricades. Thus they had three walls built at the entrances, leaving access at the corners, in the narrowest part, and the Indians fought from the top of the barricades. In this way, when one wall and those on it were destroyed, two more remained.

eighth jornada

Having rebuilt his army with men who had come over from the Islands, Captain Cortés marched with his troops toward Mexico and entered the great city of Texcoco, the seat of a dominion almost as large as that of Mexico. The city had eighty to a hundred thousand houses, or more, and the captain and his Spaniards were quartered there in some large and very beautiful rooms and courtyards.

They entered Texcoco without war having been waged by either side. The reason for this was that the lord of the city, whose name was Cuaunacuxtli, and his brother Ixtlilxochitl, the captain general, had fortified themselves in Mexico together with their bravest warriors, so that there was no one in the city to give battle. Therefore no damage or injury was done to the people, nor was anything of theirs touched, except the provisions that they supplied voluntarily.

Then Captain Cortés ordered the brigantines constructed as quickly as possible, so that they could be used in fording the lake and entering Mexico, and they were completed in a short time. Meanwhile the captain applied himself to sending officers to the surrounding towns to persuade them to ally themselves peaceably, which they did, although all the lords and bravest warriors were in Mexico.

Upon finishing the brigantines, a deep canal was dug along a gully that went all the way to the lake. The brigantines were loaded with artillery, crossbowmen and harquebusiers, and seamen to man the oars, and after assigning captains to the ships Cortés went by land around the shore of the lake. He arrived with some of the men at the causeway that is called Coyoacan, and there with about two hundred men he made his camp. At the Tlatelolco causeway he stationed Captain Gonzalo de Sandoval, and at the Tacuba causeway Don Pedro de Alvarado, with a goodly number of men and Tlaxcalan Indians.

In this manner, with forces encircling the city, and with the brigantines which were a great help on the lake, the city began to be battered by land and by water. In addition great trouble was taken to cut off the fresh water supply from the springs of Chapultepec, which reached the city by conduits, and these were fiercely defended from all sides.

The Christians wounded some of the Indians, and great numbers of Indians were killed in the assaults on horseback and by the guns, harquebuses and crossbows. In spite of all this they put up their strong barricades, and opened causeways and canals, and defended themselves courageously. During the course of the war they also killed some of the Spaniards and captured alive one of them called Guzmán, who was Cortés' aide.

It happened that as some of the Spaniards were retreating the Indians forced them into a canal, where most of them died. Captain Cortés, who found himself alone, ran to help them and began pulling out those he could with his hands. So many Indians had rushed to the attack that they laid hold of him and were pushing him into the canal to drown him, when a brave soldier named Olloa appeared at his side. He cut off the hands and arms of the Indians who were holding the captain, and thus freed him and pulled him out.

The war was sustained fiercely by both sides, since on our side we had the help of many Tlaxcalan warriors, while the Mexicans [had the advantage of] their rooftops and high buildings from which they battered us, and by turns we were forced to retreat or were able to take the offensive. The brigantines and their captains and men fought very hard on the lake, and this was a pleasure to see because the Indian canoes, which covered the water, boldly attacked the brigantines. As soon as the Spaniards took any of the houses, which were all on the water,[28] they had the Tlaxcalan Indians demolish and level them, for this gave more freedom to maneuver. And so they fought bravely, and the Indians defended themselves and killed or wounded some of the Spaniards.

When some of the Indian lords inside the city began to see the danger they were in, and the scarcity of supplies and lack of water, they decided to escape by night. One in particular was Ixtlilxochitl, captain general of Texcoco and brother of Cuaunacuxtli the lord of Texcoco. He appeared before Captain Cortés and offered himself and his allies, promising to aid him and the Christians in the war against his fellow people; and since he was very valiant, this was a great blow to the Mexicans. It must also have hurt them when on another night the lord who ruled Xochimilco and Cuitlahuac came over to our side, because his people, with their canoes, fought most cruelly against the Mexicans and contributed largely to their destruction. In addition to this, when the Christians were exhausted from war, God saw fit to send the Indians smallpox,[29] and there was a great pestilence in the city because there were so many people there, especially women, and they had nothing more to eat. We soldiers could scarcely get about the streets because of the Indians who were sick from hunger, pestilence and smallpox. Also for these reasons they began to slacken in their fighting. Moreover, as they gradually retreated to some fortified houses on the water, we held the advantage, and our allies were able to devote themselves to leveling houses and buildings, which made it possible for us to take the whole city, since we could run our horses on level ground.

The Mexicans, almost vanquished, withdrew to their fortresses on the water, and since a great number of women were left among them, they armed them all and stationed them on the rooftops. The Spaniards were alarmed at seeing so many of the enemy again, whooping and shouting at them, and when they began killing them and saw they were women, there was dismay on both sides.

Captain Hernando Cortés, and Alderete the first royal treasurer, and the scrivener who was named Orduña, and several other gentlemen, reached the fortified house where Cuauhtemoc had already taken refuge. Cuauhtemoc, youthful lord of about eighteen years of age, was a person of great valor and courage. They sent word to him saying that since there was no place further to which he could retreat, he should surrender, and that the king would pardon him and grant him many privileges. He replied with great conceit and little shame: "I do not care to give myself up, for I prefer to see you all killed." And so at night we retired to our camp.

On the following morning they began fighting again, and a requisition was sent to Cuauhtemoc, but once more he refused to surrender. But two days before the requisition, the women and children had begun to come and give themselves up to the Spaniards, for they could see they were lost. Cuauhtemoc took to a small canoe, with only one paddler, and since it was night it happened that his canoe met with a brigantine commanded by Captain García Holguín. García Holguín captured him and presented him to Captain Hernando Cortés, thereby effecting a reconciliation with Cortés, who had not borne him good will.

This done, the Spaniards seized the house that had been Cuauhtemoc's stronghold, where they found a great quantity of gold and jewels, and other plunder. The Tlaxcalans who were assisting us in the war and the people who had left the city knew its ins and outs, so that when they went home again they were rich with the spoils they took. This house was seized on the day of Saint Hippolytus, which ended the war for the city, and we left to go to our camps. Captain Cortés was requested to settle in Tacuba, or Coyoacan or Texcoco, but he would never agree.

After the conquest of Mexico was over, Captain Hernando Cortés commanded that the Spaniards stay there in Mexico, where in a short time he began building a very beautiful and great city, which is the city of Mexico. A few days later he sent some men with Don Pedro de Alvarado to settle the land of Oaxaca, where he settled a city that is called Oaxaca and gave the soldiers allotments of land.[30] From there Cortés ordered him to Guatemala, which he settled, receiving from the emperor the title of *adelantado*.[31] Captain Cortés also sent Gonzalo de Sandoval, an excellent captain, with certain men to settle the land called Medellín, where a good hundred allotments were made. Then he sent another captain, Villafuerte, to settle the land of Zacatula with certain other soldiers, who were given allotments. The rest of the soldiers who remained received allotments in Mexico and its surroundings.

Captain Hernando Cortés himself, with a number of men, left for the conquest of Pánuco, which he won, and all the other towns surrendered peaceably. Here he established a city and gave allotments to the settlers. Some days later he assembled an armada, commissioning Cristóbal de Olid as captain, and sending him to settle the land of Yucatan.[32] After he had arrived there Olid took possession of the land and usurped it. Hernando Cortés found ways and means of sending certain wellborn gentlemen, and two close friends of Cristóbal de Olid, who killed him while they were sitting down to table with him.[33] Captain Hernando Cortés, moved by passion or anger that blinded him, decided to go overland with his best soldiers, taking with him the Indian lords of the land; therefore only a few were left in the city of Mexico, and these were traders and men who knew nothing of war. It almost cost the captain's life, and the lives of everyone in Mexico, because Cuauhtemoc the lord of the land, whom Cortés took with him, and who was brave and astute in spite of his youth, planned one night with his own people to remove the horses' bridles and take the lances and kill the Spaniards. But Our Lord saved Cortés, for the conspiracy became known, and when it was discovered the evildoers were punished and killed.

At the time that he set out for Yucatan, Captain Hernando Cortés left the treasurer, Alonso de Estrada, and the comptroller, Albornoz, to govern in his place. Because he became wary of them, from Coatzacoalcos he secretly sent Gonzalo de Salazar the factor, and Chirinos, the inspector, authorizing them to act on his behalf in the event that the treasurer and comptroller should attempt any insubordination. However, Salazar and Chirinos were troublemakers, and meddled by claiming allegiance to the king, when the comptroller and treasurer had not attempted anything at all. Great wrongs resulted from this, because there were people hanged, and flogged, or unjustly maligned.

In the interval the king learned of these disturbances and sent Luis Ponce as governor or investigator, who brought Luis Ponce, or I should say Marcos de Aguilar, as chief justice. Also while Captain Hernando Cortés was away, Nuño Guzmán became governor here in Mexico, and since he was not on good terms with Cortés he took many Indians away from him and gave them to whomever he pleased; in particular he took Cuauhnahuac[34] and gave it to Villarroel, servant of Cortés. This Nuño de Guzmán had been sent by the king to conquer and govern Jalisco. Captain Hernando Cortés sailed back from Honduras by way of Cuba instead of coming back by land. And while Captain Cortés was in Pánuco the emperor named him governor of all of New Spain, so that when he came back to Mexico he governed it; then His Majesty granted him favors and made him Marqués del Valle.

The person responsible for the armada that was sent to conquer this land was Don Diego Velázquez, governor and *adelantado* of the island of Cuba, who resided in the city of Santiago, and who entrusted it to Hernando Cortés as captain. Nevertheless, Hernando Cortés went to great pains in soliciting loans among his friends, and he procured more soldiers than Don Diego Velázquez had given him, as well as securing provisions, salt pork and cassava, and another caravel and ships, with which he properly outfitted his armada. The emperor contributed absolutely nothing toward this armada, except that his officials in Cuba provided swords, daggers and other weapons, and oil, vinegar, and shirts, thereby making a tradesman of him; and the soldiers of the armada who were in need of swords, daggers, cheeses and other supplies, were charged much higher prices than these articles had cost. Also the king collected from the conquistadors when they took some gold to be smelted, for it was all taken away from them; whereupon I say that the least of the conquistadors merited being highly rewarded, since at their own expense and effort they gave the king this large new world. Therefore the least of all these men was greatly deserving, yet most of them were impoverished.

Having related briefly the things that truly happened in the taking of this land, and the multitudes of people there were, I shall tell about the best parts of the land, from Coatzacoalcos to Veracruz, which is a distance of about sixty leagues, and from there to Pánuco, which I journeyed over. On the coast of Veracruz there are large provinces, and I shall mention the best of them, leaving other towns aside. First, at six or seven leagues from the sea there is a very large province which was given as a grant to Gonzalo de Sandoval, who came to settle this land, and who was informed by the Indians that it was a great kingdom, as large as Texcoco. It was very rich in cacao, gold, cloth, fish and many other products. It could have had, by my estimate and according to what the Indians told me, some eighty thousand houses. Now it has two hundred houses, or even less.

Close by, at eight or nine leagues, there was another province almost as large, where about twenty allotments were made, which I visited. Near this province was another large one called Tlatlatelco; it had twenty thousand houses or more, and there are not two hundred left. Further on was one called Secotuxco, which had many people. Down the coast was Tlapaniquito Cotaxtla, where there were towns with many people and a great number of houses, and now there is nothing. Further on is the province of Cempoala, as mentioned before, whose town had twenty thousand houses and now has less than twenty. I omit mention of cities, villages and numerous towns in the foothills and mountains where there are still people left because the climate ranges from temperate to cold; but the rest of the coastal land is now uninhabited. From here on, to

Pánuco, it must be about fifty leagues. On the coast as well as inland there were large cities, towns and provinces, all of them thickly populated and very pretty, full of fruit trees; and now it is all deserted, with very few Indians.

The best part of the land is now in the cold country, like the province of Tlaxcala, which has many people, though not as many as formerly; there are some Christian settlers there. The city of Cholula now has about ten or twelve thousand tributaries; before there were over a hundred thousand. Tepeaca, a very large town, has many people; however, not nearly so many as it had. The same can be said of all the other provinces.

The city of Huexotzingo has ten thousand tributaries more or less; it used to be larger than Cholula. Texcoco, a large province and kingdom that was not subject to Mexico, had a great amount of land and subjects, but it has diminished severely. There are Spanish settlers here also. In Mexico very few Indians remain in comparison to the number there were. Chalco was also a very large province, subject to the king from the first and friendly toward the Spaniards. Tacuba, when we first came, was also a kingdom in its own right, and had the fealty of the many Otomí provinces and towns. The city of Xochimilco used to be a great province, and if it has ten or twelve thousand houses left it is a great deal. Coyoacan is a large place and a good one.

There are many other very large cities and towns (and places) which the Marqués Hernando Cortés could have distributed among the men who had helped him win so much land, but which were given to many persons who had never heard or seen combat; because the least of his men deserved much, for they had fought hard at their own expense and effort, and not the king's.

I should like to say something about the many things I saw concerning these people's form of worship and their rites. I shall say, then, that as a child and youth I began reading many histories and antiquities of the Persians, Greeks, and Romans. I have also read about the rites performed in Portuguese India, and I can truthfully say that in none of these have I heard of such abominable forms of worship as they offered to the Devil in this land. To my manner of thinking there is no other kingdom on earth where such offense and disservice have been rendered Our Lord, or where the Devil has been more honored and revered.

The natives of this land had very large temples, enclosed by merloned walls, or sometimes a fence made of logs piled one on top of the other, which they took to make the fire for their sacrifice. They had large towers with a house of worship at the top, and close to the entrance a low stone, about knee-high, where the men or women who were to be sacrificed to their gods were thrown on their backs and of their own accord remained perfectly still. A priest then came out with a stone knife like a lance-head but which barely cut anything, and with this knife he opened the part where the heart is and took out the heart, without the person who was being sacrificed uttering a word.

Then the man or woman, *having been killed in this fashion, was thrown down the steps, where the body was taken and most cruelly torn to pieces, then roasted in clay ovens and eaten as a very tender delicacy; and this is the way they made sacrifices to their gods.*

The priest took the heart in his hand and entered the house of worship, where there were stone and wooden idols, with an altar. With his hand he let blood drop on the idols and in the corners of the house of worship, then he went out and faced east where the sun rises, and did the same thing. He turned also toward the west, and the north and south, repeating the act.

These priests practiced very severe penances, for they let blood from their tongues and arms and legs, and whatever God gave them, until they had bled themselves, and with this blood they sacrificed to their gods. They went about very dirty and blackened, and wasted and haggard of face. They wore their hair hanging down very long and matted, so that it covered them, and went about infested with lice. They could not touch a woman, or they would be put to death for it. At night they walked like a procession of phantoms to the hills where they had their temples and idols and houses of worship.

All the people, whether noble or plebeian, removed their sandals in the courtyard before they entered to worship their gods; and at the door of the church they all squatted on their heels and very reverently sobbed and wept, asking forgiveness for their sins. The women brought pies made of poultry. They also brought fruits, and paintings done on the native paper. In my opinion they were paintings of their sins. There was such a silence, broken by sobbing and weeping, that I was spellbound with wonder and terror.

And now that they are Christians, and as though in retribution for our sins, most of them come to church by force, and with very little fear and reverence; they gossip and talk, and walk out during the principal part of the Mass and the sermon. In their time, therefore, great strictness was observed in the ceremonies to their gods, but now they feel neither fear nor shame. I could cite many more particularities; but to avoid verbosity, and because what I have said is sufficient, I shall say no more.

Soli Deo Honor et Gloria.

the chronicle
of the
anonymous conquistador

Not all of Cortés' soldiers who took up the pen felt compelled to record their war experiences. An interesting document that has come down to us describes the manners and customs of the Indians, as well as their houses, temples, and markets, and contains many acute observations that are not elsewhere found in the literature of the period.

This first-hand account originally appeared in print in the second half of the sixteenth century, in the famous collection of the Italian geographer Gian Battista Ramusio, *Navigationi e Viaggi*. The diligent Ramusio compiled as many of the Spanish and Portuguese accounts of voyages as he was able to obtain, and translated them into Italian. The author of the account in question was identified by Ramusio simply as a companion of Cortés: *un gentil'huomo del Signor Fernando Cortese*.

In the eighteenth century Francisco Javier Clavijero acknowledged this document as one of the sources for his *Ancient History of Mexico*, and dubbed its author The Anonymous Conquistador. By this name he remains known.

The nineteenth-century scholar Joaquín García Icazbalceta translated the account into Spanish for inclusion in his *Collection of Documents for the History of Mexico* (Volume I, 1858). He also studied the question of whether the author might be Francisco de Terrazas, Cortés' majordomo, as had been suggested by other Mexican historians.

García Icazbalceta concluded that there was no evidence to prove that Terrazas wrote the account, but that on the other hand there was in support of such a theory the circumstance that Terrazas was reputed to have written about the events of the Conquest.

Whoever the author may have been, unmistakably he was someone who knew the city of Tenochtitlan before its destruction by Cortés, and who had actual experience of Indian warfare.

The Anonymous Conquistador made no profound revelations, nor was he a trained observer in the modern sense, but he was remarkably objective and, for the most part, avoided pronouncing moral judgments.

The country of New Spain is similar to Spain in that it has almost the same kind of mountains, valleys and fields, except that its mountains are more formidable and rugged, and cannot be climbed without the greatest difficulty. Also there are ranges known to extend more than two hundred leagues. In this province of New Spain there are large rivers and very good fresh-water springs; extensive forests, over mountain and plain, of very tall pines, cedars, oaks, cypresses, *encinos*[1] and many varieties of mountain timber.

The hills in the central portion of the province are very pleasant, and near the coasts there are ridges extending from one sea to the other. The distance between seas at the narrowest point is one hundred and fifty leagues, while at other points it is one hundred and sixty, two hundred, three hundred and more and even close to five hundred. Further up [north] the distance is so great that the number of leagues is not known, since no Spaniards have seen it nor are they likely to in the next hundred years, although new things are being discovered every day.

In this province there are mines of gold, silver, copper, tin and iron ores. There are many kinds of fruit that look like the fruit in Spain but lack their perfection of color and flavor. However, there are many that are excellent, and as good as the Spanish fruits, but this is not general. The fields are delightful and full of very beautiful plants, as high as a man's knees. It is very fertile country, producing anything that is planted, and yielding in some regions two or three crops a year.

the animals

There are many different kinds of animals, such as lions, tigers and wolves; and also jackals, some of which are between a fox and a dog, and others between a lion and a wolf.[2] The tigers are about the same size or perhaps a little larger than the lions,[3] but they are heavier and stronger, and more fierce. Their bodies are covered with white spots. While they do no harm to the Spaniards, they do not fawn on the natives but are more likely to eat them.

There are also wild deer and foxes, fallow deer, rabbits and hare. The pigs have their navel on the crest of the spine.[4] There are many other different kinds of animals, especially one that is slightly larger than a cat, and has a pouch in its belly where it hides its young[5] when it wants to keep them out of harm. It carries them in there without showing signs of carrying anything at all, and when it flees with them it runs up a tree.

This province of New Spain is for the most part thickly populated. It has large cities and towns on the plains as well as in the mountains, and the houses are built of masonry, or mud and adobe, and all have flat roofs. This applies to the interior of the country; near the coast almost all the houses are adobe and mud with wooden beams and thatched roofs.

The people used to have very beautiful mosques with large towers and chambers where they honored their idols and made sacrifices to them, and many of their cities were more orderly than ours, with very handsome streets and squares, where they had their market places.

the soldiers

The people of this province are well proportioned, tending to be tall rather than short; they are swarthy or brownish, of good features and mien. For the most part they are very skillful, stalwart and tireless, yet they sustain themselves with less food than any other people. They are very warlike and fearless of death. They used to have great wars and differences among themselves, and all those who fell prisoner in war were either made slaves or eaten. When the enemy laid siege to some town, if the besieged surrendered without offering resistance they merely became vassals, but if they were taken by force they were all made slaves.

They have their military system, for they have captains general and also captains of four hundred and two hundred men. Each company has its standard-bearer with the insignia on a staff tied to his back in such a way that it neither hinders him in fighting nor in doing whatever he wishes, and it is so securely bound to his body that it cannot be untied or taken from him unless his body is cut in pieces.[6]

It is their custom to reward a man very highly who serves well in war or performs some outstanding feat. Even though he may be the lowest slave among them, they make him a captain and lord, giving him vassals and honoring him. Wherever he goes they serve him and show him the respect and reverence due a lord. Since they do not use caps, the warrior's hair is dressed to indicate that he has distinguished himself, as a sign for all to see and recognize. Every time he performs some notable action he wears another such sign in testimony of his valor, and the lords always reward him with other favors.

the offensive and defensive arms they use

The armor they use in warfare are certain shirts like jupons, of quilted cotton the thickness of a finger and a half and sometimes two fingers, which is very strong. Over these they wear suits all of one piece and of a heavy cloth, which they tie in back; these are covered with feathers of different colors and look very jaunty. One company of soldiers will wear them in red and white, another in blue and yellow, and others in various ways.

The lords wear certain smock-like coats which among us are of mail but theirs are of gold or gilt silver, and the strength of their feathered garments is proportionate to their weapons, so that they resist spears and arrows, and even the sword. To defend the head they wear things like heads of serpents, or tigers, or lions or wolves, and the man's head lies inside the animal's jaws as though it were devouring him. These heads are of wood covered on the outside with feathers or incrustations of gold and precious stones, and are something wonderful to see.

They carry shields of various kinds made of strong solid cane woven with heavy double cotton, and decorated with feathers and round plaques of gold. The shields are so strong that only a good crossbow can shoot through them, but arrows do not damage them. Although some of these shields have been seen in Spain, I should say they are not the kind used in warfare but in their dances and ceremonies.

The offensive arms are bows and arrows, and spears which they throw with crossbows made of another pole.[7] The spearheads are of hard stone, or a fishbone that is very strong and sharp, and some spears have three points. Their maces have three points inserted in the same manner, so that in one thrust they produce three wounds. They have swords that are like broadswords, but their hilts are not quite so long and are three fingers wide; they are made of wood with grooves into which they fit hard stone blades which cut like a Tolosa blade. One day an Indian I saw in combat with a mounted horseman struck the horse in the chest, cutting through to the inside and killing the horse on the spot. On the same day I saw another Indian give a horse a sword thrust in the neck that laid the horse dead at his feet.

They have slings with which they shoot very far, and many if not most of the warriors carry all these kinds of weapons in combat. It is one of the most beautiful sights in the world to see them in their battle array because they keep formation wonderfully and are very handsome. Among them are extraordinarily brave men who face death with absolute determination. I saw one of them defend himself courageously against two swift horses, and another against three and four, and when the Spanish horsemen could not kill him one of the horsemen in desperation hurled his lance, which the Indian caught in the air and fought with for more than an hour, until two foot soldiers approached and wounded him with two or three arrows; he turned on one of the soldiers but the other grasped him from behind and stabbed him.

During combat they sing and dance and sometimes give the wildest shouts and whistles imaginable, especially when they know they have the advantage.

Anyone facing them for the first time can be terrified by their screams and their
ferocity. In warfare they are the most cruel people to be found, for they spare
neither brothers, relatives, friends, nor women even if they are beautiful; they
kill them all and eat them. When they cannot take the enemy plunder and booty
with them, they burn everything.

It was forbidden to kill the lords but they were taken as prisoners under good
custody. Afterwards a festival was prepared in the plaza of the city, at the
center of which were certain enclosures with stone-masonry walls one and a
half *estados* high, which were reached by steps. On the top was a round court
like that for quoits, and in the middle of the court there was a round stone with
a hole in its center. The captive lord ascended and was tied by the ankle with
a long thin cord, then given a sword and shield. The warrior who had captured
him came forward to fight him, and if he defeated the prisoner again he was
held to be extremely valorous; he was given an emblem for his brave trial and
received a favor from the lord. If the captive lord defeated him and six others,
or seven in all, he was set free and given back all that had been taken from him
in war.[8]

It happened once that in a battle between the warriors of Huexotzingo and
Tula, the lord of Tula was separated from his men in the thick of the enemy
ranks, and though he performed wonderful feats with his weapons the enemy
overpowered him and took him captive to their city. They prepared the customary festival, tying him to the stone in the court, and seven men came forward to fight him, whom he killed one by one. When the Huexotzingans saw
this they thought that if they released him, such a brave and spirited warrior
would never rest until he had destroyed them; so they decided to kill him, which
they did. The deed marked them as treacherous and disloyal, for in failing to
observe all that was usual with those who were lords they had broken the
law and custom.

how the men dress

Their dress consists of cotton mantles like sheets, though not so large, finely
worked in a variety of ways, and with decorated bands and borders. Each person has two or three, and they are knotted over the chest.[9] In winter time they
cover themselves with cloaks woven of tiny feathers. They are similar to
cremesino,[10] and like our fur hats. They have them in red, black, white, purple
and yellow. They cover their private parts, in front as well as in back, with very
showy cloths like the large kerchiefs they put on their heads on journeys; they
are of various colors, with trimmings of diverse colors also, and tassels that
hang front and back. They wear shoes[11] without vamps but only soles, and

highly decorated heels. Long laces run from the toes to the instep and are fastened there with buttons. They wear nothing on their heads except in combat or in their festivals and dances, and wear their hair long and tied in various ways.

how the women dress

The women wear sleeveless cotton blouses like the garment called *sobrepelliz* in Spain; they are long and full, with a great amount of fancywork and decorated borders, and very handsome. They wear two or three, or even four of these, one of them longer than the others, to make them look like skirts. From the waist down they wear another kind of dress of pure cotton which reaches to the knees, also very showy and finely worked. They wear nothing on the head, particularly in the cooler regions. They have very beautiful hair, either black or brown, which they wear long. With their dresses, and their long flowing hair covering their backs, they are a beautiful sight. In the tropical regions near the sea the women wear a kind of veil made of tan-colored netting.

the yarn they work

The yarn they work is made of hair from the rabbit and hare's belly. They dye it on racks to whatever color they want, doing it with such perfection that nothing better could be desired. Afterwards they spin it and do fancywork almost as fine as with our silk. It never loses its color after being washed, and the cloth made from it lasts a long time.

the foods they have

The grain they make bread from is something like a chickpea; some grains are white, others are red, black or purple. It is planted and grows to a tall cane about half a lance high like millet, and bears two or three ears containing the grains. Their way of making bread is to put a large pot on some firewood, with four or five jugfuls of water, then to light the fire under it and boil the water. It is removed from the fire, and the grains, which they call *tlaolli*, are put in the water with a little lime over them to loosen the skins. Next day, or else three or four hours after it has cooled, they wash it very well in the river, or at home in quantities of water, to clear away the lime, and afterward they grind it with stones made for this purpose. As it is being ground they add water to make a paste, and thus grinding and kneading they make it into bread. They cook it on some things like large earthen pans,[12] somewhat larger than a cribble, and they eat the bread as quickly as it is made because it tastes better hot than cold.

They also have another way of making it, which is to make rolls of the dough and then wrap them in leaves. These are put on the fire in a large pot with a little water, and covered tightly, and in this way they cook. They also cook them in pans with the various things they eat.

They have many large fowl[13] in the manner of peacocks, which are very tasty; also four or five species of quail, some of which are like partridges. They have many geese and ducks of all kinds, domesticated as well as wild, from whose feathers they make their battle and ceremonial dress. These feathers are used for many things, because they are of diverse colors, and every year they pluck them from these fowl. They have large and small macaws, which they keep in their homes, and also make use of the feathers. They kill deer to eat, and rabbits and hare, since these are abundant in many places.

They have various kinds of vegetables of which they are very fond and which they eat in many ways, raw as well as prepared in various dishes. They have a kind of pepper for seasoning that is called *chilli*, and nothing is eaten without it. They are a people who live on little food, and eat less than any other people in the world.

The lords dine sumptuously on many kinds of foods: sauces and soups, cakes and pies of every kind of meat, fruits and vegetables, and fish which they have in abundance. All these kinds of food are brought to the lords, but first they are brought dishes and bowls on palm mats. They have these mats in every room, and there are also chairs made in different ways, on which they sit. These are so low that they rise scarcely a span above the floor. The foods are set before the lords together with some cotton towels with which they clean their hands and mouth, and they are served by two or three chief stewards. They eat whatever most pleases them, and afterward what is left is given to the vassal lords who are there paying them court.

the beverages they drink

They make various kinds of wines, but their principal and finest drink is called *cachanatl* and is made from the seeds of a tree fruit that is like a watermelon, but has large grains[14] inside that are almost the size of date pits. The tree bearing this fruit is the most delicate of all the trees; it grows only in a warm climate, and before they plant it they plant two or three other trees that have large leaves. When these are two *estados* high they plant this other tree between them that bears the aforementioned fruit, so that the two can protect this delicate tree from the sun and wind and provide a covering for it. They hold this tree in great esteem, because its grains are the principal money circulated in this country, each one being worth about half a *marchetto*.[15] It is the most commonly used coin, but very unhandy after gold and silver.

how cacao is made

These seeds, which they call almonds or cacao, are ground and made into powder, and some other small seeds they have are also ground, and the powder put into certain vessels that have a spout. Then they add water and stir it with a spoon, and after it is well mixed they pour it back and forth from one vessel to another until it is foamy. The foam is gathered and put in a cup, and when they are ready to drink the beverage they beat it with some small spoons made of gold, or silver or wood. To drink it one must open the mouth wide, for since it has a froth it is necessary to make room for it to dissolve and go in gradually.

This drink is the most wholesome and substantial of any food or beverage in the world, because whoever drinks a cup of this liquor can go through the day without taking anything else even if he is on a journey, and it is better in warm weather than in cold, since it is a cold drink.

another kind of wine they have

There is a certain tree, or rather, something between a tree and a teasel, that has leaves the thickness of a knee and the length of an arm, more or less, depending on its age. From its center it sprouts a trunk that grows about two or three *estados* high and as big around as a boy of six or seven. At a certain time of year, when this tree is ripe and in season, they bore a hole at the bottom from where it distills a juice that they preserve in a certain tree bark. After a day or two they drink it, to such excess that they do not stop until they fall to the ground drunk and senseless, and they consider it some great honor to drink very much and get drunk.[16]

This tree is so useful that they make wine, vinegar and syrup from it; also men and women's clothing[17] and shoes, as well as cord, house beams, roof tiles, needles for sewing and for stitching wounds and other things. In addition they gather the leaves of this tree or teasel which they cultivate like we do vineyards and which they call *maguey*,[18] and they put these leaves to cook in underground ovens. Then they crush the cooked leaves with a wooden instrument, removing the peels or roots, and they drink so much of this liquor that they get drunk. There is another kind of wine, made from the grain they eat, which is called *chicha*,[19] and this is of different kinds, red and white.

the manner of government

These people had a great lord who was like an emperor. They also had, and still have, others like kings, dukes, counts, governors, knights, squires, and men-at-arms. The lords have their governors, administrators and other officials in their own lands. So feared and respected are the lords that all they lack is to be worshipped as gods. There was great justice among the Indians, for if they committed the slightest offense they were killed or made slaves. Murder or robbery were punished very severely, particularly when someone trespassed on the property of another to steal the fruits or grain; a trespasser entering a field and stealing three or four ears or heads of grain was made the slave of the owner. If someone committed treason or any other offense against the person of the emperor or the king, he was killed together with all his relations to the fourth generation.

their religion and worship, and their temples

They had very large and beautiful buildings for their idols, where they honored them and prayed and sacrificed to them, and where there were religious persons dedicated to their service. These were like bishops, canons, and other dignitaries, who served in the temple and lived in it the greater part of the time, since the temples had large and good living quarters. Here all the sons of the lords were educated, serving the idols until they reached the age of taking a wife. In all the time they were there they never left the premises nor cut their hair, but they cut it when they left to marry.

These mosques or temples had revenues designated for the support and necessities of the priests who served in them. The idols they worshipped were certain statues the height of a man or taller, made of a paste of all the seeds they have and eat, kneaded with the blood of human hearts; and this was the substance of their gods. They had them seated in chairs that were like cathedras, holding a shield on one arm and a sword in the other, and the places where they kept these idols were towers like the one shown in the following drawing.[20]

the kind of towers

The buildings of the towers are made square, and about one hundred and fifty paces long by one hundred and fifteen or twenty paces wide. They make this building solid at the base, and when it reaches a height of two *estados* they leave a passage two paces wide around three sides of it, and begin a flight of steps up the long side. Then they build it up another two *estados,* again leaving a passage two paces wide around three sides of it, and continuing the steps up the other side. The construction is all solid, made of stone and mortar, and they keep raising it so far in this manner that they go as high as one hundred and twenty to one hundred and thirty steps. At the top they leave a square court of reasonable size, in the center of which they begin two towers that rise ten or twelve *estados* high, and at the very top they put their windows.

In these high towers they place their idols, which are well arranged and adorned, as is the chamber where they are placed. In this chamber they have their principal idol (whose name differs according to the region). The principal god of the great city of Mexico is called Horchilovos,[21] and in a city called Chennuila it is Quecadquaal,[22] and in other cities they have various other names. No one is permitted to enter the chamber where this idol is except the supreme pontiff. And every time they hold festivals for their idols they sacrifice many men and women, and little girls and boys, and when they are in need of something like rain, or want it to stop raining when it rains too much, or they are besieged by their enemies, they make sacrifices in the following manner.

the manner of sacrifice

First the person who is to be sacrificed is finely adorned and led with much gaiety and festivity through the streets and squares, where the people tell him their wants, saying that since he is going where their god is he can ask him to help them. They give him food or some other gift, and in this way he gathers many things, as is apt to occur with those who carry the heads of wolves;[23] but everything goes to the sacrificers.

They take him to the temple, where they hold a great festival with dances, in which he also joins. Later [one of the priests] who is to kill him undresses him and leads him to one side of the temple stairs where there is a stone idol. He lays him on his back, tying his hands on either side and then his feet. Again they all start singing and dancing around him, telling him the message he is to carry to their god. Next comes the sacrificer, whose office is not the least among them,[24] and he takes a stone blade that cuts like steel and is the size of a large knife. In the time it would take one to make the sign of the cross he thrusts the knife into the victim's chest and opens it, and takes out the heart while it is still hot and beating. It is immediately taken by the supreme pontiff, who anoints the mouth of the principal idol with the blood, and, without pausing, casts some of the blood toward the sun or a star (if it is night); then the mouths of the other stone and wooden idols are anointed, and the cornice of the chapel door where the principal idol is. After this they burn the heart, keeping the ashes as a relic, and also burn the victim's body, the ashes of which are kept in a different vessel from those of the heart.

At other times they sacrifice them without these preliminaries, and burn the heart and the bones of the arms or legs and keep them wrapped in many folds of paper as great relics. In each province the inhabitants have their own kind of ceremonies, idolatries and sacrifices, for in some places they worship the sun, in others the moon, or the stars, or serpents, or lions and similar wild beasts, of which they have images and statues in their mosques. In other provinces, particularly in Pánuco, they worship the member of the body that is between a man's legs; they have it in the mosque, and also set in the square,[25] together with figures in relief showing all the kinds of pleasures that can exist between men and women, and they have these pictured with legs raised in various ways. In the province of Pánuco the men are great sodomites, idlers and drunkards. When they have their fill of wine and can no longer drink it through the mouth they lie down and, raising their legs, have the wine introduced from beneath through a tube, until the body can stand no more.[26]

It is very well known that these people saw the Devil in the figures they made and regarded as idols, and that the Devil got inside these idols and talked to the people, ordering them to make sacrifices to the idols and provide human hearts, for the gods ate nothing else; and for this reason the people were so solicitous in sacrificing men and offering their hearts and blood. He also ordered many other things that they obeyed promptly. They are the most devout people in the observance of their religion that God ever created, to such an extent that they offered themselves voluntarily to be sacrificed, thinking to save their souls in this way, and they bled their own tongues and ears, and arms and thighs, to sacrifice and offer the blood to their idols. On the outskirts and along the roads they have many temples where pilgrims go to shed their blood and offer it to their idols. They also have these temples on high mountain tops, which were places of great worship and sacrifice to their idols.

the cities there are, and what some of them are like

There are large cities, especially the city of Tlaxcala, which in some ways is like Granada and in other ways like Segovia, but more populated than either. It is a dominion governed by several lords, although in a way there was one who was looked up to more than the others, and who had a captain general for war. It is good country with hills and plains, and populous, and it produces much grain.

Six leagues away there is another city on a plain, which is very pretty, and looks like Valladolid. In this city[27] I counted one hundred and ninety towers, including mosques and the houses of nobles. It is also a dominion, governed by twenty-seven officials, one of whom was highly respected and venerated. He was more than a hundred and twenty years old and was carried in a litter. The region is very beautiful, with many fruit trees, especially apple and cherry, and it produces many foodstuffs. Six leagues from here there is another city called Huexotzingo, at the foot of a hill, which looks like Burgos; it is also a dominion, governed by consuls, and the countryside is very beautiful, with fertile plains and rolling hills that are productive.

the lake of mexico

The city of Tenochtitlan Mexico is surrounded by mountains to the east and west. On one side it has some very rugged mountains, one of which is the volcano Popocatepetl. It has the appearance of a round mountain and is four leagues high or more. At the top of this mountain, which is a quarter of a league around, there is a crater from which a great column of smoke issues furiously twice a day and sometimes at night. No matter how strong the wind is, the smoke rises as high as the first bank of clouds without dispersing, and mixes with the clouds forming a solid mass. This mountain is eleven leagues from Mexico, and near the city are other mountains almost as high as this one, some of which are ten leagues away and others seven or eight.

All these mountains are covered with snow most of the year. At the foot of them are very beautiful cities and villages. The rest of the mountains are not so high, but more like foothills, and over all of them extended beautiful forests of pine, *encino* and oak. These mountains are the source of a fresh-water lake that grows so large it measures thirty leagues around. The half of the lake that is near the mountains is good fresh water, and the waters flow from their source toward the north into the other half which is salt water.

Around the fresh-water lake there are reed fields and many beautiful towns, like Cuetanaca, now called Venezuela, which is a large and good place. There is another large town called Mixquic, and another just as large as these or a little less so called Caloacan. There is also another called Xochimilco which is larger than all the others; it is outside the water and nearest of all to the lakeshore. There is another town called Huichilusbusace, and one called Mexicalcingo that is between the fresh-water and salt lakes. All these towns are on the fresh-water lake, as I have said, and most of them are in the middle. The fresh-water lake is long and narrow, and the salt lake is almost round. In this part of the fresh-water lake there are certain small fish and in the salt part the fish are smaller.

the great city of tenochtitlan mexico

This great city of Tenochtitlan Mexico is built within the salt part of the lake; not in the middle but near the edge, about a quarter of a league from the mainland on its nearest side. The circumference of this city is from two and a half to three leagues approximately. Most of the persons who have seen it judge it to have sixty thousand inhabitants or more.[28]

The city is entered by three high causeways built of stone and earth, each one of which is thirty or more paces long. One of these extends across the lake to the city for more than two leagues, and another a league and a half. These two causeways cross the lake, enter through the center of the city, and meet each other, so that it can be said they are one. The [third] causeway comes into the city from the mainland a quarter of a league away. Along this causeway a water conduit runs from the mainland to the city, carrying very good fresh water; it is bigger around than the body of a man and reaches the center of the city. All the residents drink this water, whose source is at the foot of a rock on a hill[29] where it forms a large spring, and from there it is carried three quarters of a league to the city.

the streets

The great city of Tenochtitlan Mexico has many beautiful and wide streets, although except for two or three main streets all the avenues are water on one side and earth on the other. The people walk on the dirt side or ride canoes on the water. The canoes are of concave wood, and large enough sometimes to carry five people comfortably. And so they go about, some on land and others on the water, conversing with each other.

There are many other main thoroughfares which are all water and can only be traveled by canoe in the manner I have already described, for without these they would not have access to their houses. All the other towns mentioned that are on the fresh-water part of the lake are built in this same way.

the squares and market places

The city of Tenochtitlan Mexico has large and very beautiful squares where every article in use among the people is offered for sale. The main square in particular, which is called Tutetula, is about three times the size of the square in Salamanca. There are porticos around it, and every day about twenty to twenty-five thousand people are there buying and selling. On market day, which is held every five days, there are forty to fifty thousand people.

There is an orderly arrangement of wares, so that each kind is sold separately in its proper place. The merchants who sell gold are on one side of the square, and on the other side next to these are the ones who sell different kinds of stones mounted in gold, in the shape of birds and animals. In another part they sell mirrors and beads, and in another they have plumes and feathers of every color for sewing onto the dresses they wear for festivals and warfare. In another part they cut the stones for knives and swords, which is something very interesting to see, and they also make swords and shields. In another place they sell mantles and various kinds of men's dress, while women's dresses are sold elsewhere. There is a place for the sale of shoes, another for tanned deer hides and other animal hides, and devices made of hair that all the Indian women use for the head. Cotton is sold in yet another place, and grain here and bread there, of various kinds. They sell pies, turkeys, chickens and eggs, and, nearby, hare, rabbits, deer, quail, ducks and geese. There is another place for wines of several kinds, and a place for various kinds of herbs. On one street they sell pepper, on another medicinal roots and herbs, of which they have a great number. There is a place for fruits of all kinds; another where they sell wood for houses, and nearby they have lime and stone. In short, everything is sold separately and systematically.

In addition to this great square there are others, and other markets throughout the city where foodstuffs are sold.

the temples and mosques

There were in this great city many large mosques or temples in which the idols were honored and sacrificed to. The main temple was something marvelous to behold, because it was as large as a city. It was surrounded by a high masonry wall with four main entrances. At each entrance was a building like a fortress, filled with the different kinds of weapons they use in warfare, and kept there for that purpose by their great lord Moctezuma. He also had a garrison of ten thousand picked warriors who accompanied him as his personal guard. When there was some alarm or revolt in the city or surrounding country this garrison, or part of it, went into action. If more men were needed they were soon recruited in the city and its confines. Before leaving, they all went to the main temple and armed themselves with the weapons stored there at the gates; then they made a sacrifice to their idols, and when they had received the idols' blessing they went off to war.

Within the temple compound there were large rooms and halls of various kinds. Some of these halls could easily accommodate a thousand people. There were more than twenty towers in the compound, which were as I have described them, although the principal one was longer, wider and taller, and housed the most important and revered of their idols. The idols were in the upper part of the towers, while the priests who lived in the temple occupied the other rooms and halls, and the sacrificers lived in some other chambers.

In the mosques of other cities they chant at night, as though saying matins, and many times during the day, dividing themselves into two groups and singing their hymns, then giving the responses as though they were saying vespers or complins. Inside the mosque there were fountains and washing places for the service of the temple.

the dwellings

In this city there were and still are many beautiful houses belonging to the lords. They were so large and had so many rooms, and gardens on the rooftops as well as below, that they were a sight to behold. I went inside one of the houses of the great lord [Moctezuma] more than four times for no other reason than to look at it, and each time I walked so much that I became tired, but I never saw all of it. It was the custom in all the lords' houses to have very large rooms and halls around a courtyard, and in one of the houses there was a hall large enough to hold more than three thousand people comfortably. And the house was also so large that on the roof of its upper gallery thirty men on horseback could have played a game of cañas[30] as if they were on a great square.

This great city of Tenochtitlan is somewhat longer than it is wide, and at the heart and center of it, where the main temple and the lords' houses were, the Spaniards rebuilt the city. It is as well laid out and has as beautiful streets and squares as any other city in the world. The streets are wide and spacious, with beautiful buildings and magnificent stone and brick houses. The houses are all the same height, except for some that have towers, and because of this sameness they look much better than these others.

In this Spanish city or center there are more than four hundred main houses. No city in Spain has its houses over such a large area, nor does it have better or bigger ones. They are all like fortresses since they are of block stone. There are two large squares, one of which has many handsome porticos around it; here the main church—a very good one—has been built. There is a Franciscan monastery that is a very beautiful building, and a Dominican monastery that is as good, solid and large as any building in Spain. These monasteries house friars who live exemplary lives and are great scholars and preachers. There is a good hospital and other sanctuaries.

The Indian dwellings are around this Spanish castle, city or citadel, and are therefore closed in on all sides.[31] They have more than thirty churches where they hear mass and are instructed in our faith. The natives of this city and its surroundings are very skillful in everything, and the most clever and industrious people in the world. Among them are masters of all kinds of trades, and they need see a thing made only once to be able to make it themselves.

Of all the people in the world they have the least regard for women; they never let the women know what they are doing, even though they may realize it could be to their own advantage. They have many wives, like the Moors, but one is supreme and the children she bears are the ones who inherit.

marriage

They have many wives, as many as they can support, like the Moors; but as I have said, one is the principal wife and her children inherit whereas the others do not, since they cannot because they are considered bastards. At the wedding of this head wife they have certain ceremonies that are not observed at the weddings of the others. The men have a custom of urinating sitting down, like our women, and the women standing up.[32]

the burials

They make a grave lined with stonemasonry and put the deceased in it, seated on a chair, with his sword and shield to one side, and some gold jewelry. Once I helped remove from a tomb three thousand *castellanos* worth, more or less.

They also put in enough food and drink to last several days, to sustain the dead person on his journey. If the deceased was a woman they left by her side her spindle and distaff and all her working instruments, for they said that where she was going she had to occupy herself at something. Often they burned the dead and buried their ashes.

All the people of this province of New Spain, and even those of neighboring provinces, eat human flesh and value it more highly than any other food in the world; so much so, that they often go off to war and risk their lives just to kill people to eat. The majority of them, as I have said, are sodomites and they drink to excess.

two letters
of pedro
de alvarado

Tonatiuh, the sun god, as the Mexicans called Pedro de Alvarado, sailed first with the Grijalva expedition, as captain of one of the vessels. He then joined Cortés' expedition in 1519, also with the rank of captain.

In the city of Tenochtitlan, when Cortés decided to imprison Moctezuma and hold him as hostage, he chose Pedro de Alvarado as one of the men to accompany him to Moctezuma's palace. At the time that Cortés set out for the coast against the forces of Pánfilo de Narváez, Alvarado was left in charge of Moctezuma and the Spanish garrison. He also played a vital part in the siege of Tenochtitlan.

The city fell to the Spaniards in August of 1521. Alvarado went on to the conquest of the Mixtec region of Oaxaca, and subjected Tehuantepec. (These expeditions are mentioned in the third letter of Cortés, which appears in the present volume.) After several other campaigns, by order of Cortés he left the city of Mexico in December of 1523 to undertake the conquest of Guatemala.

The two letters of Pedro de Alvarado, addressed to Hernán Cortés from Guatemala, are military dispatches sent in accordance with Cortés' instructions to keep him informed of the progress of the expedition. Perhaps for this reason Alvarado wrote in such matter-of-fact terms of the Indians he killed. At one point, for example, he speaks of their destruction with outright enthusiasm. Had Alvarado, like Bernal Díaz del

Castillo, left us his memoirs, written long after the fact, and in the consciousness that he would be judged for his actions, a more dimensional and less brutal Pedro de Alvarado might have emerged. But Alvarado's letters suggest that he had the assurance of Cortés' approval—as an old friend and fellow soldier—and that he expected to be judged only as to whether his mission was accomplished.

Alvarado's preoccupation, in the letters, was that Cortés was not giving him due credit at court, for he had received no recognition or favors from the king, whereas Cortés, by royal decree of October 22, 1522 had been made governor of New Spain and of all territories he might conquer in the future. It was not until 1526, in his fourth dispatch to the king, that Cortés reported Alvarado's services, and in 1527 Alvarado sailed for Spain, where he secured the title of governor and captain general of Guatemala.

Alvarado was still campaigning at the age of fifty-six (he was thirty-four, the same age as Cortés, at the beginning of the Conquest) when he was crushed by a falling horse, and died several days later in Guadalajara.

Dispatch sent by Pedro de Alvarado to Hernando Cortés, reporting the battles and wars sustained in the pacification of the provinces of Zacatula, Quetzalte-nango and Utatlán; the burning of their chieftain and designation of his sons to succeed him; and the discovery of three mountains of copperas, sulphur and alum.

SIRE:

From Soconusco I wrote Your Grace all that had happened to me on the way to that province, as well as something of what could be expected further on.[1] I sent messengers ahead to inform the people of this land [of Utatlán] that I was coming to conquer and pacify the provinces that refused to submit to His Majesty's rule. I requested their aid and assistance as vassals of His Majesty, since they had offered themselves as such to Your Grace, and said that if they complied they would be acting as loyal and good vassals, and would receive justice and consideration from me and the Spaniards under my command; but if they did not, I thereby declared war on them as traitors and defaulters against the service of the emperor our lord, and would moreover consider as slaves all who were taken alive in war.

After doing this and dispatching the native messengers, I assembled my horse and foot soldiers for review. On the next morning, a Saturday, I set out in quest of their land, marching for three days through an uninhabited forest. After I had encamped, the sentries I posted caught three spies from a town called Zapotit-lán, and when I asked them what brought them they replied they were gathering honey, although it was plain that they were spies. Nevertheless I did not care to press them, but used persuasion instead and gave them another requisition like the first one, to take back to the lords of their town; but they never sent me an answer of any kind.

On approaching the town I found they had left the highroad and crossroads open, but had closed the roads leading into the main streets, and I judged that their reason for doing this was to make war on us. Some Indians who had been sent out to me came there and spoke to me from a distance, telling me to enter the town to take lodging. Inside the town they could more conveniently make war on us, as they planned to do, so that day I made camp outside in order to reconnoiter the land. By afternoon they could no longer disguise their bad intentions, and they killed and wounded some of the Indians in my company. On learning of this I sent horsemen out in the field, and they met numerous warriors who fought with them and injured several of the horses.

Next day I went over the road we were to follow, and I also saw warriors, and found the country so thick with cacao trees and forest that it provided a better stronghold for them than for us, so I returned to camp. On the day after, I left camp with all of the men to enter the town. On the way was a river that was very dangerous to cross. It had been taken by the Indians, but we fought them and won it from them. I then waited on a plain above the river canyon to be sure the rear guard got over, because the crossing was very dangerous and I took every precaution I could. As I waited there many more warriors appeared from all sides to attack us, and we fended them off until all the baggage had been taken across the river.

When we reached the houses of the town we encountered warriors and the battle continued until we had passed the market place and half a league beyond. Afterwards we returned to make camp in the market place, and here I remained two days reconnoitering the land. Then I left for another town called Quetzaltenango, and had to cross two dangerous rivers full of jagged rocks, which we forded with great difficulty. After that we began to climb a pass six leagues long, and made camp that night at the halfway point. This pass was so steep that we could barely take the horses up. The next morning I continued on my way, and at the top of a steep slope I found a woman and a dog who had been sacrificed. According to the interpreter, this was a challenge. Further on I found a strong wooden barricade in a narrow gap, but there was no one in it.

When we had finished climbing the long pass the foot soldiers and crossbow-men were all ahead of me, because the way was so rough the horses could not be reined. About three or four thousand warriors attacked from a ravine, striking our Indian allies and forcing them back down, but we defeated the attackers. Then as I was at the top reassembling my troops I saw more than thirty thousand men coming toward us. It pleased God that we found some plains there, and although the horses were tired from the climb we waited for the enemy until their arrows reached us; then we charged. Since they had never seen horses before, they became very frightened and we made good pursuit, dispersing them and killing many.

I waited for all my men to reassemble, and when they were together again I went to make camp a league away from there where were some springs. There was no water where we had been, so we were suffering from thirst, and besides, when we were tired we usually stopped wherever we found a convenient place. As we were on some plains, I went ahead with thirty horsemen, many of us leading spare horses, while the rest of the men followed in a body. Then we dismounted to drink water, and while we were drinking we saw many warriors approaching over the wide plains. We let them approach us, then we charged, making another good sally. Some of these Indians stood their ground against the horses, taking on two horses per man. We pursued the enemy for all of a league until they came to the foot of a ridge; here they faced about [to meet our attack], but since we wanted to get them out in the open, we turned our horses pretending to flee, and the Indians came after us. When they were almost touch-

ing the horses' tails we turned upon them and closed in, inflicting severe punishment on them. In this engagement we killed one of the four lords of the city of
Utatlán, who was acting as captain general for all the land.

I withdrew to the springs where, very weary, with wounded Spaniards and
horses, we made camp for the night. Next morning I left for the town of Quetzaltenango, a league away, and found it deserted as a result of our encounter the
day before. I took quarters there to reorganize myself and survey the country,
which is as thickly populated as Tlaxcala, and has as much cultivated land, but
is extremely cold. After I had been there six days, one Thursday at noon a great
multitude of warriors approached from all sides. They told me themselves that
there were twelve thousand from this city, and that they could not even count
the number from the surrounding towns. As soon as I saw them I put my men in
good order and went out with ninety horsemen to give battle in the middle of a
plain that was three leagues long. I left men to guard our camp, which was no
more than a crossbow shot from the field, and we charged through the enemy,
scattering their forces. I pursued them for two and a half leagues until they were
all dispersed and no more remained ahead, then I turned back on them. In a
gully our allies and the foot soldiers were causing the greatest destruction in the
world; they also surrounded a flat hill on which the enemy had taken refuge,
and they climbed it and took every last man.

On this day many enemy troops were killed and captured. Among them were
many captains, lords and persons of rank. When the lords of the city were informed that their warriors had been routed, they convoked the other provinces,
and offered their enemies tribute to attract them to their side in order to join
forces and kill us. Their plan was to send word that they wanted to be good and
would give fealty again to the emperor our lord, and to ask me to go to their city
of Utatlán, as they later did persuade me to go. Once they had me quartered inside the city they would one night set fire to the city, and we would all burn
without being able to offer resistance. They actually put their evil plan into
effect, only Our Lord cannot permit these infidels to be victorious over us; for
the city is very strongly fortified, and has only two entrances: one a high stone
staircase of thirty-odd steps, and the other an avenue paved with hand-laid
stones, much of it already torn up, so that on that night it could be torn up entirely to prevent the horses from running out. And since the city is very compact
and the streets narrow, we could not have resisted an attack without being cut
off, nor have escaped from the fire without throwing ourselves down the em-
bankment.

When we had climbed to the city and found ourselves inside, I observed that
it was a great fortress and that we could not make use of the horses because the
streets were very narrow. Therefore I decided to leave at once. The lords of the

city tried to persuade me to stay, and asked me to sit down to eat first, so that they could carry out their purpose; but as soon as I became aware of the danger we were in I sent some men ahead to take the avenue and bridge in order to have access to level ground. The avenue was already in such condition that the horses were barely able to go over it, and there were warriors all around the city.

When they saw that I had reached level ground they became somewhat apprehensive, but this did not prevent them from doing me considerable damage. However, I overlooked the matter because I wanted to seize their lords, who had absented themselves; and with tact on my part, and the offer of certain remuneration, I was able to seize them, and I then held them captive in my quarters. Nevertheless, their warriors continued to besiege me, and to kill or wound our Indian friends who went out to gather pasture. One of the Spaniards who went for some grass was killed within crossbow shot of the camp by a stone they rolled down on him from the edge of a gully. The countryside is full of ravines, some of which are two hundred *estados* deep, and because of these we could not maneuver to give them the punishment they deserved. I knew that if I could overrun their land and burn it I could submit them to His Majesty's service, so I decided [first] to burn the lords. They said before they were burned, as it can be seen from their confessions, that they had been the ones who ordered war made on us, and that they had planned to burn me inside the city, and for that reason had asked me to come here; also that they had ordered their vassals not to give fealty to the emperor our lord, nor to serve us or do any other good works. Therefore upon learning from them of their ill will toward His Majesty's service, I burned them for the sake of the peace and welfare of this land and I gave orders that the city was to be burned and razed to its foundations, because it was so strong and menacing that it seemed more like a house of brigands than of settlers.

I sent word to the people of Guatemala, a city ten leagues from here, requisitioning them in the name of His Majesty to send me warriors, for I wanted to see whether they were well disposed toward us, and to spread fear in the land as well. They showed their good will by sending me four thousand men, and with these men and the ones I already had I made an incursion and ran all the inhabitants out of the land. When they saw the damage being done they sent me messengers to say that they wanted to be good, and that if they had erred it was because of their lords, whom they could not disobey; but now that the lords were dead, they begged me to forgive them. I granted them safe conduct and ordered them to return and occupy their homes and land as before, which they have done; so I have them now as they used to be, and in the service of His Majesty.

To further insure the land, I released two of the lords' sons and put them in their fathers' places, and I think they will act in the interests of His Majesty and the welfare of this land. With reference to the war there remains nothing to be said at present except that all who were captured were branded and made slaves, and the royal fifth[2] was delivered to the treasurer, Baltasar de Mendoza; this fifth was sold at auction to make His Majesty's revenue more secure.

As to the land itself, I inform Your Grace that it is temperate and healthful, and thickly settled with substantial towns. This city of Utitlán is well built and wonderfully strong, and has extensive cultivation. It has many subject people and towns which I am leaving under the yoke and in the service of His Majesty's royal crown.

There is in this land a mountain that has alum, and another copperas, and another with the best sulphur that has yet been found; from a piece that was brought me I made half an *arroba* of powder, without refining or mixing. Since I am sending Argueta and do not wish to delay him, I shall send you fifty pack-loads with later messengers.

I leave for the city of Guatemala on Monday, the eleventh of April, where I shall not stay long because a town called Atitlán, which is situated on the water, is at war and has killed four of my messengers. I think that with the help of Our Lord we shall soon draw it to His Majesty's service. From information that I have gathered there is much to be done further on, and for this reason I shall make haste to pass the rainy season fifty or a hundred leagues beyond Guatemala. I am told by the natives that there are great and wonderful buildings and splendid cities further on. They tell me also that this land ends five days beyond a large city that is a twenty-day march from here, and they insist that it is so. If it is true, I am very certain that it is the strait.[3]

God give me victory over these infidels, so that I may bring them to His service and that of the Crown. I should prefer not to make this report piecemeal, but rather from beginning to end, because there would be more to say. The Spanish foot soldiers and horsemen in my company have done so well in the war that they are deserving of many favors. At present I have nothing more that is worth saying, except that we are in the hardiest land of people that has been seen; and so that the Lord may give us victory I appeal to Your Grace to order services held in the city [of Mexico], by all the clerics and friars, to ask Our Lady's intercession; for we are far removed from succor unless it is to reach us from there. May Your Grace also have the kindness to inform His Majesty how we are serving him with our persons, our fortunes and efforts; firstly, to relieve Your Grace's conscience, and secondly so that His Majesty may grant us favors. May the Lord preserve your very excellent condition for a long time. From the city of Utatlán, April 11.

Inasmuch as I have a long journey ahead, I may be in need of horseshoes. If by this summer Your Grace could provide me with these it would be of great assistance, and His Majesty would be served thereby. At present they are worth one hundred and ninety pesos the dozen, and that is the price we trade and pay for them now.

Your humble servant,
PEDRO DE ALVARADO.

Disptach sent by Pedro de Alvarado to Hernando Cortés, describing the conquest of many cities, the wars, battles, treason and rebellions that occurred, and the founding of a settlement; of two volcanoes, one issuing fire and the other smoke; of a boiling river and another that was cold; and how Alvarado was wounded by an arrow.

SIRE:

Of the things that had happened to me as far as Utatlán, in war as well as the rest, I made lengthy report to Your Grace, and now I wish to report on all the lands I have traveled and conquered, and all that has happened to me.

I left the city of Utatlán, Sire, and in two days reached this city of Guatemala, where I was so well received by the lords that I could not have been more welcome in my own home, and my men and I were provided with everything we needed. Eight days after my arrival I learned from these lords that at a distance of seven leagues there was another city on a very large lake,[4] and that this city made war on Guatemala and Utatlán and other nearby cities, because of its strong position on the lake and the number of its canoes. It made night raids on its neighbors, and although the people of Guatemala were suffering damage they told me that they had not wished to make war without my permission, since they were in the service of His Majesty, but begged me to help them.

I replied that I would have their enemies summoned in the name of the emperor our lord, and that if they came I would demand that they cease making war and doing damage in this land; but if they did not come, I would set out with [the Guatemalans] to punish them. Therefore I sent two messengers who were natives of this city, and [the people of Atitlán] killed the messengers without any compunction. On learning of this, and realizing their bad intentions, I set out against them with sixty horsemen and one hundred and fifty foot soldiers, and the lords and warriors of Guatemala. I marched so far that I reached the land of Atitlán that same day. No one came out to receive me in peace or in any other way, so I went with thirty horsemen around the edge of the lake toward a rocky hill rising out of the water, on which there was a settlement. Here we saw a squadron of warriors very close to us, so we charged with the horses and pursued them until they entered a narrow causeway leading to the hill, where the horses could not follow. My companions and I dismounted and fought our way in on foot, thereby giving the Indians no time to destroy the bridges, without which we could not have entered.

Meanwhile many of the other men had caught up with us, and we took the hill, which was thickly populated. The people swam out to an islet, many of them escaping because our allies did not arrive quickly enough in the three hundred canoes they were bringing over the water. That afternoon all my men and I left the hill and made camp on a plain where there were cornfields, and there we slept the night.

Next morning we entrusted ourselves to the Lord's care and went toward the town, which was very defensible because of its many rocks and boulders, but we found it deserted. Its defenders, after losing their strength on the water, had not dared wait on land, except for a handful of them who had stayed at the edge of the town. And because of the ruggedness of the land, as I say, we did not kill many people. There I established camp at midday and began to raid the land. I captured a number of the natives, three of whom I sent as messengers to the lords, warning them that if they did not come forward to give me their fealty in the name of the Imperial Crown, the war would continue and I would raid them and search them out through the hills. They replied that their land had never before been invaded, nor had anyone ever entered it by force of arms; but that I had done so, and therefore they would be glad to serve His Majesty as I commanded. Then they came and put themselves in my power, and I told them of the greatness and might of the Emperor our lord, and said that in his royal name I forgave what had passed, but from then on they were to be good subjects and not make war on their neighbors, since all were vassals of His Majesty. Thus I left them secure and at peace, and I returned to the city of Guatemala.

Three days after my return, all the lords and nobles and captains from the lake came to me with presents and told me they were now our friends and were happy to be His Majesty's vassals, for they were free of the wars and differences among themselves. I received them very well, and gave them some of my jewels, then sent them back to their land with good will. Now they are the most peaceable people in the land.

Many lords of other provinces on the southern coast also came to give their fealty and to say they wished to be vassals of His Majesty, and did not want war with anyone, and were therefore asking me to receive them as vassals. I received them well, as was their due, and told them that in His Majesty's name I would favor and assist them. They informed me that a province called Izcuintlepec, which is further inland, tried to keep them from coming to give their fealty, and that there were other provinces disposed to come peaceably, but that this province would not let them pass; it would ask where they were going, and tell them they must be mad, and that if I wanted to go there it would wage war on me.

I was assured that this was so, not only by these provinces but also by the lords of the city of Guatemala, so I set out with all my foot soldiers and horsemen, and for the next three days slept in uninhabited country. On the following morning as we reached the boundary of Izcuintlepec, where it is densely wooded, I found all the roads closed. They were very narrow, no more than paths, for these people carried on no trade and had no communication with anyone.

I sent the crossbowmen to the vanguard, for the horses could not fight here because of the swampy ground and thick forest. It was raining so hard that the sentries and spies had gone into the town, thinking I would not reach them that day, so they were somewhat negligent and did not perceive our approach until we were in the town with them.

When I entered, all the warriors were bathing in the streams, enjoying the water, and when they tried to assemble it was too late; but some of them who stood their ground wounded several of the Spaniards and many of our Indian friends. With the thick forest and heavy rainfall they got away into the woods and I had no chance to do any damage except to burn their town. Then I sent messengers to their lords, telling them to come give me their fealty in His Majesty's name, or I would do great damage in their land and lay waste to their cornfields. The lords came, and offered themselves as vassals, and I received them and ordered them to be good from then on. I remained a week in this town, where many other towns and provinces came peaceably to offer themselves as vassals of the Emperor our lord.

Wishing to penetrate the land and learn its secrets, the better to serve His Majesty and give him more lands to possess and reign over, I decided to leave this place and go to a town called Atiepac. Its inhabitants are a different people who have their own language, and I was well received by them. At sundown, and for no reason whatsoever, the place suddenly appeared deserted, with not a man in all the town. But to avoid having the middle of the rainy season overtake me on the road, I left them thus and passed through, keeping careful watch over my men and the baggage. For my objective was to penetrate a hundred leagues further, overcoming whatever obstacles I met on the way, and then to double back and pacify the towns.

I left on the following day and reached another town, called Tacuila, where the same thing happened as in Atiepac: they received me in peace, and within an hour they had picked up and gone. Then I left for Taxisco, a good solid town of many inhabitants, where I was received as in the other towns, and slept there that night. The next day I set out for Nancintla, which is very large, but since I mistrusted these people, whom I could not understand, I sent ten horsemen to the rear, and another ten to accompany the baggage, and continued on my way. After having left Taxisco two or three leagues behind me, I learned that warriors had come after us and attacked the rear before it was able to resist, killing many of our Indian friends and taking a good part of the baggage, with all the strings for the crossbows, and the horseshoes I carried for the war.

I then sent my brother Jorge de Alvarado with forty to fifty horsemen, to go after what we had lost, and he found many armed men in the field, and fought with them and routed them, but nothing of what we had lost could be recovered because they had already torn apart the clothing and each of them was wearing a loincloth from it.

After Jorge de Alvarado reached Nancintla he turned back because all the Indians had taken to the mountains; and from here I sent Don Pedro out with foot soldiers to look for them in the mountains, so that we might draw them to His Majesty's service, but he was unable to do anything because of the thickness of the forests, and he came back. I sent some of their own Indians as messengers, with requisitions and commands, warning them that if they did not come they would be made slaves; but in spite of all this neither they nor the messengers appeared.

When I had been in Nancintla a week, some people from a town called Pazaca, which was on our way, came in peace and I received them, giving them a few of the things I had and entreating them to be good. The following morning I left for their town and at the entrance I found the roads barred, and arrows planted in the ground. On entering the town I saw that some Indians were quartering a dog in a form of sacrifice. From inside the town a cry was given and we saw a multitude of warriors. We attacked, pursuing them until we ran them out of the town, and following as far as we could.

From here I went to another town called Mopicalco, where I was received neither better nor worse than in the others, and when I got inside the town I found not a single person there. I left for the town of Acatepec, where I found no one, for it was deserted. And pursuing my objective, which was to penetrate the land for a hundred leagues, I went on to Acaxual on the shore of the South Sea.[5] Half a league before reaching the town I saw the fields full of warriors with their plumage and insignia, and their offensive and defensive arms. They were waiting for me on a plain, and I halted within crossbow shot of them to await the rest of my company. As soon as we were all together I advanced half-way toward the warriors, but they made no movement that I could observe. It seemed to me that they were somewhat close to a hill where they could take refuge, so I ordered the retreat of all my forces, which consisted of one hundred horsemen, one hundred and fifty foot soldiers, and about five to six thousand Indian allies. As we withdrew I remained in the rear guard commanding the retreat.

The enemy was greatly pleased, and followed behind us until they almost touched the horses' tails, while their arrows flew through our forward troops; and since we were on a plain there were no obstacles to impede either one of us. When I had retreated a quarter of a league to where they could not resort to flight but would have to rely on their arms, I turned back upon them with all my men. We broke through them, causing such destruction that in a short time none of them remained alive, for they were so heavily armed that when they fell to the ground they could not get up again. They wore cotton breastplates three fingers thick, and armor down to their feet, and carried long spears and arrows, and as they fell our foot soldiers killed them all.

In this encounter they wounded many of the Spaniards, injuring me among them, for one of their arrows pierced my leg and went through to the saddle. I remain crippled from this injury, having one leg a good four fingers shorter than the other.

We were forced to stay five days in this town treating our wounds, after which we left for a town called Tacuxcalco. I sent Don Pedro and other companions ahead to scout the country, and they caught two spies who told them there were warriors waiting for us from Tacuxcalco and other neighboring towns; what is more, [our scouts] even saw these warriors, of which there were a great multitude. Then Gonzalo de Alvarado, who was in the vanguard because I was injured, arrived there with forty horsemen, and he waited until we had all arrived.

When we were all assembled I mounted a horse somehow, the better to give orders for the attack, and I saw a body of warriors all formed as an enemy *batalla*.[6] I sent Gómez de Alvarado with twenty horsemen to attack the left wing, and Gonzalo de Alvarado with thirty horsemen to attack the right, and Jorge de Alvarado with the rest of the men to break through the center. The enemy were frightening to see from afar, for most of them had lances thirty spans long, and all raised high.

I stationed myself on a hill to watch the engagement, and saw that all the Spaniards got as far as an Indian ball court, and that the Indians did not flee nor did the Spaniards attack. I marveled that the Indians had the boldness thus to stand their ground. The Spaniards had not attacked because they thought that a grassy place lying between them and the Indians might be a marsh, but as soon as they found it to be firm they broke through the Indians and routed them, then pursued them past the town for more than a league. In this engagement there was much slaughter and punishment.

When the towns further along the way saw that in the field we were able to rout them, they decided to pick up and abandon the towns, and after I had rested here two days I left for Miahuaclán, whose people had also gone off to the hills. I went on to Atehuan, where messengers were sent me by the lords of Cuzcatlán to give fealty to His Majesty and to say that they wished to be his vassals. And so they gave their fealty to me in his name, and I received them thinking they would not deceive me as the others had.

On reaching the outskirts of this town of Cuzcatlán I met many Indians who came to receive me, but I found that the town had been evacuated; and after we were settled in our quarters not one of these Indians was left in the town; they had all taken to the hills. When I saw this I sent my messengers to the lords to tell them not to be treacherous, and to recall that they had given their fealty to His Majesty, and to me in his name. I gave them my assurance that I would not make war on them nor take what was theirs, but wished only to bring them into the service of God our Lord and of His Majesty.

They sent back word that they recognized no one, and would not come; that if I wanted anything of them they were awaiting me with their arms. When I saw their ill intentions I sent a command and requisition in the name of the emperor, ordering them not to default or break the peace, for they had given themselves as vassals; but if they did not obey I would proceed against them as defaulters and traitors against the service of His Majesty, and would make war on them, and all who were taken in war would be made slaves and branded. If they were loyal, they would receive my favor and protection as His Majesty's vassals.

To this there was no answer, nor did the messengers return. As I saw their wicked intention, and could not let it go unpunished, I sent men into the hills and mountains to look for them. These men found them ready for war and fought with them, and there were Spaniards and Indian friends of ours wounded. Also one of the lords of this town was captured. As further justification I again sent a command, and the lords replied as before, so then I instituted proceedings against them and against the lords of the other provinces that had made war on me, and summoned them by crier, but still they would not come.

Inasmuch as they failed to appear, the case was closed and the lords of these provinces sentenced to death as traitors, while all other persons taken or yet to be taken in war, until such time as fealty was given, were to be made slaves and branded, and their value applied to the cost of the eleven horses killed, and any more that might be killed in the course of the conquest, as well as to the cost of weapons and other things that would be necessary to said conquest.

Despite the incursions I made and the messengers I sent during the seventeen days that I spent in Cuzcatlán, I was not able to prevail over these Indians because of the mountains, ravines, thick forests and other defenses they had.

Here I learned of very extensive lands and of cities built of masonry, further inland, and I was informed by the natives that there is no end to this land. Because of its size and great cities its conquest requires much time, and inasmuch as the rainy season is in full force I decided not to go on and conquer it but to return instead to the city of Guatemala, and pacify again the land I had been through. But no matter what I did, or what efforts I made, I never was able to bring them to His Majesty's service, because all this southern coast that I went over has very dense vegetation and mountain ranges that are close together.

I returned to this city of Guatemala, therefore, because of the heavy rains; and here, to facilitate the conquest and pacification of this large and populous land, I founded and built a Spanish city in the name of His Majesty, which is called the city of Santiago. It is situated at the heart of all this land, where there are better and more abundant resources for undertaking the conquest and pacification, and for settling the land that lies ahead. I also chose two magistrates and four councilmen, as Your Grace will see by the nominations.

After the remaining two months of the rainy season have passed, which are the heaviest, I shall set out in quest of the province of Tlapallan. According to the information I have received, it is a fifteen-day march inland from here, and its city is as large as that of Mexico, with great buildings of stonemasonry having flat roofs. There are many other cities besides this, four or five of which have come to me here to give fealty to His Majesty. It is said that one of them has thirty thousand householders, and it would not surprise me, judging from the size of the cities on the coast, if the inland cities were as large as they say.

During the coming dry season, the Lord willing, I plan to continue two hundred leagues further, where I expect His Majesty will be well served and his estate augmented, and Your Grace will receive word of other new things. From the city of Mexico to as far as I have gone and conquered, it is four hundred leagues; and may it be known to Your Grace that this land has more settlements and people than all the land governed by Your Grace until now.

In this land we have found a ridge where there is a volcano that is the most terrifying thing ever seen. From its mouth it hurls rocks as big as a house, burning in flames, and when they fall they shatter in pieces, covering the mountain with fire.

Sixty leagues beyond this one we saw another volcano which throws terrible smoke that rises to the sky, in a mass half a league wide. The water carried by the rivers descending from here cannot be drunk because it tastes of sulphur. One particular and very beautiful river is so burning that it could not be crossed by some men in my company who were out making an incursion. In looking for a ford they came to another river that was cold, and where the two rivers met they found a lukewarm place where they were able to cross.

Nothing more remains to be told Your Grace about this land except that the Indians tell me that from the South Sea to the North Sea it is a winter's and a summer's march.

Your Grace favored me with the lieutenancy of Tenochtitlan and I helped take the city, and defended it when I was inside, at the risk and danger Your Grace is aware of. Had I gone to Spain, His Majesty would have confirmed the services I have rendered him and would have granted me greater favors. I have been told that His Majesty has issued his decree,[7] and I am not surprised, for he knows nothing of me, and no one is to blame for this but Your Grace for failing to report to His Majesty how I have served you: for it is you who sent me here. I beg Your Grace to inform His Majesty who I am, how I have served him in these parts, where I am, and what new conquests I have made; also my willingness to serve in the future, and how I have received a leg injury in his service, and what small pay these squires and I have earned, and what little benefit we have so far received. May the Lord increase Your Grace's life and excellent condition for a long time to come.—The City of Santiago,

28 July 1524.

PEDRO DE ALVARADO

the chronicle
of
garcia del pilar

Hernán Cortés was somewhere in Honduras
when Nuño Beltrán de Guzmán sailed to the Indies from Spain in 1525. Guzmán was newly-
appointed governor of Pánuco, a region of some
forty or fifty leagues along the Gulf coast north of
the port of Veracruz. Previously, Pánuco had
been a dependency of New Spain, under Cortés'
command.

In 1528 Nuño de Guzmán was appointed president of the first royal *Audiencia* of Mexico, re-
placing the governor Gonzalo de Salazar. Guzmán
and two of the *oidores* or jurists who were members of the *Audiencia,* Matienzo and Delgadillo,
assisted by one of the first conquistadors, García
del Pilar, governed the colony so corruptly that
they in turn had to be replaced. Before the appointment of the members of the second *Audiencia,* however, Nuño de Guzmán had absented
himself from the city of Mexico and had embarked on his conquest of the northwest.

The cruelties and abuses committed against the
Indians by Guzmán and his army subsequently
came to the attention of the second *Audiencia,*
whose members held an investigation during the
course of which many of Guzmán's henchmen
were questioned. Among these was García del
Pilar, whose account of the expedition is offered
as the final selection in the present volume.

Though primarily an indictment of Guzmán,
the document is a terrible confession of García
del Pilar's complicity, for Pilar was a willing

enough intermediary for Guzmán, and the fluency he had acquired in the Nahuatl language made his services doubly valuable. This facility for the language was first displayed when Pilar was a member of Cortés' company, and is mentioned by Bernal Díaz del Castillo in one of the last chapters of his history, in which he lists the conquistadors who came over with the great captain.

Pilar himself, in a petition to the king dated the year before the Guzmán expedition, emphasizes that his ability to speak Nahuatl permitted him—presumably unassisted—to convince many of the Indian peoples to surrender peaceably and give fealty to the Spanish king. In his testimony against Guzmán, however, he makes himself as shadowy as possible, seemingly intent on appearing as a mere bystander at the scene of his master's crimes.

Nuño de Guzmán's conquest of the west and northwest of Mexico, while not comparable to Hernán Cortés' achievement, was hardly negligible in the eyes of the Spanish Crown. The New Kingdom of Galicia, as this territory became known, encompassed the present states of Colima, Jalisco, Nayarit, Aguascalientes, Sinaloa, and part of Zacatecas, Durango, Querétaro and San Luis Potosí.

Because Your Lordship and Graces already know the number of men, Indians as well as Spaniards, who left this city [of Mexico] with Nuño de Guzmán, and when he left, I shall not state the particulars in this Memoir, but shall only say that he left in the year 1529, three days before Christmas.

He went to the city of Uchichila,[1] which is the seat of the province and dominion of Mechuacan. Before Nuño de Guzmán entered the city, Don Pedro, governor of this province and dominion, came out to receive him with many Indians in their war attire, to provide him with every service and convenience. And with these attentions Nuño de Guzmán entered the city, and as soon as he arrived he summoned the lord of the city, whose name was Don Francisco,[2] and commanded him to muster eight thousand men from all the land, and Don Francisco replied that he would do as he was commanded.

Three days after issuing this command, Nuño de Guzmán had Don Francisco seized and put in irons, then imprisoned in an alcove between two walls, next to his bedroom, alleging that Don Francisco did not supply enough provisions for the men. He also ordered Antonio de Godoy and me to ask Don Francisco why he did not have ready the silver and gold demanded of this city, to which he replied that it was being collected and we could go to see it. Godoy and I then went to the house where Don Francisco lived, and we saw a profusion of gold and silver plates and shields, but I am not certain how much there could have been.

Nuño de Guzmán kept him thus for about two weeks. One night when he was angry with Don Francisco, and dissatisfied with the amount he was providing, he ordered Godoy and me to take Don Francisco back to his house and put him to torture by fire or any other means we thought advisable, and make him disclose his treasure or whatever possessions he might have. We took him there and Godoy in his capacity of alcalde ordered me to stay by the door so that no Indians could get in, while he proceeded to bind Don Francisco and apply the torture. When he had Don Francisco's hands bound and was showing him the burning iron, there arrived two friars who were at that time residents of the city, and I left. Godoy stayed there with them, and then took Don Francisco back to his place of imprisonment.

About a week after this occurred, the Indians Nuño de Guzmán had demanded were brought to him, and I am not sure whether or not they were the full number. They were divided among the Spaniards, and some of them put in chains, to carry the baggage. Taking Don Francisco with us as a captive, we left the city. And because I do not remember now the other grave things committed in this city, I am not including them in this Memoir, but if Godoy and Juan Pascual the Tarascan interpreter wanted to tell the truth, or were questioned in my presence, these things would come to light.

After leaving this city we went to the river two leagues beyond the town of Villaseñor, which we named Río de Nuestra Señora.[3] Nuño de Guzmán had the flags raised over our camp, and the trumpets sounded, and ordered it proclaimed that as President of New Spain and Governor of Pánuco and Victoria Garayana, he was taking possession of these lands; and he also made known the rest of what is contained in the proclamation to which I refer. While we were there he built a sanctuary and made a wall around it, ordering all this work done just so he could stop there some day.

At this time he made accusation against Don Francisco, alleging that he had Indians waiting in ambush to attack us. He also submitted him to questioning about having many Spaniards killed in the province of Mechuacan, and again had him put in irons. Then he ordered the constables Cristóbal de Sepúlveda, Cristóbal Romero, and Antón Galeote to build a hut outside the camp area. There he took two Nahuatl interpreters who were from the city of Mechuacan, one called Avalos and the other Juárez, and inflicted the cord and water torment[4] on them, asking them what Christians had been killed in the city of Mechuacan, and when, and where Don Francisco's treasure was, and his jewels and women. Since he asked all this through the Tarascan interpreter Juan Pascual, there were things I could not understand, but I do know that they refused to confess, so the fire torment was inflicted on them, and their feet burned all the way to the ankles, but they never confessed anything.

On the following day Don Alonso, who is said to be married to Don Francisco's daughter, was taken to the hut, where they inflicted torture on him to make him answer the same questions, but they did not inflict the fire torture. It did not appear to me that he confessed anything, but I refer the matter to the interpreter Juan Pascual who understood the language. The next day Nuño de Guzmán had Don Pedro, the governor of Mechuacan, taken there, and he was asked the same questions and tortured, but not by fire. Then on the following day he took Don Francisco there, and I am not certain that he tortured him, but I believe he did; this can be learned from the aforementioned constables and Nahuatl interpreters, and from Don Pedro and Don Alonso.

I do not know what was said during the questioning of Don Francisco, but Nuño de Guzmán immediately dispatched men, saying they were going for the bodies of some Christians who had been killed. On this expedition he sent his steward Pedro de Guzmán,[5] accompanied by three or four other horsemen who were servants of his; I do not remember the particulars, but these could be learned from Godoy who, I think, had something to do with the matter since he was in the province of Mechuacan. When they returned it was rumored in camp that they had brought a large sum of gold and silver, and the interpreter Juan Pascual told me this himself.

Then Nuño de Guzmán condemned Don Francisco as a traitor and ordered him dragged by a horse, then tied to a stake where he was burned alive and his ashes thrown downstream.

We left there after spending twenty-five days more or less, suffering hunger and want, and we took along Don Alonso, Don Pedro and the Nahuatl interpreters, who were so disabled from the torture inflicted on them that they could travel only in hammock litters. We followed the river downstream through uninhabited country for seven or eight days, until we reached a town called Cuynao, where we made war and burned the town, and all the people fled to the hills. From there we also made raids on the surrounding towns. After we had been in Cuynao about two weeks the people came to give themselves up peaceably, and we departed leaving it at peace. While we were still there some messengers returned from the city of Mechuacan, who had been sent to that city by Don Pedro and Don Alonso. I know it is a fact that they brought in by night certain packloads of gold and silver, because the interpreter Juan Pascual told me so; and it was more than they had ever offered before. The constable Juan Sánchez also told me, for he had discovered it while making his rounds. The reason why I did not see it myself was that I was talking to the aforementioned interpreter, and I withdrew to avoid interfering in these matters.

Two days after leaving this town we reached Cuitzeo,[6] where we made war on the natives. At the end of seven or eight days, during which we raided the land, a fat man who was said to be the lord came to seek peace. And because he did not bring bearers, or gold or silver as Nuño de Guzmán demanded, the latter had him thrown to the dogs. We left him, bitten all over, at the doorstep to his house, then set fire to the house and the town, although he had come to us seeking peace as I have said.

The Tarascan Indians, and the Indians we took with us from Cuitzeo and other nearby towns carried the baggage on their backs, and by order and consent of Nuño de Guzmán many of them were kept in chains.[7] Thus we marched to the province of Tonalá, which we reached in four days more or less. As we came in sight of the town two Indians appeared and said that the chieftainess of this province wanted peace, and that they all wanted to serve [the Spaniards], but that a daughter of hers and some of the lords and nobles of the towns subject to her were prepared for war, and waiting on a hill that was within sight of the chieftainess' house. We proceeded in formation, and on entering the town we saw poultry from Castile[8] and found the people in their houses, except for the ones on the hill, whom we went after and routed. At the end of twenty days more or less that we spent in this town, all the land was at peace. Here Nuño de Guzmán was given some gold and silver. It is a good town, with an abundance of everything, and in a very good region. And thus we departed.

We passed through several more towns, some at war[9] and others at peace, and in eight or nine days we reached the town of Nochistlan[10] where we stayed twenty-five days or more. From here we made many incursions but no one came to seek peace except some messengers [from the town of Xalpa]. Here in Nochistlan three Indians from Toluca were burned, accused of offering sacrifices. After staying here the aforementioned length of time, we departed from this town leaving it completely devastated.

Five days later we arrived at Teul. From here incursions were made in various places, but no one sought peace, and here also Nuño de Guzmán was informed that there were two roads leading to the province of Temoaque, which was his destination. He sent the inspector Peralmindez Chirinos with some men by one of the roads, and took the other road himself. All of us set out on the same day, and since I was not in Chirinos' company I cannot say what occurred to him on the way.

After ten days more or less, our party arrived at a small town where the Indians came out to us in peace. Here Villaroel, the *maestre de campo*,[11] hanged one of the Indian allies we had taken with us from these parts.

Two days after leaving this town we reached Ahuacatlan,[12] whose lords came out to receive us and lodge us in their houses, giving us a plentiful supply of maize and all the necessities. Nuño de Guzmán asked these Indians for a large quantity of gold and silver, and they gave him some. Besides having given these things, they also brought us about eight hundred bearers, but not satisfied with this, Nuño de Guzmán ordered the lords seized, and some of their houses were looted. Cifontes, a resident of Colima, can give fuller information on this, since he was engaged with the lords in supplying the camp.

We left this town, and in five or six days reached the town and province of Jalisco, where we found the aforementioned Chirinos who had come by the other road. At the time we arrived some of these Indians were at war and others at peace. I refer to Jalisco and Tepic. In this town Nuño de Guzmán named Cristóbal de Oñate comptroller, Francisco Verdugo treasurer, Juan de Sámano factor, and Chirinos inspector.[13] He also sent Barrios to find a place to ford the Río Grande,[14] as it is called, and he crossed to the other side and burned the land, not leaving a house standing if it could be burned down. And when he returned, he hanged two Indians from Huexotzingo, or perhaps it was one, I do not remember.

Four days after leaving this town we came to a river called the Espíritu Santo, and when we had crossed it and were mounted and at attention Nuño de Guzmán made a proclamation ordering all the scriveners and notaries, in the name of His Majesty, to give the title of Mayor España to the land that lay beyond the river, and to give it this name in the deeds they recorded.[15] Then he took his sword in his hand and cut some branches from a tree as a sign of taking possession, and had the act certified by a scrivener. Here we had an encounter with the Indians,[16] as Your Lordship and Graces undoubtedly know; and two days later we left this place.

In another two days we reached the town of Umitlan, where we stayed a month and a half more or less. After we had made many incursions from here the Indians gave themselves up peaceably. In Teul they had told Nuño de Guzmán that this was the province of Temoaque. In this town of Umitlan some Indians were taken sick and died, but they were not many.

About seven days after we left this place we reached the province of Aztatlán, which is near the South Sea.[17] Here no warriors came out against us. Because of the heavy rains Nuño de Guzmán decided to spend the rainy season here. We arrived the fifteenth or twentieth of July, and having stayed the remainder of July and the month of August, on September seventh Nuño de Guzmán received a letter from the jurists Delgadillo and Matienzo informing him of the marqués' arrival,[18] whereupon he decided to send Chirinos to the city of Mexico, accompanied by ten or twelve horsemen. On the twentieth of September a storm struck Aztatlán, with winds and torrential rains, which destroyed most of the houses. It was such a deluge that we thought we would all perish, and more than a thousand Indians who were sick in bed were drowned [in the floods].

The storm lasted two days and when it had passed the Indians were exhausted; and because they had been here so long without any reason for staying, more than eight thousand Indians and free servants were taken sick and only about two hundred were able to stand on their feet. Because of this and the hunger they were suffering, some of the healthy ones took the risk of running away, which prompted Nuño de Guzmán to hang about fifty Indians. On seeing themselves in these circumstances, Tapiezuela, the lord of Mexico,[19] and the lords of Tlatelolco, Huexotzingo and Tlaxcala, and many other lords and nobles of the land, begged Nuño de Guzmán to keep for himself all their emblems, which were of gold and very handsome green plumes, and to allow them to go back to Jalisco until the rains passed, so they would not die as so many of their men had.[20] After much argument and discussion between them, in effect he refused. All the aforementioned Indians died here, and so did many of the lords and nobles, while others died in Chiametla, the town we went on to from here. Here in Aztatlán Nuño de Guzmán hanged a [mutinous] Spaniard and punished another.

Finding himself helpless, confined in these marshes without any Indians, Nuño de Guzmán decided to send Gonzalo López to the city of Mechuacan with fifteen horsemen and twenty foot soldiers, to fetch Indian bearers to get him out of here. López was also to bring cattle, and Spanish settlers by force if necessary, or so it was said; I remit the question to Gonzalo López who received the instructions. After López had left, I went with Samaniego, custodian of the arsenal in the city of Mexico, to ask Nuño de Guzmán's permission to go and pacify the town of Chiametla. He granted us permission, and we pacified it.

When Gonzalo López had been gone forty days, Nuño de Guzmán sent me out with ten horsemen to look for him and tell him to hasten with the Indians, for without them he was powerless. In a few days I found López in the aforementioned town of Ahuacatlan, with about a thousand Indians from the province of Mechuacan, and many nobles whom he had in chains. With these Indians and his horsemen he was raiding and burning the land thereabout, and he had built a large corral where he kept a great number of Indian men, women and children imprisoned, the men with shackles around their necks and the women tied with ropes in groups of ten.

While thus raiding and destroying the land, a horseman named Alcaráz captured a noble in some town that was subject to this province, and took him before Gonzalo López, who put him in irons and told him that if he brought many Indians to carry the baggage, all those women and children would be freed. Tearfully the noble replied that he would be glad to bring them [in exchange for] the women and children, because the latter had not killed any Spaniards but had always served them. He brought one or two hundred men, I do not remember the number, and Gonzalo López then shackled them all. The women and children, as well as the bearers and lords from Mechuacan, were all kept in bonds, some of them in chains, others in neck shackles, and the smallest children tied in fives. And in this manner we departed.

At the end of six days we reached Jalisco. Through one of their nobles whom we had with us they came in peace and offered to serve us, but asked for our assurance that they would not be subjected to the destruction suffered by their neighboring towns. This assurance was given, and some two thousand men came in peace. And while they were in this state of peace, and supplying us generously with food, Gonzalo López was having a large and very strong corral made in which he planned to imprison them by some ruse. This corral was separate from the one containing all the aforementioned captives. Then because he became sick he went away, leaving me with part of the horse and foot soldiers, and taking a thousand of the Indians from Jalisco.

In two days he reached the province of Zacualpa. Since I was not with him I did not witness what happened in this town, but saw only that he brought back about five hundred souls in captivity: men, women and children. When I asked the Spaniards who had been there how they had fared, they said: "Everything is now done by trickery and deceit. When the lord and nobles came out to us in peace we surrounded and captured them; then our Indian allies killed more than two thousand people. But the most pitiful of all were the children left to die along the way." The persons who know what occurred in this town, and whose names I shall provide in a memorandum, can give Your Lordship and Graces a more extensive account.

When Gonzalo López, on returning to Jalisco, was ready to put into effect his aforementioned plan to trap the natives of this town, the latter were warned, it was said, by someone who had seen his past cruelties. Therefore no more than two hundred men were captured, and another two hundred women and children. On seeing his prey slip out of his hands, Gonzalo López immediately burned one of the great lords of Jalisco.

Then these Indians who had come to us peaceably in Ahuacatlan, Zacualpa and Jalisco were branded, and some distributed among the Spaniards. The rest were shackled or tied, and taken with us when we left. On the march, which lasted ten or twelve days, all the children of the captive mothers died,[21] and many other Indians also.

We returned to Aztatlán and loaded these Indians with the baggage left there by Nuño de Guzmán, who had gone to Chiametla, the town that Samaniego and I had pacified. Although I did not see it, it seems that the Indians of Chiametla, who had carried part of the baggage out of Aztatlán, developed huge sores on their backs and for this reason the town was in revolt. We took up the march from Aztatlán, and four of the horsemen, who were Rodrigo Ximón, Alonso Gómez and two others whose names I do not recall, went ahead cutting down from the trees the bodies of the Indians who had hanged themselves in desperation. There were more than five hundred, in my opinion, and we removed them so that the Indians accompanying us would not see them and run away. And so we reached Chiametla, where Nuño de Guzmán had gone to raid the land, and where he supposedly had hanged four lords, and had all the land in revolt.

Then all the Indians we had brought with us were distributed among the Spaniards in lots of four and ten. Each Spaniard shackled his, and the Indians were even sold among them. The slaves also were distributed, and for each slave received, a peso was paid to the Crown. And leaving this province devastated and in a state of war, we departed.

After four days we arrived at a village that is subject to a province called Quezala. Here two Spaniards died who had left Chiametla sick and had been refused permission to go back with Francisco Verdugo.[22] Nuño de Guzmán punished a Spaniard here, and stayed three or four days expecting some town to offer itself peaceably, but the people were more inclined to flee from him because of the cruelties committed in Chiametla. And so we left.

Four days later we came to the village of Frisoles. We stayed two weeks here searching for the way ahead, because there were lagoons and thickly wooded mountains all around. After leaving this place we came in five days to the province of Piaxtla which is near the South Sea. We were here five or six days and they did not come to us in peace, so we departed leaving it burned and devastated. In this town all our Indian friends wanted to be allowed to go back. [By order of Nuño de Guzmán] one was roasted alive and some of the others, I do not remember how many, were hanged.

After ten days of passing through towns that made war on us and would not submit peaceably, we reached Cihuatlan, which is said to be the city of women.[23] Since we had no interpreter who could understand them well enough, we did not find out whether they lived alone or had husbands, but we saw many women and very few men. The town is on the bank of a river near the sea. Here Nuño de Guzmán hanged a Spaniard. And during all this march our Indian friends who carried the baggage were kept chained by the neck.

We left this place at war, and during the next ten days passed through many other towns at war, then we reached Culiacan where we had an encounter with the Indians. We routed them, and it was God's will that although these Indians use poison they did not wound any of the Spaniards. They wounded several of the horses, who died of the poison. This province is well supplied with maize, fish and fruits, and has settlements along the river as far as the sea. We followed the river down to the last of the towns, where we searched in two parties for the way ahead, but were unable to find it because a mountain range descends to the sea, and the country ahead is uninhabited except for some savages who eat roots and wear deerskins.

Not being able to go further, we went back up the river, thinking that if we followed it inland it would take us through the mountains. But after following it for ten days it became narrower and we could not pass, so we had to find our way back to Culiacan, and this was a detour of forty leagues. Here the Indians asked us where we thought we were going, for all the coast ahead and the land in the interior were uninhabited. Samaniego set out with twenty horsemen and explored for forty leagues up the coast but never found any settlements; nor did the forty foot soldiers who went north over the mountains, though they walked a hundred leagues there and back. Having made these explorations, which took about three months, we left.

In ten days we reached a town called Guamóchiles, situated in a valley twenty-five leagues from Culiacan. From here Gonzalo López set out with ten horsemen and some foot soldiers, across the mountains toward the North Sea.[24]

With many difficulties he was able to cross the mountains in forty days, and found on the other side a village of about thirty houses, where two Spaniards were killed. From there he wrote to Nuño de Guzmán telling him how he had reached the plains.

Having been taken sick, Nuño de Guzmán was carried in a litter by the nobles and other Indians of the city of Mexico, and in this way we marched over forty-five leagues of mountains. When we had crossed all the mountains and thought our difficulties were at an end, Gonzalo López arrived with his men, and they were all very thin. López told Nuño de Guzmán how he had covered a hundred and fifty leagues of plains without finding a settlement or a trail or road, and that if it had not been for some maize they had left buried they would all have died, and were even thinking of killing a horse to eat. He said he had left eighty bushels of maize back there with six horsemen guarding it, and that if Nuño de Guzmán went on, he and all his men would die, since it was uninhabited desert except for a few wild Indians, and he should therefore consider the matter carefully.

There were many altercations, we were running short of food and supplies, and it was seventy leagues back to the province of Culiacan. On seeing this, about two hundred of the Indians ran away; it was heard later that they went to the city of Mexico. Nuño de Guzmán therefore decided to talk to the men, telling them that he wanted to establish a Spanish settlement in Culiacan, another in Jalisco, and another in Teul, and was satisfied that we should go back. And so we left.

The Spaniards ate nothing but meat, and the Indians ate whatever greens they could find, therefore many of the Indians died. After many difficulties, and losing about thirty horses and mares down the precipices, we got back to the province of Culiacan, where all the rest of the Indians died that we had taken with us from these parts.

Two months later Nuño de Guzmán founded and built his city here, and gave Indians to all the Spanish settlers. I was told by persons close to Nuño de Guzmán that he gave them permission to brand Indians and use them for mining gold.[25]

We left, retracing the route we had come over, and found only three towns that were pacified. We reached the town of Zapotes where we learned that Your Lordship and Graces had authorized Don Luis de Castilla to settle Jalisco, so on the next morning Nuño de Guzmán arrived in Tepic and named alcaldes and councilmen, and founded his city.

I wish to make known to Your Lordship and Graces that in the town of Culiacan many Indians from the city of Mexico remain in chains, crying out to the

Lord God, and asking why they were left behind as slaves after two years of carrying the baggage on their backs, from which they were worn out; that they wanted to go back to their wives and children. In particular, of the one thousand and two hundred Tlaxcalans who went with us, no more than twenty survived, and these are in chains except for two who are with Gonzalo López, as Your Lordship and Graces can inform themselves. And all that I have said here, I have seen with my own eyes, with the exception of the things I state my uncertainty about in this account.

GARCIA DEL PILAR

notes

J U A N DIAZ

1. Cuba.

2. These were the temples, erected on a pyramidal base, and usually with
   steps on one side leading to the temple proper, the whole finished in
   cream-white stucco. The pyramid as an architectural form was common to
   many of the cultures of Meso-America, from Zacatecas in the north to
   Nicaragua in the south, and the number of such buildings throughout the
   Mexican "empire" was estimated by Torquemada at more than forty thousand. Originally natural mounds selected possibly because of the ideolog-
   ical association of *height* with *sky,* they gradually evolved as stone con-
   structions fitted over an artificial mound of dirt and rubble. In some instances a larger and more splendid pyramid was built over an older one,
   as was the case at Tenayuca near Mexico City, excavation of which disclosed five pyramids lying inside the outer one—like the layers of an onion,
   as J. Eric S. Thompson has expressed it.

3. A term of Caribbean origin transplanted by the Spaniards who had lived in
   the Antilles.

4. Mutilations and deformations of the body have occurred in all parts of the
   world, surviving today among certain primitive people. It can reasonably
   be assumed that these practices are religious in origin, even though they
   sometimes appear to be a question of aesthetic preference, as in the Mayan
   elongation of the head. Cranial deformation, however, did not exist among
   the other civilizations of Meso-America. Tattooing was common, and incrustations of the teeth; also piercing of the nose, lips and earlobes for or-
   namental studs, usually signifying rank. Other mutilations can be traced
   directly to religious penitences, since they involve the letting of blood—a
   vital fluid and magic essence indispensable to the sustenance of the gods.
   The earlobes and tongue most frequently suffered the prick of the flint

knife or cactus spine, to such an extent that the Spaniards found the Totonacs' ears virtually shredded. Uncommon in the north, but severe among the Maya and other southern peoples were penitences connected with other parts of the body including the sexual organs. Possibly circumcision, which was practiced by the Totonac and Olmec peoples of the gulf coast, had some relation to these penitences.

5. Various kinds of pipes were described by early observers, and a number of aromatic or narcotic substances besides tobacco were found to be inhaled by the Indians of the Antilles and the American continent. The pipes referred to here by Juan Díaz were short lengths of hollowed reed filled with a mixture of ground substances, and smoked in the manner of a cigarette. In the city of Mexico-Tenochtitlan these were commonly seen in the market place, either undecorated or painted with gold, or else with flowers, eagles, fish and other designs. The long tubular pipe is known to have been used by the Maya as early as the second century A.D., as depicted in a sculpture at Palenque showing a priest smoking. At Chichén Itzá a pipe was discovered which is remarkably like those of the prehistoric North American Indians. Clay pipes with bowls have been found in many parts of Mexico, and there is one from Oaxaca almost identical to the modern pipe. Cigar smoking was observed in the Antilles at the time of Columbus' voyage of discovery; however, it was the cigar itself which the natives of Haiti called tobacco, and not the leaves or plant. In Mexico the priests used tobacco in pellets to produce a state of trance for receiving divine revelation, but the simple pleasure of after-dinner smoking was enjoyed by Moctezuma who, Bernal Díaz del Castillo tells us, selected one of three gilt and painted pipes, took some smoke but not very much, and on this went to sleep.

6. Indian corn, which of course is not a root but a plant of the grass family, and indigenous to America. Díaz may have been thinking of cassava bread, made by the Indians of the Antilles from the root of the yucca. This was regularly carried by Spanish ships leaving the islands. According to Fray Bartolomé de las Casas, fifty pounds of cassava could sustain a man for one month. Maize was reported by explorers from Canada to Patagonia and was the principal crop of ancient American civilizations many centuries before Columbus. The bread referred to by the Spanish chroniclers has survived to this day as the *tortilla*, while *tamales* and *atole*, also made of ground maize, are of equally remote origin.

7. This amusing bit of insularity nevertheless states the Spaniards' general surprise and admiration at discovering indications of a true civilization, such as they had not seen in the Antilles or along the Spanish Main. Maya cities had their principal structures built around courts or plazas, and in the larger centers there were so-called palaces as well as the temples, which were rows of chambers on long low platforms, and probably occupied by the priests and nobility. The vaulted roof, though not the true arch with a keystone, was characteristic of these narrow rooms. In the Mexican Period at Chichén Itzá, about the year 1150, wide rooms were attained by the use of columns and wooden beams to support the vaults. The Maya used limestone, and burned and slaked it to make mortar which held together a mass of broken limestone. This was covered with facing stones polished on the outside but left rough on the inside in order to adhere to the mortar. The palaces were sometimes two and three storied, the upper stories usually receding and built over a solid core rather than over the lower rooms. Besides pyramids and palaces, a Maya city might contain stone-lined reservoirs, sweathouses, underground passages, and a court for the sacred ball game. Remains have been found of houses with stone foundations for the walls, such as those described by Juan Díaz, and probably they belonged to the nobility while the peasants and workers lived in settlements away from the center. The thatched huts of the latter have not changed materially since the Conquest.

8. A holy drink called *balche,* made from the fermented honey, was used as an offering to the gods and drunk for the purpose of cleansing the body of evil.

9. Peccaries.

10. Campeche.

11. Also called Champoton.

12. Fernández or Hernández de Córdoba personally suffered twelve arrow wounds at Potonchán, and lost fifty-two or nearly half of his men in a desperate retreat to the ships pursued by Indian warriors and canoes. He never recovered from his wounds, and died shortly after returning to Cuba.

13. The Spanish word *canoa* is of West Indian origin, and not Mayan nor Mexican. Bernal Díaz del Castillo called this boat piragua—also of Ara-

wakan and Cariban origin—describing it as a dugout. Judging by Juan Díaz' observations, the war canoe of the Indians in Tabasco carried up to thirty men, while according to Bernal Díaz it held forty and fifty in a standing position. A mural at Chichén Itzá depicts the three-man dugout canoe, probably the most commonly used.

14.   Spain.

15.   The author says *un mármol.*

16.   Jaguars and serpents are the two creatures most frequently represented in Meso-American art. Worship of the jaguar (ocelot), a god of the underworld or interior of the earth, reached obsessive proportions among the Olmecs of the lower Gulf of Mexico. The Toltecs of central Mexico, and later the Aztecs, had military orders of the eagle and the jaguar, symbolizing the sun in the sky and in the underworld.

17.   War prisoners were taken primarily to be offered in sacrifice, a practice which ensured the supply of human blood for the gods without depleting the home population. (See Note 24 to the Chronicle of Andrés de Tapia.)

18.   A beautiful and rare example of this art, also discovered at the Island of Sacrificios, may be seen in the National Museum of Mexico. The Mexican variety of alabaster, known as *tecali*, was found only in the Mixtec region of southern Puebla and northern Oaxaca, and exported to other regions. Since Sacrificios was a pilgrimage center, it is likely that the stones mentioned by Díaz were deposited as offerings by people of various parts. The most precious of stones were jade or jadeite, called *chalchíhuitl* by the Mexicans.

19.   While the Spanish ships had been exploring this part of the coast, the peoples of which were dominated by the Mexicans or Aztecs, a native of the town of Mictlancuautla ran to the city of Mexico-Tenochtitlan to tell Moctezuma of the strange apparitions he had seen on the water. The Mexican king received the news in some agitation, believing it to mean the return of Quetzalcoatl and the end of his own reign. Quetzalcoatl, one of the oldest gods of Meso-America, possibly antedating the birth of Christ, and known to the Maya as Kukulkan, was god of the wind; he was the morning star or Venus; the creator of man as well as his sustenance of maize; the discoverer of the science of the stars, and inventor of the calendar. Ce Acatl, the high

priest of this god, who took the name Quetzalcoatl as was customary, became king of the Toltecs in the tenth century and though he was a great
ruler he was eventually ousted by partisans of the more violent and blood-
thirsty god Tezcatlipoca. When Quetzalcoatl the priest-king left the Toltec
capital of Tula—considered by the Aztecs their cultural and spiritual home
—he went toward the east, promising to return and rule once more. The
year he would return would be Ce Acatl, the name of the year of his birth,
and which was his own given name. Ce Acatl-Quetzalcoatl, then, if it was
he who had appeared on the eastern shore, must be received in submission
and with the attention he merited, so Moctezuma sent emissaries to the
coast to receive him. These were the people the Spaniards saw on the
mainland at the Ximapan River, which they called the Banderas because
of the white banners the Indians raised and lowered. They had no idea, of
course, of the meaning of their welcoming, since verbal communication
was mutually unintelligible though voluble enough, each side thinking
whatever it found most suitable. When the Spaniards sailed away again,
Moctezuma's emissaries returned to Mexico to report that the god-men had
been persuaded to allow Moctezuma to finish out his days.

20. The soldiers were eager to obtain these because they thought them to be
made of gold, and according to Antonio de Herrera, official historian appointed by Philip II of Spain, they took back six hundred pieces. Copper
in Meso-America was used for certain simple tools such as hatchets, small
knives, hooks and awls, but for the most part flint and stone implements
were in use, some of them surviving long after the Conquest. On the other
hand metals were worked into astonishingly beautiful and intricate jewelry
and ornaments.

21. Havana.

22. The cross was a very common sign indicating the four cardinal points.
Among the Maya it was also a sun symbol, representing not only the four
quarters but the sun's rays. Cross bones appeared on many sculptures as a
death symbol, Maya religion being dualistic and preoccupied with good
and evil, life and death. In the Toltec representation of Quetzalcoatl this
god carried a shield with a symbol in the form of the Saint Andrew's cross,
which gave rise to the hopeful but mistaken notion that Quetzalcoatl had
been an early Christian apostle in disguise.

23. This observation is pure fantasy, although the hypothesis of a lost tribe of
Israel in America was taken seriously by some students, and has only in

modern times received a decent burial. The peoples of the Totonac and Olmec civilizations on the Mexican gulf coast circumcised male infants approximately one month after birth. According to one current theory, the practice may have been related to the religious penitences of the sexual organs, mentioned in Note 4 above. Fray Diego Duran went to considerable lengths in his work to showing parallels between the customs and histories of the Jews and Indians. (Duran, *The Aztecs: Historia de las Indias de Nueva España,* translated and annotated by Doris Heyden, introduction by Ignacio Bernal, Orion Press, New York, 1963.)

ANDRES DE TAPIA

1. The title of Marqués del Valle de Oaxaca was conferred on Cortés after the Conquest, on a return visit to Spain in 1529. It elevated him to the hereditary nobility, with a rank second only to that of duke. In colonial Mexico in the sixteenth century no further titles of nobility were conferred, but the seventeenth century saw the creation of nine marquises, nine counts, three viscounts, and two lords. The first dukedom was conferred in the eighteenth century. After Mexico's independence from Spain, both the constitutions of 1857 and 1917 explicitly disavowed titles of nobility or hereditary honors and prerogatives. (*Bravo Ugarte; Atienza*)

2. As a notary and then alcalde in Cuba, Cortés had years of experience in practical affairs, and with the connections he had made he was able to raise additional capital for outfitting the armada. Tapia has glossed over the more unsavory aspects of these activities, but Cortés himself laughingly told Fray Bartolomé de las Casas that during this period he had been rather an elegant corsair. The stern Las Casas was not amused.

3. Cozumel.

4. Lineal measure of 1.85 yards, originating as the approximation of a man's height.

5. In ordinary religious observance quail substituted for human hearts as an offering. Other offerings to the various gods included plants and flowers, precious stones, plumes, and dishes of food. Most common was copal incense, which was burned in every household.

6. Jerónimo de Aguilar.

7. A word of Caribbean origin.

8. Ancient measure of ship capacity, equivalent to five-sixths of a metric ton.

9. Tales of the miraculous and supernatural appear frequently in the six-teenth–century chronicles. See also the chronicle of Fray Francisco de Aguilar included in this volume.

10. They counted in units of twenty, the progression being as follows:

$$1 \times 20 = 20$$
$$20 \times 20 = 400$$
$$400 \times 20 = 8000 \ (xiquipilli \text{ in Nahuatl}; \ pic \text{ in Maya})$$
$$8000 \times 20 = 160,000$$
$$160,000 \times 20 = 3,200,000$$
$$3,200,000 \times 20 = 64,000,000$$

The *xiquipilli* or 8000 value could be multiplied by all the values from 1 to 8000 itself, the latter also giving the figure of 64,000,000. For astro-nomical calculations, particularly among the Maya, the progression was carried infinitely further.

11. The Indian woman referred to is Malinche, who became Cortés' mistress and the mother of his bastard son Martín Cortés. Her native tongue was Nahuatl, spoken by the peoples of the central plateau and other parts, but in Tabasco she had learned the Maya language. She and Jerónimo de Agui-lar communicated in Maya, which he translated to Spanish for Cortés. In addition to her charms and linguistic abilities, Malinche possessed a shrewdness that helped the Spaniards in many a knotty situation. Today the term *malinchismo* is used in a derogatory sense, meaning an abject preference for foreigners or things foreign.

12. Tapia and Cortés give the spelling as Muteczuma, and Bernal Díaz del Castillo as Montezuma. Correctly it is Motecuhzoma, "he who becomes enraged, or haughty," but for the sake of consistency I have chosen to use the more commonly accepted spelling Moctezuma throughout this book. Two *tlatoani* or "kings" of Mexico had this name, though they were not father and son; the one concerning us here was known to his people as Moctezuma the Younger.

13. In a most obscure sentence Tapia attempted to explain that the Mexicans, or Aztecs, had founded their city of Tenochtitlan on a small island of the densely populated Valley of Mexico, after many years of wandering in search of the land promised by their god Huitzilopochtli. This was a mere two hundred years before the Conquest. At first they subsisted by catching fish and other edible marine life, trading these to the older communities of the lakeshore for the things they needed. Gradually they enlarged their islet by constructing flats of cane wattling which they filled with earth, where they did their planting. These were the so-called floating gardens, intersected by canals, as they can be seen today at Xochimilco.

14. Tribute paid by one prince to another in recognition of superiority.

15. Villa Rica de la Veracruz. In 1525 it was moved to a point now called *la Antigua*, and in 1599 to its present site.

16. Since some of the ships belonged to Diego Velázquez, and there were other creditors in Cuba, Cortés needed the mates' testimony as legal justification for destroying the ships. Alonso Puerto Carrero and Francisco de Montejo, who sailed the remaining caravel to Spain, were officially questioned on this matter at La Coruña in 1520. They deposed that the ships' pilots and mates had sworn to the unseaworthiness of the vessels, and that "Hernando Cortés paid or undertook to pay their owners for them."

17. Charles V.

18. The cleric Juan Díaz was one of the conspirators, but Cortés did not punish him. Juan Escudero and Diego Cermeño were hanged, two others flogged, and Gonzalo de Umbría had his toes cut off.

19. Son of Christopher Columbus.

20. Now part of the Bahamas.

21. The more accepted version is that Hernández de Córdoba abandoned the idea of going for a cargo of slave labor, persuaded by his pilot Antón de Alaminos to sail west. Alaminos had been cabin boy on one of Christopher Columbus' voyages, and remembered that the Admiral was convinced there was land in that direction, but had not the ships to attempt the exploration. Since these were uncharted waters Hernández de Córdoba

sailed cautiously, furling the ships' sails by night (there were two caravels and a brigantine, carrying 110 soldiers). A hurricane tossed them about for two days, and after twenty-one days of navigation they sighted the tip of Yucatan. Credit for the discovery of New Spain belongs in a very real sense to Alaminos, for he was chief pilot on all three voyages: those of Hernández de Córdoba in 1517, Grijalva in 1518, and Cortés in 1519.

22. The Totonac people of Cempoala and surrounding towns.

23. Cortés had sent ambassadors to the independent state of Tlaxcala, asking to be received as a friend, at the suggestion of the Cempoalan allies accompanying him. The four chieftains of Tlaxcala heard the ambassadors with mixed feelings, then decided among themselves to play the game both ways. While the ambassadors were detained with one excuse and another, Xicotencatl, son of one of the chieftains, was to march toward the border with a great army and try to stop the Spaniards. If he succeeded, Tlaxcala would have defended her honor, but if he failed they could blame the attack on the fierce Otomí Indians whom they allowed to live on their borders, and there would be time enough to make amends later.

24. However much our latter-day romantics minimize this aspect of Indian reality, the chilling fact is that an agreement existed among these neighbors whereby both sides were assured of a supply of sacrificial victims. Tlaxcala, Huexotzingo, and Cholula on one side of the bargain, and Mexico, Texcoco, and Tacuba on the other, met by turns in a ceremonial combat called, prettily enough, *xochiyaoyotl* or flowery war. This took place during the first days of their twenty-day religious "month." Each side endeavored not to kill but to take captive as many of the opponents as possible, to be appropriately offered in due course to their respective gods. But the Tlaxcalans held the short end of the stick, for at the same time that they owed their existence to the pact, they were kept by the Mexicans from developing their trade. Alliance with the Spaniards against the Mexicans therefore seemed to hold out the promise of freedom and revenge.

25. Copal, from the Nahuatl *copalli.*

26. Captain Diego de Ordaz is the first man known to have climbed to the crater of Popocatepetl ("smoking mountain"), 17,888 feet above sea level. The Indian guides and bearers refused to go more than halfway, saying no human steps had ever penetrated its fastnesses. The other nine Spaniards

reached intermediate points, none but Ordaz climbing all the way. During the descent the volcano erupted but the party saved itself by getting under a boulder. The Indian people attributed Ordaz with the qualities of a god, coming to him to offer gifts and kiss his garments. (*Orozco y Berra.*)

27. Not slaves but *tlameme*, who were trained from childhood for the occupation of bearer. Pack animals were unknown to the inhabitants of Meso-America. Normally the *tlameme* traveled at a steady jog for fifteen miles a day carrying a load of fifty pounds, and made journeys as long as three hundred and fifty miles. They moved the freight of the empire: cotton, maize, beans, cacao, rubber, paper in rolls, gold, precious stones and feathers (more highly valued than gold), tobacco, building materials, and copal, most of which flowed into the city of Tenochtitlan in the form of tribute.

28. The pass between the summits of Ixtaccihuatl and Popocatepetl.

29. Huitzilopochtli, a solar diety, was the tribal god of the Aztecs, and his worship by subject nations was obligatory. Of the two temples at the top of the great pyramid of Tenochtitlan, which faced west, the one on the right was dedicated to Huitzilopochtli, and the one on the left to Tlaloc, god of rain. Three lesser pyramids within the sacred compound were dedicated to the sun, to the god Xipe, and an earlier temple of Huitzilopochtli.

30. Pulque.

31. Obsidian.

32. There is no good reason to be skeptical of this figure, considering that in four days alone, on the occasion of the consecration of the temple in 1486, it was estimated that King Ahuizotl had 72,344 victims sacrificed. Another estimate put it at 64,060. Allowing for exaggeration, it is still possible that in the intervening years up to 1519 the *tzompantli* or skull rack could have gained the proportions given by Tapia.

33. Huitzilopochtli.

34. Honorary municipal post entailing certain civil functions.

CORTES

(These notes are by Francis A. MacNutt)

1. Said to have been introduced by a negro slave who came with Pánfilo de Narváez (Torquemada, lib. iv., cap. lxxx.).

2. Texcoco.

3. Tezmulocan: present name is San Martin Tesmelucan, in the state of Puebla.

4. This was the usual flag of truce. It was in the form of a square of netting. Cortés, with Israelitish rapidity, calculated its money value at four *marks*, and Bernal Díaz was equally quick at estimating it to be worth eighty *dollars:* eight ounces went the mark.

5. Coanacochtzin succeeded his brother Cacamatzin who was strangled by order of Cortés on the Sorrowful Night. He had long aspired to his brother's crown, and, with his younger brother Ixtlilxochitl, shared in the betrayal of Cacamatzin when he was seized in his palace at Texcoco and carried by boat to Mexico. Ixtlilxochitl had already met Cortés on the road from Tlascala and Tlepehuacan, bearing likewise his flag of truce, and offering his friendship and alliance.

6. Coatlinchan and Huexothla. From Chiantla and Texcoco the villages and haciendas extended in an unbroken succession to Coatepec.

7. Now called Tenango Tepopula.

8. These people came begging forgiveness for their part in the former hostilities and offering assistance; thus one by one, the adjacent cities and tribes abandoned the capital to its fate.

9. Cortés misses this name entirely; which is not to be wondered at, as the boy was called Ahuaxpitcatzin.

10. Meaning Coanacochtzin.

11. He is described, by the historian Ixtlilxochitl, as being as white as a Spaniard, tall, graceful, and of genial manners. He spoke Castilian fluently, and

almost every evening after supper he spent much time in discussion with Cortés, who became very fond of him. The lad was placed on the throne of Texcoco, and Antonio de Villareal and Pedro Sánchez Farfan had charge of his education, while Prince Ixtlilxochitl, who had also been baptised under the name of Fernando, had command of Texcocan military operations.

12. Already mentioned as alguacil mayor of Veracruz; he was a fellow townsman of Cortés from Medellin and one of the bravest and most competent captains in Mexico, being also extremely popular with his men, and always faithful to his commander. In temperament, he was a happy contrast to Pedro de Alvarado. His death at an early age, which took place in 1528 at Palos, was a great grief to Cortés, who attended him in his last hours.

13. Chalco was tributary to Mexico but under a ruler of its own.

14. Juan Yuste came originally with Pánfilo de Narváez, passing later into service under Cortés. He started with five horsemen and twenty-five foot to bring some gold from Veracruz, and at Tlascala he was joined by three hundred natives. Ignorant of the events which had followed upon Alvarado's massacre in Mexico, he and his party proceeded with entire confidence, and were surprised with the consequences Cortés describes.

15. Aiutecatl and Teutepil.

16. History hardly records a greater *tour de force* than the construction, transport, and launching of these brigantines: the glory of the conception belongs to Cortés, but the merit of its execution was due to the Tlascalans. Martin López, a ship-carpenter, was in charge of the work, assisted by a few other Spaniards, but the brunt of the work and the cost were borne by the Tlascalans.

Prescott recalls two instances of similar undertakings but on a smaller scale with less distance to cover: the first was during the siege of Taranto by Hannibal, and the second at the same place, seventeen centuries later under Gonsalvo de Córdoba. Balboa also built four small boats on the isthmus of Darien, two of which he succeeded in carrying to the coast and launching successfully. For magnitude of the undertaking, distance of transport, number of men engaged, with no beasts of burden to help them, and the importance of the issue at stake, the achievement of Cortés and the Tlascalans stands alone. The arrival of the convoy at Texcoco was rightly made the occasion of a triumphal entry, to the sound of music and salutes, while the crowds enthusiastically cheered for Castile and Tlascala. It was found necessary to build a canal in which to join the parts of the brigantines together, and from which to launch them safely on the waters of the lake. In the *Voyage de Thomas Gage*, the author, who travelled in Mexico in 1626, says that, as the tallow and oil required in the ship building were very scarce in Texcoco, they were obtained from the dead bodies of the Indians slain in the daily skirmishes. As the fat of dead Indians was found useful for dressing wounds, there is no reason why it should not do equally well as ship's tallow. Cortés had previously built two brigantines on the lake, bringing the cordage, sails, and iron, from the dismantled ships in Veracruz, just to show Moctezuma what the "water houses" were like, but he had also counted on using them in case of need; they had, however, been destroyed during the fighting with Alvarado, while Cortés was absent.

17. Xatlocan: a place near Zumpango surrounded by a lake of the same name: it was a dependency of Texcoco.

18. Cuauhtitlan, three leagues from Mexico.

19. Tenayucan.

20. Atzcapotzalco, barely one league from Mexico; called the town of Silversmiths as it was famous for its metal work.

21. Huaxtepec.

22. Ayachapichtla; Sandoval was not disposed to attack because of his own extreme weariness, and the exhausted condition of his men and horses, but the captain Luis Marin counselled him on no account to withdraw, as upon the Chalcans, who were watching only to see which side was the stronger in order to give their alliance to the victor, the moral effect would be bad.

23. Santiago (St. James) was the patron Saint of Spain, and from the times of the Moorish wars his name had been their battle cry. Bernal Díaz naively relates that this battle was fought and won by the Indians of Tlascala and Chalco, the Spaniards being more interested in capturing Indian women and collecting booty than in slaying the enemy, adding also that the cruelties of the Indians were so shocking that the Spaniards tried to save the enemy from their own allies. Bernal Díaz attacks Gomara's ac-

count of the stream being red with blood, and says that, while some wounded Mexicans did make their way down to the water, in seeking to escape, and it may have been discoloured for the length of time required to say an "Ave Maria," it is untrue that anyone suffered from thirst on that account, as the town possessed several fountains of the finest water.

24. Bernal Díaz relates that Quauhtemotzin was so enraged when he heard of the defection of the Chalcans and of the hostilities against him, in which they had taken part with the Spaniards, that he despatched a force of twenty thousand warriors against them, which was transported across the lake in two thousand canoes. Sandoval had barely got back to Texcoco and had not even had time to make his report to the commander, when an express arrived from Chalco with the news that things were in a worse state than ever. Cortés, hastily assuming that Sandoval had returned too soon, leaving his mission only half accomplished, fell into a rage, and ordered Sandoval's instant return to Chalco, without hearing a word of what he had to say in explanation. Sandoval was so much hurt at this injustice that on his second return to Texcoco bringing the prisoners, he would have nothing to say to Cortés in spite of the latter's apologies and protests. The two men did afterwards make up this quarrel, and became as good friends as ever. There was also much grumbling over the partition of the slaves; first His Majesty's fifth was deducted, then the fifth belonging to Cortés, then the officers took their shares, so that by the time it came to allotting any to the soldiers there was not much of any value left. Bernal Díaz says that those who were in favour with Cortés, bought their slaves privately and had them branded, paying the price to him: many slaves also escaped or disappeared, but the soldiers were credited with their value, which was charged against them in the division of the spoils.

25. Bernal Díaz speaks of but one ship, on board which came Julian de Alderete, royal treasurer; also Fray Pedro Melgarejo de Urrea, a Franciscan, of whom further mention will be made, and many others. The welcome news was brought that Juan de Fonseca, the Bishop of Burgos, was out of favour with the Emperor.

26. Tozopan, Mexicalzingo, and Nautlan.

27. Tlamanalco: a little more than one league from Chalco.

28. Xiuhtepec.

29. Cuauhnahuac: the present Cuernavaca. This town, the ancient capital of the Tlahuica tribes, situated on an isolated sort of promontory at an elevation of over five thousand feet, and surrounded, save on one side, by a narrow but profound cañon which was impassable, was defended by a strong garrison under Coatzin, its lord. The feat of the Tlascalan, to which Cortés does scanty justice, was indeed remarkable, and is described by Bernal Díaz, who claims also to have followed on the heels of the intrepid warrior. Two immense trees growing on opposite sides of the ravine, inclined towards one another until their branches met; seeing this the bold Tlascalan conceived the plan of crossing by this aërial bridge, and, with an agility worthy of his conception, he safely passed on the swaying boughs over the dizzy height, and slid down the tree trunk on the other side, while the garrison of Cuernavaca were fighting elsewhere, and unobservant of his achievement. About thirty Spaniards and a number of Tlascalans followed his example, three of whom lost their balance and fell into the stream below. Bernal Díaz says that it was a frightful undertaking, and that he himself became quite blind and giddy from the great height and danger. Indeed it was no small thing for a man, weighted with arms and armour, to essay such a feat, and if the credit of the invention belongs to the Tlascalan, we cannot withhold our admiration from the thirty Spaniards who had the hardihood to follow him.

Cuernavaca is the present capital of the State of Morelos, and is one of the most beautiful and interesting towns in Mexico, while its situation is hardly excelled in picturesqueness and grandeur by any other in the world. The palace, which Cortés afterwards built there, still stands, and a charming villa, with luxuriant gardens overhanging the great *barranca* which was built by a Spaniard, Laborda, in the XVIIIth century, became a favourite resort of the unfortunate Emperor Maximilian during his brief and luckless reign.

30. The name Xochimilco signifies "field of flowers": the town was situated on the left bank of the lake of the same name.

31. Cortés searched in vain for this Indian who saved his life, but, as he could never be found dead or alive, he finally declared that he was persuaded that it was not an Indian but his holy patron St. Peter who had rescued him. Clavigero pertinently notes that, in this battle as in many others, the Indians might easily have killed Cortés had they not determined to take him alive and sacrifice him. Bernal Díaz attributes the rescue of Cortés to a Castilian soldier, Cristóbal de Olea, who led a body of Tlascalans to

his relief, but makes no mention of any one particular Tlascalan. Cortés may, however, be supposed to know better, and he refers to Olea as "a servant of mine who helped raise the horse." Olea received three frightful wounds from the deadly *maquahuitl,* a weapon which the Mexicans wielded with great address.

The fighting in and around Xochimilco lasted from the 15th of April until the morning of Friday the 20th, when the Spaniards arrived in Tlacopan (Tacuba), and, though Cortés says little about the events of those days, his men suffered considerably. While a small division was engaged in pillaging some storehouses near Xochimilco, the Mexicans attacked them; wounding a number and taking Juan de Lara, Alonso Hernández, and two other soldiers of Andres de Monjaraz's company prisoners. These men were carried in triumph to Temixtitan where, after being questioned by Quauhtemotzin, they were sacrificed and their arms and legs taken to be exhibited in the neighbouring provinces as a forecast of the fate awaiting the remainder of the white men (Bernal Díaz, cap. cxlv.).

Cortés wished to leave behind the spoils taken at Xochimilco rather than be cumbered with them, but yielded to the clamours of his men, who declared they were able to defend what they had taken. The arrival in Tlacopan was marked, as Cortés relates, by the capture of two more Spaniards, Francisco Martin Vendabal and Pedro Gallego, and the commander, on this occasion, made a rare display of feeling which led to the composition of a romance or ballad, long in popular vogue—

> "En Tacuba está Cortés
> Con su escuadron esforzado,
> Triste estaba y muy penoso,
> Triste y con gran cuidado,
> La una mano en la mejilla
> Y la otra en el costado," etc.

Standing on a lofty teocalli, a group of the leaders, including Julian de Alderete and Fray Pedro Melgarejo, surveyed the country, with the great capital floating on the waters of its lake, and one Alonzo Perez, noting the pensive sadness of the commander's mien, begged him not to feel dejected, for losses and destruction were incident to warfare, but that of him it could never be said that like Nero he had watched the burning city, quoting the couplet—

> "Mira Nero de Tarpeya
> A Roma come de ardia."

Cortés answered, calling him to witness how often he had begged the Mexicans to make peace and save themselves, adding that his sadness was not for any one cause alone, but from thinking of all the hardships still to be endured in reconquering the city, which with God's help they must now undertake.

32. Huitzilopocho is the present Cherubusco. Cuitaquaca was Cuitlahuac and is now called Tlahua; the last town mentioned should be Mixquic.

33. Citlatlepoc.

34. Acolman, where Cortés first learned that reinforcements had arrived from Veracruz.

35. Chinantla: the lance heads of black obsidian which are frequently mentioned were chiefly manufactured here, and were called by the same name. Chinantla now forms part of the state of Oaxaca.

36. The feast fell upon Sunday April 28th, and was chosen for the launching of the brigantines. All the Spaniards received the sacraments; Fray Olmedo said Mass at an altar erected near the lake and blessed the boats. Amidst salvos of artillery, strains of music from the Christian and Indian bands, and the enthusiastic cries of *"Castilla! Tlascala!"* from the crowds, the brigantines glided gracefully into the lake. A solemn *Te Deum* closed the ceremony.

37. Pedro de Alvarado was one of four brothers all of whom fought under the command of Cortés; Jorge served afterwards in Guatemala, and died in Madrid in 1540; Gómez died in Peru, and Juan, a bastard brother, died at sea while going to Cuba to bring horses. Pedro was one of the most daring and cruel of the Spanish captains; two exploits gained him a conspicuous place in the annals of of the conquest, the first being the massacre of the nobles during the religious dance in the great temple, which provoked such terrible consequences, and the second his renowned leap which still holds its place amongst the heroic feats of history under the name of *El Salto de Alvarado,* a street in Mexico near the spot of the alleged jump perpetuating the legend.

Bernal Díaz denies the fact, and bluntly explains that the story took its origin from a libellous refrain or *pasquinade* composed by a soldier who had a sharp faculty for such rhyming. This represented Alvarado as deserting his two hundred and fifty men during the retreat of the *Noche Triste,* saving himself by jumping his horse over a canal, and it passed, according to Díaz, into the common stock of camp stories and jokes. This desertion was one of the accusations presented in his trial (record published by D. José Ramírez, Mex. 1847) to which Alvarado answered that he had held his men together as long as he could, but that it was they who deserted him, leaving him wounded, with his horse killed, and that he escaped only by a soldier taking him up behind him on his horse in the fight; nothing is said about any "leap." Cortés likewise never mentions it. The legend will never die, for it is of those which please popular fancy and become enshrined in the historical folk-lore, which is imperishable.

After the conquest, he was made governor of Cuauhtemallan and Chiapa, but his restless spirit spurred him to other adventures, and he fitted out an expedition in 1535, by royal licence, composed of some five or more ships, carrying fifteen hundred men, and the necessary horses and arms, bound for Peru, where he landed at Puerto Viejo, marching thence to Quito. His arrival was unwelcome to Pizarro and Diego Almargo, who solved the difficulty by buying out his armament for 100,000 *castellanos* said at the time to have been an enormous price. He returned to Mexico, and undertook other ventures to the Spice Islands and California, and was finally killed in 1541 by a kick from a horse. When dying, he was asked where he suffered, to which he replied "In my soul."

Alvarado was called *Tonatiuh* (the sun) by the natives, on account of his high colouring and red beard; he was handsome, physically strong and brave, a typical swashbuckler of his period, cruel to the Indians, faithless to his friends, of quick temper, poor judgment, and known as a confirmed liar. Bernal Díaz fought in Alvarado's division during the siege.

38. Although a number of the men had been sailors or fishermen, and consequently knew something about handling boats, none of them wanted to act as rowers for the brigantines, and it was with difficulty that Cortés completed his crews. Many of the natives of Palos, Triana, and other seaports, whom he ordered to take the oars, even objected on the score of their gentle birth, but the commander enforced his orders in spite of all excuses and protests. Each brigantine displayed the royal standard as well as its own particular ensign (Bernal Díaz).

39. According to Bernal Díaz, who was in Alvarado's division, Olid had taken possession of all the available houses in Acolman for himself and his troops, marking the houses thus appropriated with green branches, so that when

Alvarado's division reached the town there were no quarters for them. The soldiers of the two divisions almost fell to fighting, and the two commanders had challenged one another, but several of the cooler-headed officers interfered and restored a semblance of peace; but Alvarado and Olid were never afterwards friends. Cortés sent the Franciscan, Fray Pedro Melgarejo and Captain Luis Marin, as his peace-makers.

Another incident occurred at this time, which Cortés passes over in silence. This was the desertion of the Tlascalan general, Xicotencatl, who left the army, accompanied by a few followers, and returned to Tlascala. Various reasons are given for his action; Bernal Díaz attributes it to jealousy of Chichimecatl, and a perfidious plan to get possession of his lands while the latter was absent, fighting against Mexico. Herrera ascribes his desire to return home, to a love affair (lib. i., cap. xvii.). There had been a quarrel between a Spanish soldier and a Tlascalan chief, in which the latter was badly wounded; the matter was hushed up, so that Cortés should not hear it, as he was very strict in such matters; thus the soldier remained unpunished and as Xicotencatl was a relative of the wounded chief he left (Prescott, lib. vi., cap. iv.). Cortés first sent some Tlascalans to seek to induce him to return, and, this failing, he despatched some Spanish horsemen, with orders to arrest the general and bring him back. He simultaneously sent news of the affair to the Senate of Tlascala, informing the senators that amongst Spaniards, desertion was punishable by death. The versions of Xicotencatl's end do not agree. Herrera describes his death by hanging in public at Texcoco, while Bernal Díaz says he was executed where he was captured. Xicotencatl had always mistrusted the Spaniards, nor could the blandishments of Cortés nor the popular sentiment in Tlascala ever change his opinion. He was opposed to the alliance, and after fighting the Spaniards in the field, he continued to oppose them in the councils of his people. Cortés was aware of his sentiments and conscious of the bad effect such an example of desertion would have if left unpunished; hence it is likely he was glad to be rid of an ally on whose fidelity he could not count. Xicotencatl's act of desertion was indefensible, and its penalty by the code of Tlascala was death.

40. Called Tepepolco: extensive quarries of the red porous stone *Tetzontli,* used for building purposes, were found here, and the place afterwards became the property of Cortés, and was known as Peñón del Marqués.

41. This was the small fortress called Xoloc, which stood at the junction of the causeways leading to Itztapalapan and Cuyoacan respectively. It con-

sisted of two small towers surrounded by a wall, and was not large enough to hold a numerous garrison, and hence was easily captured by the Spaniards. It was just after passing Xoloc that the first meeting between Moctezuma and Cortés took place.

42. *Como iban más que retraiendose* is the quaint device of Cortés to avoid saying that the Spaniards were in full flight.

43. The Mexican historian, Ixtlilxochitl, is authority for the story that Cortés and his Texcocan ally, Prince Ixtlilochitl, headed this assault upon the great teocalli, penetrating into the sanctuary of the idol; and that Cortés himself tore away the jewelled mask of gold from the idol's face while the Prince of Texcoco struck off its head with his sword. In the absence of any mention of these details by Cortés or any other witnesses, this version seems unworthy of credence.

44. It seems incredible that neither Spaniards nor allies should have sustained any loss in this long day's fighting, which, though it ended to their advantage, had witnessed their utter rout and the capture of their gun on the square. Bernal Díaz, who was fighting under Alvarado, on the causeway from the Tacuba side, gives a more convincing description of the daily losses and the wounds which the men had to dress as best they could when they returned at night to their camp. There was a soldier Juan Catalan, who was reputed to have the gift of healing by prayer and charms, who had his hands full, as the Indians also placed faith in him, and brought him all their wounded. "I say," he piously adds, "that it pleased our Lord Jesus Christ in his mercy to give us strength and to speedily heal us."

45. The Mexican historian, Ixtlilxochitl, contradicts Cortés on this point, affirming that the boy-king Fernando was already dead, and that his brother Ixtlilochitl reigned. Both these princes bore the same Christian name of Fernando, hence the natural and unimportant confusion of their identity, but, as Cortés says nothing of the first one's death, which he could have no motive in misrepresenting, and distinguishes very clearly between the two, his version, given at the time, must prevail over that of a later writer. The same chronicler claims that Ixtlilochitl fought throughout the siege with the Spaniards, performing prodigies of valour, and he reproaches Cortés for suppressing all mention of these services in his despatches, and for failing to recompense him and his people after the victory to which their valour so largely contributed (Orozco y Berra, lib. iii., cap. vi.).

46. Otomís: tribes inhabiting the mountain regions to the west. Orozco y Berra gives June 11th as the probable date of their arrival in the camp.

47. The perfidy of these people dealt a terrible blow to Quauhtemotzin and the defenders of Temixtitan, for to their defection they added treachery of the blackest complexion. Their chiefs appeared before the Emperor with offers of assistance, which were gratefully accepted by the hard-pressed sovereign. Their troops were assigned places, and, when the fighting began, made a feint at first of attacking the Spanish allies, but afterwards suddenly turned their arms against the Mexicans who were of course taken completely by surprise; their chiefs quickly rallied, however, and bringing up fresh troops the traitors soon got the worst of it, and, leaving many dead, and others prisoners, the remainder fled from the city. The prisoners were upbraided by Macehuatzin, lord of Cuitlahuac, who decapitated four of the principal ones with his own hand and delivered the others to Quauhtemotzin, who ordered them to be sacrificed in the temples of Mexico and Tlatelolco (Sahagun, lib. xii., cap. xxxiv.; Torquemada, lib. iv., cap. cxiii.). One of the worst effects of the defection of the lake towns was to cut off the supplies of fresh water and food, which, in spite of the vigilance of the brigantines, they had found means to transport into the beleaguered city. Henceforth hunger was added to the horrors of the siege, while the Spanish camp was enriched by supplies of fresh provisions.

48. Cortés says nothing of the losses suffered by the Spaniards during the operations of these days, though they were considerable enough to merit notice. The Mexicans had arranged a clever device for capturing the brigantines, which was partially successful. They stationed thirty of their largest canoes, full of warriors, amongst some rushes, and drove a number of stakes into the bottom of the lake in such wise as to impede the movements of the brigantines. Some smaller canoes, such as usually carried supplies, were then sent into the open, where they were quickly discovered by the Spaniards, who gave chase, allowing themselves to be drawn into the trap, where the stakes interfered with their movements. The captain of one of the brigantines, Portillo, was killed, and Pedro Barbo was mortally wounded; many others were wounded, and the Mexicans carried off one brigantine in triumph. They paid dearly for this victory, for Cortés was so much mortified by this disaster, that a counter ambuscade was prepared, which drew the Mexicans successfully, and in which they suffered severe loss of many canoes, a number of slain, and others prisoners. The Aztecs had one formidable warrior of giant stature, called Tzilacatzin, who

was wonderfully skilful with his sling, every stone he sent bringing down its man. He was made the aim of all the Spanish archers, and musketeers, his great stature making him easily distinguishable, but they could never hit him. On one of these days eighteen Spaniards were captured alive and sacrificed, their bodies being afterwards cut up and distributed to be eaten. Another day a furious assault led by a daring warrior of Tlatelolco called Tlapanecatl, almost succeeded in capturing the ensign Corral who carried the Spanish standard, and did carry off no less than fifty-three Castilian prisoners, besides numerous of the allies, and four horses all of whom were sacrificed in the various temples. In the rout of Alvarado, which Cortés here briefly mentions, but which was a complete disaster, five more Spaniards were taken alive, besides many Indian prisoners; a horseman and his horse were drowned, and the survivors, all badly wounded, and utterly demoralised, drew off to their camp amidst the victorious shouts of the Mexicans. The latter followed up to the very camp, but were repulsed with loss by a small battery stationed there, which was worked by an able engineer, named Medrano. The guns were so placed that they raked the entire causeway, and as the brigantines used their guns on both sides, the camp was effectively protected (Bernal Díaz, cap. cii.; Sahagun, lib. xii., cap. xxxvi.; Torquemada, lib. iv., cap. xciii.). Alvarado was an intrepid commander, and, nothing daunted by his repulse, he continued for four days to renew his attack at the same point, until, on Friday, June 28th, he finally captured the bridge. Six more Spaniards perished in these combats, besides the wounded and allies whose dead were unnumbered.

49. *Tianguiz* or *Tianquiztli* is the Mexican word for market.

50. This was the last victorious day for the Mexicans, and witnessed their culminating effort against their foes. Quauhtemotzin was everywhere present amongst his troops, urging them to a supreme struggle, and sounding his trumpet of conch-shell, "upon hearing which signal" Bernal Díaz says, "it is impossible to describe the fury with which they closed upon us" (cap. ciii.). Dominating the shouts of "Santiago!" the screams of the wounded, the crash of arms, and the fierce war-cries of the Mexicans, was heard the lugubrious roll of the sacred *Tlapanhuehuetl* of serpents' skins which the priests beat with inspired frenzy before the war-god on the teocalli. Cortés again owed his escape from instant death to the determination which obsessed the Mexicans to take him alive for the sacrifice. His rescuer was the same Cristóbal de Olea who had once before come to his aid in a moment

of peril at Xochimilco; with one blow of his sword he cut off the arm of the warrior who held the general, falling dead himself the next moment.

Bernal Díaz says that Olea slew four chiefs before he himself fell (*loco citato*).

Seven horses were killed, seventy Spaniards were captured alive, Cortés was badly wounded in the leg; Sandoval likewise in three places and both his division and that of Alvarado suffered serious reverses. When an account came to be taken of the extent of the disaster, dismay filled the sinking hearts of the Spaniards, and the Indian allies began to doubt the power of the *teules* and to ask themselves whether they were not after all fighting on the wrong side.

Cortés threw the blame for this catastrophe on Alderete, who had disobeyed his order never to advance without first securing his retreat. Alderete denied that he had ever had any such order, and declared that it was Cortés who had urged the troops forward. Recriminations and censures were thus exchanged, for naturally nobody would accept responsibility for such a calamity; it appears certain that Cortés had not been in favour of the assault, but had allowed his better judgment to be overruled by his companions, who were weary of the daily fighting, and thought they could storm the Tlateloco market-place, and so end the siege.

While gloom reigned in the Spanish camp, there was exultation amongst the Mexicans whose waning hopes of victory were revived by their success. The priests proclaimed that the war-god was appeased by the savour of so many Spanish victims and within eight days would give his faithful a complete victory over the impious invaders. This oracle was published amongst the allies, and shook their wavering faith in the Spaniards; they saw that the city stubbornly held out, they perceived that the strangers were neither invincible nor immortal, and, as the ancient superstitious fear of their gods reasserted itself, tens of thousands quietly detached themselves from the Spanish camp and marched off homewards. Cortés used every effort to hold them and urged that they should at least wait eight days and see whether the prophecy was fulfilled before deciding against him. The Tlascalan general, Chichimecatecle, and Prince Ixtlilxochitl of Texcoco remained steadfast to their sworn allegiance. The latter was naturally an object of peculiar hatred to the Mexicans, who reviled him, and heaped imprecations on him as a renegade from his race, and a traitor to his country. If he felt these taunts, he did not betray his feelings, but day after day joined in the scenes of carnage, facing both danger and obloquy unmoved. For five days there was some respite, the Spaniards nursing their wounds and preparing for a resumption of hostilities, while

the Mexicans were engaged in making overtures to win back their faithless subjects and allies.

The situation of the Spaniards was well-nigh desperate, but that of the
Mexicans was hardly better, for famine stalked their streets, claiming as
many victims as the Spanish cannon, and terribly weakening the defenders of the city. The besiegers tenaciously held their position on the causeways, and, aided by the brigantines, on the lakes, were unceasingly
vigilant in maintaining the blockade.

Throughout the siege there were a few Spanish women—some of them
described as "wives" of the soldiers—in camp, who displayed scarcely less
courage than the men, for, not only did they occupy themselves in the
nursing which is women's natural function in wartime, but they even
mounted guard to relieve the weary soldiers, who needed rest; and instances are given of their joining in the actual fighting. Cortés had intended leaving all these women at Tlascala, but his proposed order to
that effect aroused such opposition, especially among the women themselves who declared that Castilian wives, rather than abandon their husbands in danger, would die with them, that it was never given. Little has
been said of the courage and devotion of these obscure heroines, but Herrera has recorded the names of five, Beatriz de Palacios, María de Estrada,
Juana Martin, Isabel Rodríguez, and Beatriz Bermúdez, as meriting honorable mention in the annals of the conquest.

The eight days appointed by the priests for the destruction of the besiegers expired, and the prophecy remained unfulfilled; seeing which the
vacillating allies returned to the Spanish camp in large numbers where the
politic general received them with his customary imperturbable urbanity,
and, after reproaching them for their faithless desertion in a panic of foolish superstition, declared that he pardoned their fault and accepted them
once more as vassals of Spain, and his allies.

51. Malinalco.

52. Probably Huisuco.

53. Cuernavaca again though Cortés varies his incorrect spelling.

54. A gentleman who first came to San Domingo with Columbus in 1493; he
landed on the coast, which he named Florida, in 1512, when sailing under
a commission from Don Diego Columbus, governor of San Domingo. Instead of discovering the fountain of perpetual youth he had come to seek,

he was wounded in a skirmish with the Indians from which he died in Cuba.

55. The logic of this taunt was verified later, as Cortés observes, for the work of rebuilding the city fell upon the Indian allies who had destroyed it.

56. A soldier called Sotelo, native of Seville, who claimed to have seen much service in Italy, and to know all about the construction of engines of warfare, proposed to Cortés to make this catapult. As Bernal Díaz says, he was eternally talking about the wonderful military machines he could build, with which he promised to destroy in two days the remaining quarter of the city, where Quauhtemotzin held out. The commander consented to the trial, and stone, lime, timber, cables, and all the necessary materials, were furnished, together with carpenters, and masons, to carry out Sotelo's instructions. The machine was erected on the platform of masonry known as the *Mumuztli*, a sort of theatre which stood in the square, and the process of its construction was watched with exultant expectations by the Indian allies, who foresaw the wholesale destruction of their enemies by means of the mysterious machine. They indulged in jubilant prophecies, and called on the Mexicans to observe the growth of the engine destined to accomplish their overthrow. The Mexicans were equally impressed by the strange monster, and watched its building with the feelings of one in the condemned cell, who hears the workmen building the scaffold on which he is to perish at dawn. The day of the trial (August 6th) arrived, and a huge stone was fired which instead of flying over into the Indian quarter, where it was aimed, shot up into the air, and fell back into exactly the place from whence it departed. Cortés was furious with Sotelo, and ashamed of the failure in the presence of the gazing multitude: the luckless inventor was in disgrace, and the catapult remained one of the standing jokes in the army. Infusing some gaiety into the company this invention may be said to have served some good purpose, even though not exactly the one expected of it.

57. Huitzilopotchli, also spelled Huitchilopochtli: the god of war whose statue stood in the great teocalli.

58. Cihuacoatl.

59. Quauhtemotzin, seeing that escape was hopeless, stood up in the canoe saying: "I am the King of Mexico and of this country; take me to Malintzin.

I ask only that my wife and children and the women be spared." Some twenty persons were with him, all of whom Holguin brought back to the city. There is little to add to what Cortés here says about what passed on that historic occasion, except that he gave orders that the Princess Tecuichpo, youngest daughter of Moctezuma, recently married to her cousin Quauhtemotzin should receive every consideration. Humboldt, commenting on Quauhtemotzin's choice of instant death, commends the unfortunate young sovereign's conduct in the following terms: *"Ce trait est digne du plus beau temps de la Grèce et de Rome. Sous toutes les zones, quelle que soit la couleur des hommes, le langage des âmes fortes est le même lorsqu'elles luttent contre le malheur"* (*Essai Politique*, p. 192, 4th ed.). The captive monarch was not deceived by the suave manners and honeyed words of his captor, and his forebodings were realised, when, a few days later, upon his protesting that there was no treasure left in the city, Cortés consented to his torture to force him to speak. Bernal Díaz seeks to excuse Cortés's part in this unworthy proceeding. It may be said in extenuation that he yielded to the angry clamours of disappointed soldiers, and the insinuation that he had arranged with Quauhtemotzin to conceal the treasure so as later to appropriate it for himself. The custodian of the royal fifth, Aldarete, seems to have insisted on the torture. The king bore the pain unflinchingly and rebuked his fellow sufferers who groaned aloud, saying: "Do you think I am taking my pleasure in my bath?" His feet were almost burned off, and he remained a cripple until his death. The anniversary of his capture and the fall of the city were celebrated as a public holiday all during the period of Spanish rule in Mexico, but the Republic has abolished this observance. The eleventh and last of the Aztec sovereigns was the son of Ahuitzotl; he succeeded Cuitlahuatzin and married his widow Tecuichpo. He was a young man of great personal bravery and energy, in all things the opposite of his superstitious uncle Moctezuma. He worked indefatigably to win allies, organise an effective defence, and save the tottering kingdom and city; he galvanised the timid into something like courage, confirmed the waverers, and encouraged the patriots; large stores of arms and provisions were laid in, the useless, aged men, and women and children, were sent off to safe places in the mountains, while the city was filled with warriors. The kings of Texcoco and Tlacopan joined in these plans, co-operating with their fellow sovereign. Had like zeal and harmony existed a year earlier Cortés and his men would never have reached the capital, save as victims to be offered to Huitzilopochtli. Quauhtemotzin arrived too late. Nothing could ward off the oncoming disaster. The powerful states of Tlascala, Cholula, and others, had openly gone over to the Spaniards, blind to the inevitable destruction they were preparing for themselves; the allies of Mexico were doubtful and faint-hearted,—some of them merely neutrals, awaiting the issue to declare for the victor. Never did prince die for duty's sake, choosing death with open eyes and making a last stand for a forlorn cause, more nobly than did the heroic Quauhtemotzin. His captivity and death are noted in the Fifth Letter.

60. While the brigantine with the royal captain and his fellow prisoners was returning across the lake, Sandoval came on board and demanded that Quauhtemotzin be delivered to him, as he was commander of that division of the fleet, but Holguin claimed the honour of the capture, and refused to yield to his superior. The dispute which ensued, delayed matters, but Cortés who was informed of the dissension, sent Luis Marin and Francisco Lugo with peremptory orders to cease wrangling, and bring the prisoners to him.

Bernal Díaz relates that, afterwards, the commander called the two claimants, and cited to them, by way of example, the incident from Roman history of the capture of Jugurtha and the dispute between Marius and Sylla as to the honour of that feat, which was productive of civil wars which devastated the state. He calmed them with the assurance that the circumstance should be fully laid before the Emperor, who would decide which of the two should have the action emblazoned in his arms. Two years later, the imperial decision was given, and ignored both the contestants, granting instead to Cortés himself the device of seven captive kings, linked with a chain and representing Moctezuma, Quauhtemotzin, and the rulers of Texcoco, Tlapocan, Iztapalapan, Coyohuacan, and Matolzingo.

61. Michoacan was an independent kingdom, peopled by a different race from the Mexicans, and speaking a different language, though it shared to some degree the manners, customs, and civilisation of Anahuac: the chief city was Patzcuaro on the lake of the same name. There was an almost permanent state of hostilities between the Tarasque (tribal name of the natives of Michoacan) and Aztec nations.

62. Named after Cortés's birthplace in Estremadura.

63. When the news of Narváez's summary treatment of the commissioner from the *Audiencia* of Hispaniola, Ayllon, reached Spain, proceedings were be-

gun against him, but the Bishop of Burgos, always active in Velázquez's interests, secured their suspension until fuller information might be had, and also the release of Narváez from the prison in Veracruz, where Cortés had confined him. Cristóbal de Tapia, an inspector of the royal smelting operations in Hispaniola was therefore despatched to Veracruz, with full powers to deal with the matter; he was hardly the man for the mission, and was as little able to cope with Cortés as Narváez had been.

64. He was a Franciscan friar, empowered to administer the *Bulas de la Cruzada*. The indulgences provided by such bulls were granted on the usual conditions required for obtaining an indulgence, and were applicable to the living and the dead. This usage originated, as the title indicates, with the Crusades, and after it had fallen into disuse elsewhere, was continued in Spain owing to the long centuries of warfare against the Moors and the later conflicts with the Barbary pirates. It became therefore a peculiarly Spanish institution, and was extended to all countries under Spanish rule.

65. This man was a private soldier who had come to Mexico in Narváez's company; not Cortés alone but also Sandoval, Alvarado, and Olid were to be killed, and the commandership given to Francisco Verdugo, brother-in-law to Diego Velázquez, who was said, however, to be ignorant of the conspiracy. The plan was for several of the conspirators to stab the four leaders while they were seated at table. Cortés displayed a wise self-restraint in going no further in the affair than the execution of Villafaña, though he had the list of other names, the finding of some of which surprised and pained him greatly. He spread the report that Villafaña had swallowed the paper containing the list of the guilty ones.

66. This is an error; after Don Fernando's death, the young prince Ahuaxpitzcatzin, an illegitimate son of Nezahualpilli, who had received the name of Carlos upon his baptism as a Christian, was chosen King, but Cortés had refused to recognise the election, and had prevailed on the electors to annul it in favour of his ally, the ambitious Ixtlilxochitl, whose Christian name was also Don Fernando. The confusion of the two Fernandos, Kings of Texcoco has already been noticed.

67. The volcano of Orizaba which was mentioned in the First Letter. The Indian name was Citlatepetl, meaning *Star Mountain*. Humboldt gives the height as 17,368 feet; the crater is now extinct.

AGUILAR

1. The Dominicans, known in England at first as Black Friars.

2. In the sense used here, a stage or phase of a military expedition. *Jornada* can also mean a day's march.

3. She was given the name Marina in Christian baptism.

4. Umbria was not hanged but had his toes cut off as punishment. Andrés de Tapia mentions him as the companion who helped him count the skulls of the *tzompantli* in front of the Great Temple.

5. An armor made of strong quilted cotton and kapok, which the Spaniards later adopted.

6. Here Captain Hernando Cortés showed the greatest courage and resoluteness, and so did his men. *Aguilar's Note.*

7. Later it was called the Hill of Victory. *Aguilar's Note.*

8. Cortés did not admit any casualties either in his dispatch to the emperor. But Bernal Díaz del Castillo mentions that they buried the dead under the temple rooms so that the Indians would not discover they were mortal. Bernal did not specify number beyond writing *los muertos.*

9. This valorous and generous act of Hernando Cortés and his soldiers equals the great acts of any captain and his soldiers ever known to the world. *Aguilar's Note.*

10. Chieftain of one of the four districts of Tlaxcala, and general of the army.

11. There were often sorcerers among these emissaries, sent to bewitch the Spaniards, and they justified their failure by complaining that they could never catch the Spaniards asleep. They were not being untruthful: Bernal Díaz wrote, as an old man, that he was unable to learn again to sleep the night through, or use a mattress.

12. From his ascent of Popocatepetl.

13.   These bridges, occurring at intervals along the causeway, could be re-moved for defensive purposes, whereupon the water served as a moat. The breaks in the causeway also permitted the canoes to circulate about the lake.

14.   Spanish writers garbled the name of the city of Tenochtitlan in a variety of ways, since they had nothing to go on but sound. Aguilar spells it Tenustitlan, but I have corrected this and other important names in the text to conform with currently accepted spelling.

15.   The site now occupied by the National Palace.

16.   Kapok, the hairy seed-covering of the ceiba tree. In Nahuatl, *pochotl*.

17.   Aguilar gets ahead of his story here. He relates Moctezuma's captivity on a subsequent page.

18.   Those who had seen action in the Antilles.

19.   The decision of a brave captain, comparable to the best of the Romans, by which he and his men earned great distinction. His men were so few against so many, and the enemy had good artillery and more than one hundred horsemen. And though they were advised of our coming, we defeated and forced them to surrender, whereas we had neither artillery nor horse but were virtually unarmed. *Aguilar's Note.*

20.   Presumably in the interval between setting off the charge and the actual discharge.

21.   This was Cuitlahuac, who ruled only eighty days before he died of small-pox. He was succeeded by Cuauhtemoc, last king of the Mexicans and heroic defender of the city of Tenochtitlan.

22.   Knight commander of a military order.

23.   Two days before he said this, it happened that a soldier who was im-prisoned in the church we had, punished for some mischief, ran out at midnight shouting that he had seen dead men jumping around the church; also the heads of dead men, among them his own. The sentries on duty came running, as well, to say that they had seen dead men's legs and heads

falling into the canal. All this turned out to be true, for as Botello had said he was to die that night, and the soldier had seen his own head, and the sentries had seen what they said, so all of them died the night that we retreated . . . *Aguilar's Note.*

24. Aguilar was writing in 1560, whereas the events narrated took place in June, 1520.

25. Later Aguilar says they left at midnight. This is corroborated by Bernal Díaz del Castillo.

26. On this day Captain Cortés distinguished himself very much indeed, matching the prowess and the forcefulness of Augustus Caesar and the greatest captains of the world; and not only he but the other captains as well, who were few, whereas the enemy were more than five or six hundred thousand selected men. *Aguilar's Note.*

27. In this battle Don Pedro de Alvarado stood out as a valiant captain, gaining all that he had lost the day before. I give faith also that Cristóbal de Olid, Gonzalo de Sandoval and others conducted themselves courageously. *Aguilar's Note.*
     ". . . gaining all that he had lost the day before." ". . . *y ganó lo que el día antes había perdido.*" He had lost all but four of his men the day before; Aguilar probably means that he more than made up for his defeat. *Translator's Note.*

28. The island city was crisscrossed with waterways, and the houses were built along these canals. The only roads were the main causeways converging at the heart of the city.

29. Credit for bringing smallpox and a few other peculiarly European diseases to these shores is due more rightly to the Spanish expeditionary forces than to the Lord. Motolínia, one of the twelve first Franciscan friars to come to Mexico, wrote in his *Historia de los Indios de la Nueva España* that smallpox was carried here by a Negro in the armada of Pánfilo de Narváez. The disease struck first in Yucatan, then Cempoala, from where it spread rapidly to the interior.

30. *Repartimientos,* which entailed the obligation on the part of the grantee

to protect and provide education for the Indians living on his allotment, in exchange for exacting tribute from them.

31. Military and political governor of an outlying province.

32. He was sent to the Gulf of Honduras, in obedience to the king's desire to find a strait connecting the Atlantic and Pacific.

33. Aguilar says they were *compadres*: the relationship between godfather and father of a child; or, more loosely, cronies. In any event the expeditionary force was led by Francisco de las Casas, and he failed in carrying out his mission. Cristóbal de Olid held him prisoner in his house, together with Gil Gonzalez de Avila, and one night at supper the two attacked the unarmed Olid with knives. Olid escaped and hid in an Indian hut, but was found and brought to trial by Casas and Avila. These two had meanwhile persuaded most of Olid's men to rejoin Cortés. Olid was beheaded in the public square of Naco.

34. Now Cuernavaca.

THE ANONYMOUS CONQUISTADOR

1. A member of the oak family.

2. The Mexican *coyotl* (coyote) and *cuetlachcoyotl* respectively.

3. Puma. In Nahuatl, *miztli*.

4. The peccary, indigenous to America and closely allied to the true swine, has a cutaneous gland on the rump, which secretes a fatty substance. The Spaniards at first believed this gland to be the navel.

5. Opossum. *Tlacuatzin* in Nahuatl.

6. The Indians attached great significance to their standard, and its capture meant defeat.

7. A mechanical arm or spear-thrower called *atlatl*.

8. Although the Spaniards called these rituals "gladiatorial combats" they

were of a sacrificial nature and were held during the first religious festival of the Mexican year. According to Fray Diego Durán and other early writers, as soon as the prisoner was wounded the temple drums sounded and he was taken to the sacrificial stone nearby, where his heart was cut out and offered to the sun. The Anonymous Conquistador is the only writer who says that captives were sometimes given their liberty, a statement that is doubtful in view of the circumstance that warriors considered themselves dishonored if they were not permitted to die fighting, and would in any event be ostracized or put to death as cowards by their own people.

9. More often at the shoulder, leaving the other shoulder bare.

10. This is the word in Ramusio's Italian text, which Garcia Icazbalceta translated in Spanish as *carmesi*, a red silk or woolen cloth.

11. *Cactli*, a sandal.

12. *Comalli*, a griddle.

13. The *huaxolotl*, or turkey.

14. Cacao beans, from the Nahuatl *cacahuatl*. The drink was *chocolatl*.

15. Italian copper coin bearing the likeness of Saint Mark.

16. On this subject there is the contradictory testimony of the jurist Alonso de Zurita, who reported to the Crown that drinking had not been a problem until the post-Conquest disintegration of Indian social order. Formerly the drinker had been despised by the community and punished in accordance with its laws. A warrior or other person of rank guilty of drunkenness was publicly degraded by having his head shaved, which amounted to stripping him of his insignia. Persons over thirty were allowed to drink in moderation on festive occasions, and anyone over fifty was permitted three cups of pulque with meals, on the theory that at that age the blood began to run cold.

17. From cloth of the woven *ixtli* fiber, worn by the common people.

18. Agave; the so-called century plant.

19. A beer made of maize.

20. The text published by Ramusio was illustrated with several highly imaginative but unauthentic drawings which were also included by Clavijero in his *Ancient History of Mexico* (1780). Today they are regarded as mere curiosities.

21. Huitzilopochtli.

22. Quetzalcoatl, in the city of Cholula.

23. In rural Spain the man who killed a wolf carried the animal's head around to show to the neighbors, and these rewarded him, according to their means, for ridding the countryside of such a menace.

24. Often there were six priests in attendance. Four of the priests held the victim's hands and feet, one the head, and the sixth, who was the highest in rank, performed the sacrifice.

25. Indications of phallic worship exist also at Uxmal and Chichén Itzá in Yucatan. The cult was probably imported from the Gulf Coast, but it is believed by Mayanists (Thompson, Spinden) that it did not gain any importance, and in fact was repellent to the majority of the Maya people.

26. Undoubtedly the author was pandering to his readers' taste for sensationalism. The references to homosexuality, however, are founded on fact, although it was considered an offense grave enough to carry the death penalty.

27. Cholula.

28. Three hundred thousand inhabitants is the number given by most writers. Fray Francisco de Aguilar, whose chronicle appears in this book, and who had a liking for statistics, stated there were one hundred thousand houses. This is taken to mean families, and would also indicate approximately three hundred thousand inhabitants.

29. Chapultepec.

30. An equestrian sport introduced into Spain by the Arabs, in which the players threw their spears at one another, simultaneously warding off their opponents' spears with leather shields.

31. The author assumed it was understood that the Spaniards also controlled the lake and the approaches to the island.

32. Apparently this was intended as a witticism.

ALVARADO

1. This letter was referred to in one of the dispatches of Cortés but has never been found.

2. Conquests were undertaken at private expense, and the Crown received one-fifth of total revenue. In the case of seagoing expeditions, the ship-owner or outfitter was entitled to two-thirds of the revenues, after deducting the royal fifth. The other third was divided among the conquistadors.

3. The sought-for passage to the Spice Islands.

4. Atitlán.

5. On the Pacific coast of the present Republic of El Salvador.

6. A "battle" in the now obsolete sense of a division of an army.

7. The matter of the decree is taken up in the introduction to this volume.

PILAR

1. Tzintzuntzan, in the State of Michoacán.

2. Tzimtzincha Tangaxuan, lord of Tarascans, who received the name Francisco in Christian baptism.

3. The Lerma River.

4. In the cord and water torture, a strong thin cord was tied around the victim's temples and the fleshy parts of the arms and legs. A heavy rod was placed under the cord next to the body, and turned so as to slowly tighten the cord, which cut deeper and deeper into the bleeding flesh. Then cold water was dropped onto the cord, making it contract and tighten further.

5. Nuño de Guzmán was a native of Guadalajara, Spain, and Pedro de Guzmán was from Alcalá de Henares, but it is thought that they may have been related. There was also Pedro Núñez Guzmán, a resident of Toledo, listed among the thirty-one attendants accompanying Nuño in 1526, when he sailed from Spain with the title of Governor of Pánuco.

6. In the present State of Jalisco.

7. Chained together by their necks.

8. Livestock and domestic fowl had been brought to America in large numbers since the beginning of the Spanish colonization. The earliest reference is contained in a memoir written by Columbus to Ferdinand and Isabella, dated January 30 of 1494: ". . . sheep, lambs . . . and heifers are needed, and should be sent by every caravel that is dispatched; also male and female asses, and mares for work and for breeding purposes, since there are none of these animals here . . ." On the mainland, after the discovery of Florida, the Spanish observed the bison or buffalo and called them *vacas de la tierra* (native cows). These were never domesticated. The Spanish brought pigs to Mexico, among the other livestock, and the pigs seem to have been bred so successfully that thousands of them were herded along on the expeditions as a source of fresh meat. By 1530—nearly ten years after Cortés' conquest of central Mexico—European domestic fowl could very well have preceded Nuño de Guzmán's expedition into western Mexico through the activities of traders.

9. *De guerra.* This is to say they had not given fealty and therefore, technically, were belligerents. Furthermore, as belligerents they could be taken as slaves and either used or sold on the market. This gave rise to many abuses and, rightly, the indignation of the missionaries and responsible colonists.

10. In the State of Zacatecas.

11. A high ranking officer in the militia, second to general.

12. In the State of Nayarit.

13. In an effort to reorganize his conquest.

14. The Tepic or Santiago River.

15. The Crown did not accept this name, but ordered the province to be called Nueva Galicia.

16. Further ahead there were warriors waiting under cover. In the attack they injured a number of Spanish soldiers, and fifty or sixty horses.

17. The Pacific.

18. Cortés reached Veracruz on July 15, 1530 on his return voyage from Spain. Nuño de Guzmán's friends in the *Audiencia* of Mexico, Delgadillo and Matienzo, feared that Cortés, with his commission of Captain General of New Spain and his great personal popularity, might attempt to reinstate himself. Rumors of his return had reached Nuño sometime before, since Cortés had delayed his voyage as long as he was able, in the hope of timing his arrival in Mexico to coincide with the appointment of the new *Audiencia*.

19. Moctozomatzin, chieftain of the Mexicans, called Tapia or Tapiezuela by the Spaniards.

20. They were being ravaged by malaria and dysentery. Other contemporary writers mention that "many" Spaniards also died, but it is safe to assume that the soldiers received better care than the Indians, as well as priority in the matter of food supplies, which were alarmingly short. The swollen river, as it innundated the countryside, carried away fifteen hundred pigs, numerous deer and other game, and ruined the local crops. The Indians whom Guzmán had brought by force from Mexico, Tlaxcala, and other cities of the central plateau, could not acclimate themselves to the humid tropics, and for this reason begged to be permitted to recuperate in the more healthful climate of Jalisco.

21. Abandoned along the roads by Gonzalo López.

22. Verdugo was sent to found and settle Santiago de Compostela.

23. The legend of a city of wealthy Amazons had lured many of the Spaniards into joining Nuño de Guzmán's expedition.

24. He was sent to find a route from the Pacific to the Gulf of Mexico.

25. The Crown forbade making slaves of Indians who were serving peaceably.

bibliography

EARLY HISTORY AND DOCUMENTS

Acosta, Joseph de. *Historia natural y moral de las Indias.* Seville: 1590. Mexico: Fondo de Cultura Económica, 1962.

Aldana, Cristóbal de. *Crónica de la Merced de Mexico.* 1770? Mexico: Biblioteca Nacional, 1953.

Benavente, Toribio de (Motolinia). *Historia de los indios de la Nueva España.* Barcelona: Juan Gili, 1914.

Casas, Fray Bartolomé de las. *Historia de las Indias.* 1527-1561. 3 vols. Mexico: Fondo de Cultura Económica, 1951.

Clavijero, Francisco Javier. *Historia antigua de Mexico.* 1780. 4 vols. Mexico: Editorial Porrúa, 1958.

Columbus, Christopher. *Four Voyages to the New World.* (Letters and selected documents.) 1493-1503. Bilingual edition. New York: Corinth, 1961.

Cortés, Hernán. *Cartas de relación.* 1519-1526. Mexico: Editorial Porrúa, 1960.

Díaz del Castillo, Bernal. *Historia verdadera de la conquista de la Nueva España.* 1568. 2 vols. Mexico: Editorial Porrúa, 1955.

Herrera, Antonio de. *Historia general de los hechos de los Castellanos en las islas y tierrafirme de el Mar oceano.* 1601-1615. 10 vols. Asunción: Editorial Guarania, 1944-1947.

Humboldt, Alexander, Freeherr von. *Essai Politique sur le royaume de la Nouvelle Espagne.* 5 vols. Paris: F. Schaell, 1811.

Ixtlilxochitl, Fernando de Alva. *Horribles Cruel-dades de los Conquistadores de México*. Mexico: A. Valdés, 1829.

López, de Gómara, Francisco. *Historia general de las Indias*. 1540-1551. 2 vols. Barcelona: Editorial Iberia, 1954.

Muñoz Camargo, Diego. *Historia de Tlaxcala*. 15?? Mexico: Lauro Rosell, 1948.

Oviedo y Valdés, Gonzalo Fernández de. *Historia general y natural de las Indias*. Seville: Iuam Cromberger, 1535.

Paso y Troncoso, Francisco del (ed.). *Epistolario de Nueva España*. 1505-1518. 16 vols. Mexico: Robredo, 1939-1942.

Pomar, Juan Bautista. *Relación de Texcoco*. 1582. Mexico: Chávez Hayhoe, 1941.

Prescott, William H. *History of the Conquest of Mexico*. Philadelphia: J. B. Lippincott Co., 1899.

Sahagun, Fray Bernardino de. *Historia general de las cosas de Nueva España*. 1547-1585. 4 vols. Mexico: Editorial Porrúa, 1956.

Torquemada, Juan de. *Monarchia Indiana*. Madrid: N. Rodriguez Franco, 1723.

Zurita, Alonso de. *Breve relación de los señores de la Nueva España*. Mexico: Chávez Hayhoe, 1941.

MORE RECENT WORKS

Carcer y Disdier, Mariano de. *Apuntes para la historia de la transculturación Indoespañola*. Mexico: Instituto de Historia, 1953.

Carreño, Alberto Maria. *La iniciación de la vida jurídica y municipal en Nueva España*. Vol. IX, No. 1 of "Memorias de la Academia Mexicana de la Historia," 1950.

Caso, Alfonso. *El pueblo del sol*. Mexico: Fondo de Cultura Económica, 1953.

Chapman, Anne. *Puertos de intercambio en Meso-

américa prehispánica. Mexico: Instituto Nacional de Antropología e Historia, 1959.

Krickeberg, Walter. *Las antiguas culturas mexicanas.* (Translated from the German.) Mexico: Fondo de Cultura Económica, 1961.

López Austin, Alfredo. *La constitución real de Mexico-Tenochtitlan.* Mexico: Universidad Nacional Autónoma de Mexico, 1961.

Mariéjol, Jean Hippolyte. *The Spain of Ferdinand and Isabella.* (Translated from the French by Benjamin Keen.) New Brunswick: Rutgers University Press, 1961.

Orozco y Berra, Manuel. *Historia antigua y de la conquista de Mexico.* 4 vols. Mexico: Editorial Porrúa, 1960.

Ricard, Robert. *La conquista espiritual de Mexico.* (Translated from the French.) Mexico: Editorial Jus, 1947.

Spinden, Herbert Joseph. *Maya Art and Civilization.* 1912. Colorado: Falcon's Wing Press, 1957.

Thompson, J. Eric S. *The Rise and Fall of Maya Civilization.* London: Gollancz, 1956.

SOURCES OF THE TRANSLATIONS

Juan Díaz
Itinerario de Juan de Grijalva. Published in *Crónicas de la Conquista.* University of Mexico. 1950. Reproduced from the García Icazbalceta text.

Andrés de Tapia
Relación de Andrés de Tapia. Published in *Crónicas de la Conquista.* University of Mexico. Reproduced from the García Icazbalceta text.

Fray Francisco de Aguilar
Relación breve de la conquista de la Nueva España. José Porrúa e Hijos Sucs. 1954. Edition limited to 250 copies.

Anonymous Conquistador
*Relación de algunas cosas de la Nueva España
y de la gran ciudad de Temestitan Mexico.*
José Porrúa e Hijos Sucs. 1961. Edition limited
to 250 copies. Containing a facsimile reproduc-
tion of Ramusio's Italian text.

Pedro de Alvarado
*Relación hecha por Pedro de Alvarado a Her-
nando Cortés.* José Porrúa e Hijos Sucs. 1954.
Edition limited to 250 copies.

García del Pilar
Appendix to *Memoria de los servicios que
había hecho Nuño de Guzmán, desde que fue
nombrado Gobernador de Pánuco en 1525.*
José Porrúa e Hijos Sucs. 1955. Edition limited
to 250 copies.

DICTIONARIES AND REFERENCE BOOKS

Appleton's Revised Cuyás Dictionary. 2 vols.
New York: Grolier, 1956.

Diccionario de la Lengua Española. Real Academia Española, 18th edition. Madrid. Espasa-
Calpe, 1956.

Diccionario de Mejicanismos. Francisco J. Santa-
maria, 1st edition. Mexico: Editorial Porrúa,
1959.

Encyclopedia Americana. 30 vols. New York:
Americana Corporation, 1962.

Encyclopaedia Britannica. 24 vols. Chicago: Encyclopaedia Britannica, Inc., 1947.

Funk & Wagnalls Standard Dictionary. International Edition. 2 vols. New York: Funk & Wagnalls, 1962.

Tesoro de la Lengua Castellana, o Española. Se-
bastian de Cobarruvias Orozco. Madrid. Luis
Sanchez (printer to His Majesty Philip III),
1611.

Webster's Twentieth Century Dictionary. Un-
abridged. New York: World, 1940.

index

Acapichtla (Ayachapichtla) (city),
battle of, 71–72, 221 n.22
Acapuzalco (Atzcapotzalco) (city), 69,
221 n.20
Acaxual (town, El Salvador), battle
at, 192–93
Aculman (Acolman) (city), 81
Aculuacan (province), 57
Adobe: bricks used as projectiles, 110;
use for Indian houses, 168
Agave, uses for, 173, 241 n.18
Aguilar, Fray Francisco de: account
of conquest of Mexico, 134–64; on
population of Mexico-Tenochtitlan,
162–63, 242 n.28
Aguilar, Jerónimo de (Hernando), as
interpreter for Cortés, 21, 137–38,
141, 215 nn.6,11
Aguilar, Marcos de, 161
Ahuacatlan (town), looting
by Guzmán expedition, 202,
204
Ahuaxpitzcatzin, Don Carlos,
132, 236 n.66
Ahuizotl (Aztec king), 218 n.32
Alabaster, use in making jars, 12,
212 n.18
Alaminos, Antón de, 216–17 n.21
Albinos, kept by Moctezuma as curi-
osities, 41
Albornoz (comptroller), 161
Alderete, Julian de, 101, 160,
222 n.25, 223–24 n.31, 230–32 n.50;
role in torture of Quauhtemotzin,
233–35 n.59
Alguacil mayor. *See* Sandoval,
Gonzalo de
Allies, Indian
—of Mexico-Tenochtitlan, 54, 63,
72–73, 158, 222 n.24
—of Spanish forces, 57–58, 62–63, 66,
80, 112, 220 n.13; torture and killing of Aztecs, 119, 121. *See also*
Tlaxcala
Almargo, Diego, 225–26 n.37
Alum, discovery of, 184, 188
Alvarado, Gómez, 193, 225–26 n.37
Alvarado, Gonzalo de, 193
Alvarado, Jorge de, 137, 192, 193,
225–26 n.37
Alvarado, Juan, 225–26 n.37
Alvarado, Pedro de, 3, 4, 220 n.12,
225–26 n.37
—personal account of Guatemala
expedition, 182–96
—plot by Spanish conspirators to
assassinate, 236 n.65
—role in conquest of Mexico, 182–83,
196; in Aguilar's account, 137, 139,
151, 153; in Cortés' account to
Charles V, 84, 96, 98–99, 129–30,
229–30 n.48; in Tapia's account, 17,
22, 45
—subjugation of Tututepeque province, 129–30
—wounding of, 193
Amazons, myth of among Spanish,
7–8, 206, 245 n.23
Ambuscades: set by Spanish, 70, 92,
110–12, 229–30 n.48; of Spaniards
by Indian forces, 67, 229–30 n.48;
use by Spanish in Guatemala,
185–86, 192–93
Animals, of New Spain (Mexico),
167–68
Aquçmil (Cozumel) (island), 20, 137
Aqueducts to Mexico-Tenochtitlan,
85, 178
Argueta (Spanish messenger), 188
Armada, Spanish, scuttling by Cortés,
26, 138–39
Armor, Indian, feathered coats as,
168–69
Armor, Indian (Ixcahuipiles), 139,